The Britannica Guide to
Heat, Force,
and Motion

PHYSICS EXPLAINED

The Britannica Guide to
Heat, Force,
and Motion

EDITED BY ERIK GREGERSEN, ASSOCIATE EDITOR,
SCIENCE AND TECHNOLOGY

IN ASSOCIATION WITH

Published in 2011 by Britannica Educational Publishing
(a trademark of Encyclopædia Britannica, Inc.)
in association with Rosen Educational Services, LLC
29 East 21st Street, New York, NY 10010.

First Edition

Britannica Educational Publishing
Michael I. Levy: Executive Editor
J.E. Luebering: Senior Manager
Marilyn L. Barton: Senior Coordinator, Production Control
Steven Bosco: Director, Editorial Technologies
Lisa S. Braucher: Senior Producer and Data Editor
Yvette Charboneau: Senior Copy Editor
Kathy Nakamura: Manager, Media Acquisition
Erik Gregersen: Associate Editor, Science and Technology

Rosen Educational Services
Hope Lourie Killcoyne: Senior Editor and Project Manager
Nelson Sá: Art Director
Cindy Reiman: Photography Manager
Matthew Cauli: Designer, Cover Design
Introduction by Erik Gregersen

Library of Congress Cataloging-in-Publication Data

The Britannica guide to heat, force, and motion / edited by Erik Gregersen.—1st ed.
    p. cm.—(Physics explained)
"In association with Britannica Educational Publishing, Rosen Educational Services."
Includes bibliographical references and index.
ISBN 978-1-61530-309-0 (lib. bdg.)
    1. Thermodynamics--Popular works. I. Gregersen, Erik. II. Title: Heat, force, and motion.
QC311.B835 2011
536'.7—dc22

                                                    2010018515

Manufactured in the United States of America

On page xii: The physical forces of air resistance, friction, and gravity are at play on a baseball when tossed in a game of catch. As Galileo first noted, the curved path followed by such
a projectile is a parabola. *Thinkstock Images/Comstock/Getty Images*

On page xx: The locomotive is powered by a steam engine that converts the energy from
burning coal into forward motion. *Istockphoto/Thinkstock*

On pages 1, 28, 43, 59, 106, 134, 157, 192, 206, 256, 277, 300, 351, 356, 362: A gyroscope.
Tim Simmons/Stone/Getty Images

CONTENTS

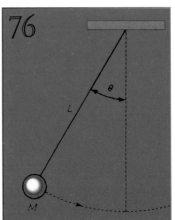

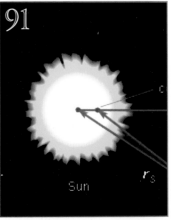

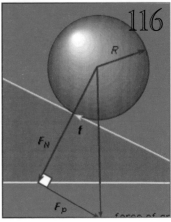

205

215

233

INTRODUCTION

Heat, force, and motion—the most fundamental parts of physics, form the beginnings of many basic physics courses. They are also part of everyday life. Everyone has felt hot or cold. Everyone has stubbed a toe or thrown a ball. The subfields of thermodynamics and mechanics, unlike more complex areas such as quantum mechanics and relativity, are the closest to everyday human experience as it has happened throughout history. This book provides readers with in-depth coverage of these physical concepts, as well as examples and simple experiments that concretize the ideas covered.

Thermodynamics, as the name reveals, is the study of heat and how it moves and changes. The exact nature of heat was not realized until the mid-19th century. Prior to that time, the dominant explanation of temperature and related phenomena was the caloric theory of heat. Caloric was an invisible weightless substance that permeated matter. Cold objects contained little caloric; hot objects contained a good deal of it. Since caloric flowed from hot to cold, caloric repelled itself.

The caloric theory had some success and did explain many aspects of heat. However, in 1798, Sir Benjamin Thompson, Count Rumford of the Holy Roman Empire, became interested in cannon making and how it related to caloric. Cannons were made by having horses turn an iron bit, which bored away the center of a metal cylinder. The bit grinding against the middle of the cylinder generated heat. By immersing the cannon in water and driving the horses for hours, Thompson was able to boil the water from the friction and so able to calculate how much caloric was transferred from the cannon to the water. However, the caloric originally must have come from the bit, but if the bit contained enough caloric to boil the amount of water necessary to cover a cannon, the bit would have melted before it even touched the cannon.

Count Rumford's experiment was ignored for the most part, and the science of thermodynamics proceeded with caloric as its foundation. The French soldier Sadi Carnot explained heat engines—machines that use heat to make something else move, such as the piston in a steam engine—using the caloric theory. It was not until the 1840s that Julius Robert van Mayer in Germany and James Joule in England disproved the caloric theory and found the true nature of heat. In a cylinder containing gas that is heated, expands, and moves a piston (Mayer) and a paddle wheel stirring water (Joule), the heat was found to be equal to the energy of the motion. Heat was a form of energy. The energy put into stirring the paddle wheel had heated the water. The energy had not been created or destroyed; it had been merely converted from one form to another. The total amount of energy was conserved. This is the first law of thermodynamics.

Thermodynamics has three other fundamental laws. The zeroth concerns the measurement of thermal equilibrium. The second states that heat cannot be converted completely into work; there is always some energy that is wasted. This wasted energy is stated in terms of a quantity called entropy, or heat energy per temperature, that always increases. The entire universe has an entropy, which, in one of the bleakest conclusions of physics, will increase until no useful work can be done anywhere. The third law sets the scale by which entropy is measured.

The other subfield of physics that is considered in this book is mechanics, which studies how bodies move. Mechanics came to fruition much earlier than did thermodynamics. In the early 17th century, the Italian astronomer Galileo used a simple experiment involving balls rolling down an inclined plane to discover the law of motion often stated as "a body in motion stays in motion."

That is, bodies have inertia. To change the movement of a body, a force must be applied to it. The same conditions apply to something sitting still. A force must be applied to an object at rest to get it moving.

This statement about bodies and how they move is the first of Newton's three laws of motion, which form the basis of the subject of mechanics. The second law defines what a force is: namely, mass times acceleration, or mathematically, $F = ma$. The third law is the well-known statement "for every action, there is an opposite and equal reaction."

These laws can be applied to many different things from an apple falling from a tree to a planet orbiting a star. One system treated in detail in many physics courses is the simple harmonic oscillator, a mass on a spring. The mass is moved; the spring stretches. A restoring force pulls the mass back, compressing the spring. The spring moves the mass in a cycle of stretching and compressing. The physics learned from the system can be applied to a pendulum in a clock, the skin on a drum, or any oscillatory system.

The subject of mechanics is filled with such generalizations from the universal to the particular. For example, in the subfield of the mechanics of solids, forces on bulk materials are studied. With the mass on the spring or the planet in its orbit, no consideration need be made of its internal structure. But in much of one's everyday life, solid objects such as cars, land masses, and houses have insides. How do Newton's laws apply to a girder in a skyscraper? To answer this question, one uses the mechanics of solids.

The basic concepts of the mechanics of solids are those of stress, strain, and elasticity. Stress is a force per area. An object sitting on a floor is pulled toward the center of Earth by the force of gravity. This force places a stress on the floor. The floor gives under the stress. This "give" is quantified by strain, how much a material moves over a unit of its length. (Strain is a dimensionless quantity, length divided by length.) When the weight is lifted from the floor, the floor rebounds. The floor's ability to return to its original state is its elasticity. A rubber band is extremely elastic and snaps right back to its original length after a force stretching it is released. A steel beam is nowhere near as elastic as a rubber band.

Every building that stands is a testament to the usefulness of the mechanics of solids. Structural engineers and architects have applied this field of physics to build ever taller and taller buildings. For millennia, the tallest structure in the world was the Great Pyramid of Giza, which is basically a giant pile of rocks standing 147 metres (481.4 feet) above the desert. The ancient Egyptians of Khufu's time did not need to know so much about the stress one block placed upon another. The tallest building of our time is the Burj Khalifa, a skyscraper standing 828 metres (2,717 feet) above the desert in Dubai. This building required much more knowledge. The builders of the Burj Khalifa had to know how the building would sway in the wind, how it would expand in the desert heat, how it would stand up to shifts in the ground (the site is near a geographical fault line), and how the foundation would hold the weight of the whole. All this they learned from the mechanics of solids.

A corresponding subject dealing with the motions of liquids and gases is called fluid mechanics. There are some stresses called shear stresses dealing with the differing motions of layers of a material with respect to each other that will not effect a solid; however, even the slightest motion of one layer of water, for example, with respect to a lower layer will cause some movement.

Fluid mechanics can be considered in both its static and its dynamic forms, that is, fluids at rest and fluids in motion. The science of static fluids is ancient, dating back to Archimedes, the ancient Greek mathematician (d. 212/211 BCE), who discovered that the force upward on a floating body is equal to the weight of the liquid it displaces. (Archimedes likely did not shout "Eureka" after discovering this in his bathtub. That story is probably a later embellishment by the Roman architect Vitrivius.) The science of dynamic fluids had to wait until the 18th century and the mathematicians Leonhard Euler and Daniel Bernouilli. They applied Newton's laws to a moving fluid. Their results can applied the flow of water in a pipe or winds in the atmosphere.

Just as skyscrapers testify to the usefulness of the mechanics of solids, the existence of much of modern technology testifies to the usefulness of fluid mechanics. An airplane wing experiences a lift force that arises from the circulation of air around it. Wind tunnels are used to study the flow of air around cars, and the results are used to make cars more efficient and thus better for the environment. The study of water flowing past a levee can have quite an effect on those living nearby who depend on that structure to hold in times of flood.

The most notable of the mechanical forces is that of gravitation. Everything from the atmosphere to the oceans to all life on Earth is held near the surface of the planet by gravity. However, gravity is not just something that large celestial bodies have. Gravity is a property of all objects with mass. Two people exert a gravitational force on each other, but it is far less than that exerted by the mass of Earth.

It is with gravity that science must go beyond the physics of Newton to that of Einstein and his theory of relativity. Gravity is not just a force, but a field. The commonly given analogy is the gravity is like the ball distorting a rubber sheet, with the sheet being space-time, the structure of the universe.

Gravity is one of four fundamental forces, with the others being the strong nuclear force that holds atoms together, the weak nuclear force that causes radioactive decay, and the electromagnetic force that is seen in electricity and magnetism. Surprisingly, gravity is the weakest of these forces; however, its range is that of the universe. All of the galaxies are attracted to all the others, and the amount of mass there is and therefore, its gravitational effects, is something that must be known if one is to understand the fate of the universe. The universe will not collapse back into a primordial fireball, but keep expanding at an ever slower rate.

Although seemingly the most quotidian areas of physics, the subjects of heat, force, and motion as can be seen from this brief introduction cover a wide range of experience. A sunbather laying on a beach on a summer's day experiences both the force of gravity and the heat of the sun. The Frisbee players nearby experience those forces, and motion as well. The universe as a whole—from its broadest expanse down to a grain of sand on a beach here on Earth—are affected by both thermodynamics and mechanics.

CHAPTER 1

THERMODYNAMICS:
THE LAWS OF ENERGY AND WORK

Thermodynamics is the science of the relationship between heat, work, temperature, and energy. In broad terms, thermodynamics deals with the transfer of energy from one place to another and from one form to another. The key concept is that heat is a form of energy corresponding to a definite amount of mechanical work.

Heat was not formally recognized as a form of energy until about 1798, when Count Rumford (Sir Benjamin Thompson), a British military engineer, noticed that limitless amounts of heat could be generated in the boring of cannon barrels and that the amount of heat generated is proportional to the work done in turning a blunt boring tool. Rumford's observation of the proportionality between heat generated and work done lies at the foundation of thermodynamics. Another pioneer was the French military engineer Sadi Carnot, who introduced the concept of the heat-engine cycle and the principle of reversibility in 1824. Carnot's work concerned the limitations on the maximum amount of work that can be obtained from a steam engine operating with a high-temperature heat transfer as its driving force. Later that century, these ideas were developed by Rudolf Clausius, a German mathematician and physicist, into the first and second laws of thermodynamics, respectively.

The most important laws of thermodynamics are:

- **The zeroth law of thermodynamics.** When two systems are each in thermal equilibrium with a third system, the first two systems are in thermal equilibrium with each other. This property makes it meaningful to use thermometers as the "third system" and to define a temperature scale.

- **The first law of thermodynamics, or the law of conservation of energy.** The change in a system's internal energy is equal to the difference between heat added to the system from its surroundings and work done by the system on its surroundings.

- **The second law of thermodynamics.** Heat does not flow spontaneously from a colder region to a hotter region, or, equivalently, heat at a given temperature cannot be converted entirely into work. Consequently, the entropy of a closed system, or heat energy per unit temperature, increases over time toward some maximum value. Thus, all closed systems tend toward an equilibrium state in which entropy is at a maximum and no energy is available to do useful work. This asymmetry between forward and backward processes gives rise to what is known as the "arrow of time."

- **The third law of thermodynamics.** The entropy of a perfect crystal of an element in its most stable form tends to zero as the temperature approaches absolute zero. This allows an absolute scale for entropy to be established that, from a statistical point of view, determines the degree of randomness or disorder in a system.

Although thermodynamics developed rapidly during the 19th century in response to the need to optimize the performance of steam engines, the sweeping generality of the laws of thermodynamics makes them applicable to all physical and biological systems. In particular, the laws of thermodynamics give a complete description of all changes in the energy state of any system and its ability to perform useful work on its surroundings.

THERMODYNAMIC STATES

The application of thermodynamic principles begins by defining a system that is in some sense distinct from its surroundings. For example, the system could be a sample of gas inside a cylinder with a movable piston, an entire steam engine, a marathon runner, the planet Earth, a neutron star, a black hole, or even the entire universe. In general, systems are free to exchange heat, work, and other forms of energy with their surroundings.

A system's condition at any given time is called its thermodynamic state. For a gas in a cylinder with a movable piston, the state of the system is identified by the temperature, pressure, and volume of the gas. These properties are characteristic parameters that have definite values at each state and are independent of the way in which the system arrived at that state. In other words, any change in value of a property depends only on the initial and final states of the system, not on the path followed by the system from one state to another. Such properties are called state functions. In contrast, the work done as the piston moves and the gas expands and the heat the gas absorbs from its surroundings depend on the detailed way in which the expansion occurs.

The behaviour of a complex thermodynamic system, such as Earth's atmosphere, can be understood by first applying the principles of states and properties to its component parts—in this case, water, water vapour, and the various gases making up the atmosphere. By isolating samples of material whose states and properties can be controlled and manipulated, properties and their interrelations can be studied as the system changes from state to state.

THERMODYNAMIC EQUILIBRIUM

A particularly important concept is thermodynamic equilibrium, in which there is no tendency for the state of a system to change spontaneously. For example, the gas in a cylinder with a movable piston will be at equilibrium if the temperature and pressure inside are uniform and if the restraining force on the piston is just sufficient to keep it from moving. The system can then be made to change to a new state only by an externally imposed change in one of the state functions, such as the temperature by adding heat or the volume by moving the piston. A sequence of one or more such steps connecting different states of the system is called a process. In general, a system is not in equilibrium as it adjusts to an abrupt change in its environment. For example, when a balloon bursts, the compressed gas inside is suddenly far from equilibrium, and it rapidly expands until it reaches a new equilibrium state. However, the same final state could be achieved by placing the same compressed gas in a cylinder with a movable piston and applying a sequence of many small increments in volume (and temperature), with the system being given time to come to equilibrium after each small increment. Such a process is said to be reversible because the system is at (or near) equilibrium at each step along its path, and the direction of change could be reversed at any point. This example illustrates how two different paths can connect the same initial and final states. The first is irreversible (the balloon bursts), and the second is reversible. The concept of reversible processes is something like motion without friction in mechanics. It represents an idealized limiting case that is very useful in discussing the properties of real systems. Many of the results of thermodynamics are derived from the properties of reversible processes.

TEMPERATURE

The concept of temperature is fundamental to any discussion of thermodynamics, but its precise definition is not a simple matter. For example, a steel rod feels colder than a wooden rod at room temperature simply because steel is better at conducting heat away from the skin. It is therefore necessary to have an objective way of measuring temperature. In general, when two objects are brought into thermal contact, heat will flow between them until they come into equilibrium with each other. When the flow of heat stops, they are said to be at the same temperature. The zeroth law of thermodynamics formalizes this by asserting that if an object A is in simultaneous thermal equilibrium with two other objects B and C, then B and C will be in thermal equilibrium with each other if brought into thermal contact. Object A can then play the role of a thermometer through some change in its physical properties with temperature, such as its volume or its electrical resistance.

With the definition of equality of temperature in hand, it is possible to establish a temperature scale by assigning numerical values to certain easily reproducible fixed points. For example, in the Celsius (°C) temperature scale, the freezing point of pure water is arbitrarily assigned a temperature of 0 °C and the boiling point of water the value of 100 °C (in both cases at 1 standard atmosphere). In the Fahrenheit (°F) temperature scale, these same two points are assigned the values 32 °F and 212 °F, respectively. There are absolute temperature scales related to the second law of thermodynamics. The absolute scale related to the

Celsius scale is called the Kelvin (K) scale, and that related to the Fahrenheit scale is called the Rankine (°R) scale. These scales are related by the equations K = °C + 273.15, °R = °F + 459.67, and °R = 1.8 K.

WORK AND ENERGY

Energy has a precise meaning in physics that does not always correspond to everyday language, and yet a precise definition is somewhat elusive. The word is derived from the Greek word *ergon*, meaning "work," but the term *work* itself acquired a technical meaning with the advent of Newtonian mechanics. For example, a man pushing on a car may feel that he is doing a lot of work, but no work is actually done unless the car moves. The work done is then the product of the force applied by the man multiplied by the distance through which the car moves. If there is no friction and the surface is level, then the car, once set in motion, will continue rolling indefinitely with constant speed. The rolling car has something that a stationary car does not have—it has kinetic energy of motion equal to the work required to achieve that state of motion. The introduction of the concept of energy in this way is of great value in mechanics because, in the absence of friction, energy is never lost from the system, although it can be converted from one form to another. For example, if a coasting car comes to a hill, it will roll some distance up the hill before coming to a temporary stop. At that moment its kinetic energy of motion has been converted into its potential energy of position, which is equal to the work required to lift the car through the same vertical distance. After coming to a stop, the car will then begin rolling back down the hill until it has completely recovered its kinetic energy of motion at the bottom. In the absence of friction, such systems are said to be conservative because at any given moment the total amount of energy (kinetic plus potential) remains equal to the initial work done to set the system in motion.

As the science of physics expanded to cover an ever-wider range of phenomena, it became necessary to include additional forms of energy in order to keep the total amount of energy constant for all closed systems (or to account for changes in total energy for open systems). For example, if work is done to accelerate charged particles, then some of the resultant energy will be stored in the form of electromagnetic fields and carried away from the system as radiation. In turn the electromagnetic energy can be picked up by a remote receiver (antenna) and converted back into an equivalent amount of work. With his theory of special relativity, Albert Einstein realized that energy (E) can also be stored as mass (m) and converted back into energy, as expressed by his famous equation $E = mc^2$, where c is the velocity of light. All of these systems are said to be conservative in the sense that energy can be freely converted from one form to another without limit. Each fundamental advance of physics into new realms has involved a similar extension to the list of the different forms of energy. In addition to preserving the first law of thermodynamics, also called the law of conservation of energy, each form of energy can be related back to an equivalent amount of work required to set the system into motion.

Thermodynamics encompasses all of these forms of energy, with the further addition of heat to the list of different kinds of energy. However, heat is fundamentally different from the others in that the conversion of work (or other forms of energy) into heat is not completely reversible, even in principle. In the example of the rolling car, some of the work done to set the car in motion is inevitably lost as heat due to friction, and the car eventually comes to a stop on a level surface. Even if all the generated heat were collected and stored in some fashion, it could never be converted entirely back into mechanical energy of motion. This fundamental limitation is expressed quantitatively by the second law of thermodynamics.

The role of friction in degrading the energy of mechanical systems may seem simple and obvious, but the quantitative connection between heat and work, as first discovered by Count Rumford, played a key role in understanding the operation of steam engines in the 19th century and similarly for all energy-conversion processes today.

TOTAL INTERNAL ENERGY

Although classical thermodynamics deals exclusively with the macroscopic properties of materials—such as temperature, pressure, and volume—thermal energy from the addition of heat can be understood at the microscopic level as an increase in the kinetic energy of motion of the molecules making up a substance. For example, gas molecules have translational kinetic energy that is proportional to the temperature of the gas: the molecules can rotate about their centre of mass, and the constituent atoms can vibrate with respect to each other (like masses connected by springs). Additionally, chemical energy is stored in the bonds holding the molecules together, and weaker long-range interactions between the molecules involve yet more energy. The sum total of all these forms of energy constitutes the total internal energy of the substance in a given thermodynamic state. The total energy of a system includes its internal energy plus any other forms of energy, such as kinetic energy due to motion of the system as a whole (e.g., water flowing through a pipe) and gravitational potential energy due to its elevation.

THE FIRST LAW OF THERMODYNAMICS

The laws of thermodynamics are deceptively simple to state, but they are far-reaching in their consequences. The first law asserts that if heat is recognized as a form of energy, then the total energy of a system plus its surroundings is conserved; in other words, the total energy of the universe remains constant.

The first law is put into action by considering the flow of energy across the boundary separating a system from its surroundings. Consider the classic example of a gas enclosed in a cylinder with a movable piston. The walls of the cylinder act as the boundary separating the gas inside from the world outside, and the movable piston provides a mechanism for the gas to do work by expanding against the force holding the piston (assumed frictionless) in place. If the gas does work W as it expands, and/or absorbs heat Q from its surroundings through the walls of the cylinder, then this corresponds to a net flow of energy $W - Q$ across the boundary to the surroundings. In order to conserve the total energy U, there must be a counterbalancing change

$$\Delta U = Q - W \qquad (1)$$

in the internal energy of the gas. The first law provides a kind of strict energy accounting system in which the change in the energy account (ΔU) equals the difference between deposits (Q) and withdrawals (W).

There is an important distinction between the quantity ΔU and the related energy quantities Q and W. Since the internal energy U is characterized entirely by the quantities (or parameters) that uniquely determine the state of the system at equilibrium, it is said to be a state function such that any change in energy is determined entirely by the initial (i) and final (f) states of the system: $\Delta U = U_f - U_i$. However, Q and W are not state functions. Just as in the example of a bursting balloon, the gas inside may do no work at all in reaching its final expanded state, or it could do maximum work by expanding inside a cylinder with a movable piston to reach the same final state. All that is required is that the change in energy (ΔU) remain the same. By analogy, the same change in one's bank account could be achieved by many different combinations of deposits and withdrawals. Thus, Q and W are not state functions, because their values depend on the particular process (or path) connecting the same initial and final states. Just as it is only meaningful to speak of the balance in one's bank account and not its deposit or withdrawal content, it is only meaningful to speak of the internal energy of a system and not its heat or work content.

From a formal mathematical point of view, the incremental change dU in the internal energy is an exact differential, while the corresponding incremental changes $d'Q$ and $d'W$ in heat and work are not, because the definite integrals of these quantities are path-dependent. These concepts can be used to great advantage in a precise mathematical formulation of thermodynamics.

HEAT ENGINES

The classic example of a heat engine is a steam engine, although all modern engines follow the same principles. Steam engines operate in a cyclic fashion, with the piston moving up and down once for each cycle. Hot high-pressure steam is admitted to the cylinder in the first half of each cycle, and then it is allowed to escape again in the second half. The overall effect is to take heat Q_1 generated by burning a fuel to make steam, convert part of it to do work, and exhaust the remaining heat Q_2 to the environment at a lower temperature. The net heat energy absorbed is then $Q = Q_1 - Q_2$. Since the engine returns to its initial state, its internal energy U does not change ($\Delta U = 0$). Thus, by the first law of thermodynamics, the work done for each complete cycle must be $W = Q_1 - Q_2$. In other words, the work done for each complete cycle is just the difference between the heat Q_1 absorbed by the engine at a high temperature and the heat Q_2 exhausted at a lower temperature. The power of thermodynamics is that this conclusion is completely independent of the detailed working mechanism of the engine. It relies only on the overall conservation of energy, with heat regarded as a form of energy.

In order to save money on fuel and avoid contaminating the environment with waste heat, engines are designed to maximize the conversion of absorbed heat Q_1 into useful work and to minimize the waste heat Q_2. The Carnot efficiency (η) of an engine is defined as the ratio W/Q_1 — i.e., the fraction of Q_1 that is converted into work. Since $W = Q_1 - Q_2$, the efficiency also can be expressed in the form

$$\eta = \frac{Q_1 - Q_2}{Q_1} = 1 - \frac{Q_2}{Q_1} \tag{2}$$

If there were no waste heat at all, then $Q_2 = 0$ and $\eta = 1$, corresponding to 100 percent efficiency. While reducing friction in an engine decreases waste heat, it can never be eliminated; therefore, there is a limit on how small Q_2 can be and thus on how large the efficiency can be. This limitation is a fundamental law of nature — in fact, the second law of thermodynamics.

Isothermal and Adiabatic Processes

Because heat engines may go through a complex sequence of steps, a simplified model is often used to illustrate the principles of thermodynamics. In particular, consider a gas that expands and contracts within a cylinder with a movable piston under a prescribed set of conditions. There are two particularly important sets of conditions. One condition, known as an isothermal expansion, involves keeping the gas at a constant temperature. As the gas does work against the restraining force of the piston, it must absorb heat in order to conserve energy. Otherwise, it would cool as it expands (or conversely heat as it is compressed). This is an example of a process in which the heat absorbed is converted entirely into work with 100 percent efficiency. The process does not violate fundamental limitations on efficiency, however, because a single expansion by itself is not a cyclic process.

The second condition, known as an adiabatic expansion (from the Greek *adiabatos*, meaning "impassable"), is one in which the cylinder is assumed to be perfectly insulated so that no heat can flow into or out of the cylinder. In this case the gas cools as it expands, because, by the first law, the work done against the restraining force on the piston can only come from the internal energy of the gas. Thus, the change in the internal energy of the gas must be $\Delta U = -W$, as manifested by a decrease in its temperature. The gas cools, even though there is no heat flow, because it is doing work at the expense of its own internal energy. The exact amount of cooling can be calculated from the heat capacity of the gas.

Many natural phenomena are effectively adiabatic because there is insufficient time for significant heat flow to occur. For example, when warm air rises in the atmosphere, it expands and cools as the pressure drops with altitude, but air is a good thermal insulator, and so there is no significant heat flow from the surrounding air. In this case the surrounding air plays the roles of both the insulated cylinder walls and the movable piston. The warm air does work against the pressure provided by the surrounding air as it expands, and so its temperature must drop. A more-detailed analysis of this adiabatic expansion explains most of the decrease of temperature with altitude, accounting for the familiar fact that it is colder at the top of a mountain than at its base.

THE SECOND LAW OF THERMODYNAMICS

The first law of thermodynamics asserts that energy must be conserved in any process involving the exchange of heat and work between a system and its surroundings. A machine that violated the first law would be called a perpetual motion machine of the first kind because it would manufacture its own energy out of nothing and thereby run forever. Such a machine would be impossible even in theory. However, this impossibility would not prevent the construction of a machine that could extract essentially limitless amounts of heat from its surroundings (earth, air, and sea) and convert it entirely into work. Although such a hypothetical machine would not violate conservation of energy, the total failure of inventors to build such a machine, known as a perpetual motion machine of the second kind, led to the discovery of the second law of thermodynamics. The second law of thermodynamics can be precisely stated in the following two forms, as originally formulated in the 19th century by the Scottish physicist William Thomson (Lord Kelvin) and the German physicist Rudolf Clausius, respectively:

1. A cyclic transformation whose only final result is to transform heat extracted from a source which is at the same temperature throughout into work is impossible.
2. A cyclic transformation whose only final result is to transfer heat from a body at a given temperature to a body at a higher temperature is impossible.

The two statements are in fact equivalent because, if the first were possible, then the work obtained could be used, for example, to generate electricity that could then be discharged through an electric heater installed in a body at a higher temperature. The net effect would be a flow of heat from a lower temperature to a higher temperature, thereby violating the second (Clausius) form of the second law. Conversely, if the second form were possible, then the heat transferred to the higher temperature could be used to run a heat engine that would convert part of the heat into work. The final result would be a conversion of heat into work at constant temperature—a violation of the first (Kelvin) form of the second law.

Central to the following discussion of entropy is the concept of a heat reservoir capable of providing essentially limitless amounts of heat at a fixed temperature. This is of course an idealization, but the temperature of a large body of water such as the Atlantic Ocean does not materially change if a small amount of heat is withdrawn to run a heat engine. The essential point is that the heat reservoir is assumed to have a well-defined temperature that does not change as a result of the process being considered.

ENTROPY

The concept of entropy was first introduced in 1850 by Clausius as a precise mathematical way of testing whether the second law of thermodynamics is violated by a particular process. The test begins with the definition that if an amount of heat Q flows into a heat reservoir at constant temperature T, then its entropy S increases by $\Delta S = Q/T$. (This equation in effect provides a thermodynamic definition of temperature that can be shown to be identical to the conventional thermometric one.) Assume now that there are two heat reservoirs R_1 and R_2 at temperatures T_1 and T_2. If an amount of heat Q flows from R_1 to R_2, then the net entropy change for the two reservoirs is

$$\Delta S = \frac{Q}{T_2} - \frac{Q}{T_1}. \tag{3}$$

ΔS is positive, provided that $T_1 > T_2$. Thus, the observation that heat never flows spontaneously from a colder region to a hotter region (the Clausius form of the second law of thermodynamics) is equivalent to requiring the net entropy change to be positive for a spontaneous flow of heat. If $T_1 = T_2$, then the reservoirs are in equilibrium and $\Delta S = 0$.

EFFICIENCY LIMITS

The condition $\Delta S \geq 0$ determines the maximum possible efficiency of heat engines. Suppose that some system capable of doing work in a cyclic fashion (a heat engine) absorbs heat Q_1 from R_1 and exhausts heat Q_2 to R_2 for each complete cycle. Because the system returns to its original state at the end of a cycle, its energy does not change. Then, by conservation of energy, the work done per cycle is $W = Q_1 - Q_2$, and the net entropy change for the two reservoirs is

$$\Delta S = \frac{Q_2}{T_2} - \frac{Q_1}{T_1}. \tag{4}$$

To make W as large as possible, Q_2 should be kept as small as possible relative to Q_1. However, Q_2 cannot be zero, because this would make ΔS negative and so violate the second law of thermodynamics. The smallest possible value of Q_2 corresponds to the condition $\Delta S = 0$, yielding

$$\left(\frac{Q_2}{Q_1}\right)_{min} = \frac{T_2}{T_1}. \tag{5}$$

This is the fundamental equation limiting the efficiency of all heat engines whose function is to convert heat into work (such as electric power generators). The actual efficiency is defined to be the fraction of Q_1 that is converted to work (W/Q_1), which is equivalent to equation (2).

The maximum efficiency for a given T_1 and T_2 is thus

$$\eta_{max} = 1 - \left(\frac{Q_2}{Q_1}\right)_{min} = 1 - \frac{T_2}{T_1}. \tag{6}$$

A process for which $\Delta S = 0$ is said to be reversible because an infinitesimal change would be sufficient to make the heat engine run backward as a refrigerator.

As an example, the properties of materials limit the practical upper temperature for thermal power plants to $T_1 \cong 1{,}200$ K. Taking T_2 to be the temperature of the environment (300 K), the maximum efficiency is 1 − 300/1,200 = 0.75. Thus, at least 25 percent of the heat energy produced must be exhausted into the environment as waste heat to avoid violating the second law of thermodynamics. Because of various imperfections, such as friction and imperfect thermal insulation, the actual efficiency of power plants seldom exceeds about 60 percent. However, because of the second law of thermodynamics, no amount of ingenuity or improvements in design can increase the efficiency beyond about 75 percent.

ENTROPY AND HEAT DEATH

The example of a heat engine illustrates one of the many ways in which the second law of thermodynamics can be applied. One way to generalize the example is to consider the heat engine and its heat reservoir as parts of an isolated (or closed) system—i.e., one that does not exchange heat or work with its surroundings. For example, the heat engine and reservoir could be encased in a rigid container with insulating walls. In this case the second law of thermodynamics (in the simplified form presented here) says that no matter what process takes place inside the container, its entropy must increase or remain the same in the limit of a reversible process. Similarly, if the universe is an isolated system, then its entropy too must increase with time. Indeed, the implication is that the universe must ultimately suffer a "heat death" as its entropy progressively increases toward a maximum value and all parts come into thermal equilibrium at a uniform temperature. After that point, no further changes involving the conversion of heat into useful work would be possible. In general, the equilibrium state for an isolated system is precisely that state of maximum entropy. This is equivalent to an alternate definition for the term *entropy* as a measure of the disorder of a system, such that a completely random dispersion of elements corresponds to maximum entropy, or minimum information.

ENTROPY AND THE ARROW OF TIME

The inevitable increase of entropy with time for isolated systems plays a fundamental role in determining the direction of the "arrow of time." Everyday life presents no difficulty in distinguishing the forward flow of time from its reverse. For example, if a film showed a glass of warm water spontaneously changing into hot water with ice floating on top, it would immediately be apparent that the film was running backward because the process of heat flowing from warm water to hot water would violate the second law of thermodynamics. However, this obvious asymmetry between the forward and reverse directions for the flow of time does not persist at the level of fundamental interactions. An observer watching a film showing two water molecules colliding would not be able to tell whether the film was running forward or backward.

So what exactly is the connection between entropy and the second law? Recall that heat at the molecular level is the random kinetic energy of motion of molecules, and collisions between molecules provide the microscopic mechanism for transporting heat energy from one place to another. Because individual collisions are unchanged by reversing the direction of time, heat can flow just as well in one direction as the other. Thus, from the point of view of fundamental interactions, there is nothing to prevent a chance event in which a number of slow-moving (cold) molecules happen to collect together in one place and form ice, while the surrounding water becomes hotter. Such chance events could be expected to occur from time to time in a vessel containing only a few water molecules. However, the same chance events are never observed in a full glass of water, not because they are impossible but because they are exceedingly improbable. This is because even a small glass of water contains an enormous number of interacting molecules (about 10^{24}), making it highly unlikely that, in the course of their random thermal motion, a significant fraction of cold molecules will collect together in one place. Although such a spontaneous violation of the second law of thermodynamics is not impossible, an extremely patient physicist would have to wait many times the age of the universe to see it happen.

The foregoing demonstrates an important point: the second law of thermodynamics is statistical in nature. It has no meaning at the level of individual molecules, whereas the law becomes essentially exact for the description of large numbers of interacting molecules. In contrast, the first law of thermodynamics, which expresses conservation of energy, remains exactly true even at the molecular level.

The example of ice melting in a glass of hot water also demonstrates the other sense of the term *entropy*, as an increase in randomness and a parallel loss of information. Initially, the total thermal energy is partitioned in such a way that all of the slow-moving (cold) molecules are located in the ice and all of the fast-moving (hot) molecules are located in the water (or water vapour). After the ice has melted and the system has come to thermal equilibrium, the thermal energy is uniformly distributed throughout the system. The statistical approach provides a great deal of valuable insight into the meaning of the second law of thermodynamics, but, from the point of view of applications, the microscopic structure of matter becomes irrelevant. The great beauty and strength of classical thermodynamics are that its predictions are completely independent of the microscopic structure of matter.

OPEN SYSTEMS

Most real thermodynamic systems are open systems that exchange heat and work with their environment, rather than the closed systems described thus far. For example, living systems are clearly able to achieve a local reduction in their entropy as they grow and develop; they create structures of greater internal energy (i.e., they lower entropy) out of the nutrients they absorb. This does not represent a violation of the second law of thermodynamics, because a living organism does not constitute a closed system.

THERMODYNAMIC POTENTIALS

In order to simplify the application of the laws of thermodynamics to open systems, parameters with the dimensions of energy, known as thermodynamic potentials, are introduced to describe the system. The resulting formulas are expressed in terms of the Helmholtz free energy F and the Gibbs free energy G, named after the 19th-century German physiologist and physicist Hermann von Helmholtz and the contemporaneous American physicist Josiah Willard Gibbs. The key conceptual step is to separate a system from its heat reservoir. A system is thought of as being held at a constant temperature T by a heat reservoir (i.e., the environment), but the heat reservoir is no longer considered to be part of the system. Recall that the internal energy change (ΔU) of a system is given by

$$\Delta U = Q - W, \qquad (7)$$

where Q is the heat absorbed and W is the work done. In general, Q and W separately are not state functions, because they are path-dependent. However, if the path is specified to be any reversible isothermal process, then the heat associated with the maximum work (W_{max}) is $Q_{max} = T\Delta S$. With this substitution the above equation can be rearranged as

$$-W_{max} = \Delta U - T\Delta S. \qquad (8)$$

Note that here ΔS is the entropy change just of the system being held at constant temperature, such as a battery. Unlike the case of an isolated system as considered previously, it does not include the entropy change of the heat reservoir (i.e., the surroundings) required to keep the temperature constant. If this additional entropy change of the reservoir were included, the total entropy change would be zero, as in the case of an isolated system. Because the quantities U, T, and S on the right-hand side are all state functions, it follows that $-W_{max}$ must also be a state function. This leads to the definition of the Helmholtz free energy

$$F = U - TS \qquad (9)$$

such that, for any isothermal change of the system,

$$\Delta F = \Delta U - T\Delta S \qquad (10)$$

is the negative of the maximum work that can be extracted from the system. The actual work extracted could be smaller than the ideal maximum, or even zero, which implies that $W \leq -\Delta F$, with equality applying in the ideal limiting case of a reversible process. When the Helmholtz free energy reaches its minimum value, the system has reached its equilibrium state, and no further work can be extracted from it. Thus, the equilibrium condition of maximum entropy for isolated systems becomes the condition of minimum Helmholtz free energy for open systems held at constant temperature. The one additional precaution required is that work done against the atmosphere be included if the system expands or contracts in the course of the process being considered. Typically, processes are specified as taking place at constant volume and temperature in order that no correction is needed.

Although the Helmholtz free energy is useful in describing processes that take place inside a container with rigid walls, most processes in the real world take place under constant pressure rather than constant volume. For example, chemical reactions in an open test tube—or in the growth of a tomato in a garden—take place under conditions of (nearly) constant atmospheric pressure. It is for the description of these cases that the Gibbs free energy was introduced. As previously established, the quantity

$$-W_{max} = \Delta U - T\Delta S \qquad (11)$$

is a state function equal to the change in the Helmholtz free energy. Suppose that the process being considered involves a large change in volume (ΔV), such as happens when water boils to form steam. The work done by the expanding water vapour as it pushes back the surrounding air at pressure P is $P\Delta V$. This is the amount of work that is now split out from W_{max} by writing it in the form

$$W_{max} = W_{max} + P\Delta V, \qquad (12)$$

where W_{max} is the maximum work that can be extracted from the process taking place at constant temperature T and pressure P, other than the atmospheric work ($P\Delta V$). Substituting this partition into the above equation for $-W_{max}$ and moving the $P\Delta V$ term to the right-hand side then yields

$$-W_{max} = \Delta U + P\Delta V - T\Delta S. \qquad (13)$$

This leads to the definition of the Gibbs free energy

$$G = U + PV - TS \qquad (14)$$

such that, for any isothermal change of the system at constant pressure,

$$\Delta G = \Delta U + P\Delta V - T\Delta S \qquad (15)$$

is the negative of the maximum work W_{max} that can be extracted from the system, other than atmospheric work. As before, the actual work extracted could be smaller than the ideal maximum, or even zero, which implies that $W' \leq -\Delta G$, with equality applying in the ideal limiting case of a reversible process. As with the Helmholtz case, when the Gibbs free energy reaches its minimum value, the system has reached its equilibrium state, and no further work can be extracted from it. Thus, the equilibrium condition becomes the condition of minimum Gibbs free energy for open systems held at constant temperature and pressure, and the direction of spontaneous change is always toward a state of lower free energy for the system (like a ball rolling downhill into a valley). Notice in particular that the entropy can now spontaneously decrease (i.e., $T\Delta S$ can be negative), provided that this decrease is more than offset by the $\Delta U + P\Delta V$ terms in the definition of ΔG. A simple example is the spontaneous condensation of steam into water. Although the entropy of water is much less than the entropy of steam, the process occurs spontaneously provided that enough heat energy is taken away from the system to keep the temperature from rising as the steam condenses.

A familiar example of free energy changes is provided by an automobile battery. When the battery is fully charged, its Gibbs free energy is at a maximum, and when it is fully discharged (i.e., dead), its Gibbs free energy is at a minimum. The change between these two states is the maximum amount of electrical work that can be extracted from the battery at constant temperature and pressure. The amount of heat absorbed from the environment in order to keep the temperature of the battery constant (represented by the $T\Delta S$ term) and any work done against the atmosphere (represented by the $P\Delta V$ term) are automatically taken into account in the energy balance.

GIBBS FREE ENERGY AND CHEMICAL REACTIONS

All batteries depend on some chemical reaction of the form

$$reactants \rightarrow products$$

for the generation of electricity or on the reverse reaction as the battery is recharged. The change in free energy ($-\Delta G$) for a reaction could be determined by measuring directly the amount of electrical work that the battery could do and then using the equation $W_{max} = -\Delta G$. However, the power of thermodynamics is that $-\Delta G$ can be calculated without having to build every possible battery and measure its performance. If the Gibbs free energies of the individual substances making up a battery are known, then the total free energies of the reactants can be subtracted from the total free energies of the products in order to find the change in Gibbs free energy for the reaction,

$$\Delta G = G_{products} - G_{reactants}. \tag{16}$$

Once the free energies are known for a wide variety of substances, the best candidates for actual batteries can be quickly discerned. In fact, a good part of the practice of thermodynamics is concerned with determining the free energies and other thermodynamic properties of individual substances in order that ΔG for reactions can be calculated under different conditions of temperature and pressure.

In the above discussion, the term *reaction* can be interpreted in the broadest possible sense as any transformation of matter from one form to another. In addition to chemical reactions, a reaction could be something as simple as ice (reactants) turning to liquid water (products), the nuclear reactions taking place in the interior of stars, or elementary particle reactions in the early universe. No matter what the process, the direction of spontaneous change (at constant temperature and pressure) is always in the direction of decreasing free energy.

Enthalpy and the Heat of Reaction

As discussed above, the free energy change $W_{max} = -\Delta G$ corresponds to the maximum possible useful work that can be extracted from a reaction, such as in an electrochemical battery. This represents one extreme limit of a continuous range of possibilities. At the other extreme, for example, battery terminals can be connected directly by a wire and the reaction allowed to proceed freely without doing any useful work. In this case $W' = 0$, and the first law of thermodynamics for the reaction becomes

$$\Delta U = Q_0 - P\Delta V, \qquad (17)$$

where Q_0 is the heat absorbed when the reaction does no useful work and, as before, $P\Delta V$ is the atmospheric work term. The key point is that the quantities ΔU and $P\Delta V$ are exactly the same as in the other limiting case, in which the reaction does maximum work. This follows because these quantities are state functions, which depend only on the initial and final states of a system and not on any path connecting the states. The amount of useful work done just represents different paths connecting the same initial and final states. This leads to the definition of enthalpy (*H*), or heat content, as

$$H = U + PV. \tag{18}$$

Its significance is that, for a reaction occurring freely (i.e., doing no useful work) at constant temperature and pressure, the heat absorbed is

$$Q_0 = \Delta U + P\Delta V = \Delta H, \tag{19}$$

where ΔH is called the heat of reaction. The heat of reaction is easy to measure because it simply represents the amount of heat that is given off if the reactants are mixed together in a beaker and allowed to react freely without doing any useful work.

The above definition for enthalpy and its physical significance allow the equation for ΔG to be written in the particularly illuminating and instructive form

$$\Delta G = \Delta H - T\Delta S. \tag{20}$$

Both terms on the right-hand side represent heats of reaction but under different sets of circumstances. ΔH is the heat of reaction (i.e., the amount of heat absorbed from the surroundings in order to hold the temperature constant) when the reaction does no useful work, and $T\Delta S$ is the heat of reaction when the reaction does maximum useful work in an electrochemical cell. The (negative) difference between these two heats is exactly the maximum useful work $-\Delta G$ that can be extracted from the reaction. Thus, useful work can be obtained by contriving for a system to extract additional heat from the environment and convert it into work. The difference ΔH - $T\Delta S$ represents the fundamental limitation imposed by the second law of thermodynamics on how much additional heat can be extracted from the environment and converted into useful work for a given reaction mechanism. An electrochemical cell (such as a car battery) is a contrivance by means of which a reaction can be made to do the maximum possible work against an opposing electromotive force, and hence the reaction literally becomes reversible in the sense that a slight increase in the opposing voltage will cause the direction of the reaction to reverse and the cell to start charging up instead of discharging.

As a simple example, consider a reaction in which water turns reversibly into steam by boiling. To make the reaction reversible, suppose that the mixture of water and steam is contained in a cylinder with a movable piston and held at the boiling point of 373 K (100 °C) at 1 atmosphere pressure by a heat reservoir. The enthalpy change is ΔH = 40.65 kilojoules per mole, which is the latent heat of vaporization. The entropy change is

$$\Delta S = {}^{40.65}\!/_{373} = 0.109 \text{ kilojoules per mole·K}, \qquad (21)$$

representing the higher degree of disorder when water evaporates and turns to steam. The Gibbs free energy change is ΔG = ΔH - $T\Delta S$. In this case the Gibbs free energy change is zero because the water and steam are in equilibrium, and no useful work can be extracted from the system (other than work done against the atmosphere). In other words, the Gibbs free energy per molecule of water (also called the chemical potential) is the same for both liquid water and steam, and so water molecules can pass freely from one phase to the other with no change in the total free energy of the system.

I n order to carry through a program of finding the changes in the various thermodynamic functions that accompany reactions—such as entropy, enthalpy, and free energy—it is often useful to know these quantities separately for each of the materials entering into the reaction. For example, if the entropies are known separately for the reactants and products, then the entropy change for the reaction is just the difference

$$\Delta S_{reaction} = S_{products} - S_{reactants}$$

and similarly for the other thermodynamic functions. Furthermore, if the entropy change for a reaction is known under one set of conditions of temperature and pressure, it can be found under other sets of conditions by including the variation of entropy for the reactants and products with temperature or pressure as part of the overall process. For these reasons, scientists and engineers have developed extensive tables of thermodynamic properties for many common substances, together with their rates of change with state variables such as temperature and pressure.

The science of thermodynamics provides a rich variety of formulas and techniques that allow the maximum possible amount of information to be extracted from a limited number of laboratory measurements of the properties of materials. However, as the thermodynamic state of a system depends on several variables—such as temperature, pressure, and volume—in practice it is necessary first to decide how many of these are independent and then to specify what variables are allowed to change while others are held constant. For this reason, the mathematical language of partial differential equations is indispensable to the further elucidation of the subject of thermodynamics.

Of especially critical importance in the application of thermodynamics are the amounts of work required to make substances expand or contract and the amounts of heat required to change the temperature of substances. The first is determined by the equation of state of the substance and the second by its heat capacity. Once these physical properties have been fully characterized, they can be used to calculate other thermodynamic properties, such as the free energy of the substance under various conditions of temperature and pressure.

In what follows, it will often be necessary to consider infinitesimal changes in the parameters specifying the state of a system. The first law of thermodynamics then assumes the differential form $dU = d'Q - d'W$. Because U is a state function, the infinitesimal quantity dU must be an exact differential, which means that its definite integral depends only on the initial and final states of the system. In contrast, the quantities $d'Q$ and $d'W$ are not exact differentials, because their integrals can be evaluated only if the path connecting the initial and final states is specified. The examples to follow will illustrate these rather abstract concepts.

WORK OF EXPANSION AND CONTRACTION

The first task in carrying out the above program is to calculate the amount of work done by a single pure substance when it expands at constant temperature. Unlike the case of a chemical reaction, where the volume can change at constant temperature and pressure because of the liberation of gas, the volume of a single pure substance placed in a cylinder cannot change unless either the pressure or the temperature changes. To calculate the work, suppose that a piston moves by an infinitesimal amount dx. Because pressure is force per unit area, the total restraining force exerted by the piston on the gas is PA, where A is the cross-sectional area of the piston. Thus, the incremental amount of work done is $d'W = PAdx$.

However, Adx can also be identified as the incremental change in the volume (dV) swept out by the head of the piston as it moves. The result is the basic equation $d'W = PdV$ for the incremental work done by a gas when it expands. For a finite change from an initial volume V_i to a final volume V_f, the total work done is given by the integral

$$W = \int_{V_i}^{V_f} PdV. \tag{22}$$

Because P in general changes as the volume V changes, this integral cannot be calculated until P is specified as a function of V; in other words, the path for the process must be specified. This gives precise meaning to the concept that dW is not an exact differential.

EQUATIONS OF STATE

The equation of state for a substance provides the additional information required to calculate the amount of work that the substance does in making a transition from one equilibrium state to another along some specified path. The equation of state is expressed as a functional relationship connecting the various parameters needed to specify the state of the system. The basic concepts apply to all thermodynamic systems, but here, in order to make the discussion specific, a simple gas inside a cylinder with a movable piston will be considered. The equation of state then takes the form of an equation relating P, V, and T, such that if any two are specified, the third is determined. In the limit of low pressures and high temperatures, where the molecules of the gas move almost independently of one another, all gases obey an equation of state known as the ideal gas law: $PV = nRT$, where n is the number of moles of the gas and R is the universal gas constant, 8.3145 joules per K. In the International System of Units, energy is measured in joules, volume in cubic metres (m^3), force in newtons (N), and pressure in pascals (Pa), where 1 Pa = 1 N/m^2. A force of one newton moving through a distance of one metre does one joule of work. Thus, both the products PV and RT have the dimensions of work (energy). A P-V diagram would show the equation of state in graphical form for several different temperatures.

To illustrate the path-dependence of the work done, consider three processes connecting the same initial and final states. The temperature is the same for both states, but, in going from state i to state f, the gas expands from V_i to V_f (doing work), and the pressure falls from P_i to P_f. According to the definition of the integral in equation (22), the work done is the area under the curve (or straight line) for each of the three processes. For processes I and III the areas are rectangles, and so the work done is

$$W_{\mathrm{I}} = P_i(V_f - V_i) \qquad (23)$$

and

$$W_{\mathrm{III}} = P_f(V_f - V_i), \qquad (24)$$

respectively. Process II is more complicated because P changes continuously as V changes. However, T remains constant, and so one can use the equation of state to substitute $P = nRT/V$ in equation (22) to obtain

$$W_{\mathrm{II}} = \int_{V_i}^{V_f} \frac{nRT}{V} dV = nRT \ln \frac{V_f}{V_i} \qquad (25)$$

or, because

$$P_i V_i = nRT = P_f V_f \qquad (26)$$

for an (ideal gas) isothermal process,

$$W_{\mathrm{II}} = P_i V_i \ln \frac{V_f}{V_i} = P_f V_f \ln \frac{V_f}{V_i}. \qquad (27)$$

W_{II} is thus the work done in the reversible isothermal expansion of an ideal gas. The amount of work is clearly different in each of the three cases. For a cyclic process the net work done equals the area enclosed by the complete cycle.

HEAT CAPACITY AND SPECIFIC HEAT

As shown originally by Count Rumford, there is an equivalence between heat (measured in calories) and mechanical work (measured in joules) with a definite conversion factor between the two. The conversion factor, known as the mechanical equivalent of heat, is 1 calorie = 4.184 joules. (There are several slightly different definitions in use for the calorie. The calorie used by nutritionists is actually a kilocalorie.) In order to have a consistent set of units, both heat and work will be expressed in the same units of joules.

The amount of heat that a substance absorbs is connected to its temperature change via its molar specific heat c, defined to be the amount of heat required to change the temperature of 1 mole of the substance by 1 K. In other words, c is the constant of proportionality relating the heat absorbed ($d'Q$) to the temperature change (dT) according to $d'Q = nc\, dT$, where n is the number of moles. For example, it takes approximately 1 calorie of heat to increase the temperature of 1 gram of water by 1 K. Since there are 18 grams of water in 1 mole, the molar heat capacity of water is 18 calories per K, or about 75 joules per K. The total heat capacity C for n moles is defined by $C = nc$.

However, since $d'Q$ is not an exact differential, the heat absorbed is path-dependent and the path must be specified, especially for gases where the thermal expansion is significant. Two common ways of specifying the path are either the constant-pressure path or the constant-volume path. The two different kinds of specific heat are called c_p and c_V respectively, where the subscript denotes the quantity that is being held constant. It should not be surprising that c_p is always greater than c_V, because the substance must do work against the surrounding atmosphere as it expands upon heating at constant pressure but not at constant volume. In fact, this difference was used by the 19th-century German physicist Julius

Robert von Mayer to estimate the mechanical equivalent of heat.

HEAT CAPACITY AND INTERNAL ENERGY

The goal in defining heat capacity is to relate changes in the internal energy to measured changes in the variables that characterize the states of the system. For a system consisting of a single pure substance, the only kind of work it can do is atmospheric work, and so the first law reduces to

$$dU = d'Q - P\,dV. \tag{28}$$

Suppose now that U is regarded as being a function $U(T, V)$ of the independent pair of variables T and V. The differential quantity dU can always be expanded in terms of its partial derivatives according to

$$dU = \left(\frac{\partial U}{\partial T}\right)_V dT + \left(\frac{\partial U}{\partial V}\right)_T dV \tag{29}$$

where the subscripts denote the quantity being held constant when calculating derivatives. Substituting this equation into $dU = d'Q - P\,dV$ then yields the general expression

$$d'Q = \left(\frac{\partial U}{\partial T}\right)_V dT + \left[P + \left(\frac{\partial U}{\partial V}\right)_T\right] dV \tag{30}$$

for the path-dependent heat. The path can now be specified in terms of the independent variables T and V. For a temperature change at constant volume, $dV = 0$ and, by definition of heat capacity,

$$d'Q_V = C_V\,dT. \tag{31}$$

The above equation then gives immediately

$$C_V = \left(\frac{\partial U}{\partial T}\right)_V \qquad (32)$$

for the heat capacity at constant volume, showing that the change in internal energy at constant volume is due entirely to the heat absorbed.

To find a corresponding expression for C_P, one need only change the independent variables to T and P and substitute the expansion

$$dV = \left(\frac{\partial V}{\partial T}\right)_P dT + \left(\frac{\partial V}{\partial P}\right)_T dP \qquad (33)$$

for dV in equation (28) and correspondingly for dU to obtain

$$d'Q = \left[\left(\frac{\partial U}{\partial T}\right)_P + P\left(\frac{\partial V}{\partial T}\right)_P\right]dT + \left[\left(\frac{\partial U}{\partial P}\right)_T + P\left(\frac{\partial V}{\partial P}\right)_T\right]dP. \qquad (34)$$

For a temperature change at constant pressure, $dP = 0$, and, by definition of heat capacity, $d'Q = C_P\,dT$, resulting in

$$C_P = C_V + \left[P + \left(\frac{\partial U}{\partial V}\right)_T\right]\left(\frac{\partial V}{\partial T}\right)_P. \qquad (35)$$

The two additional terms beyond C_V have a direct physical meaning. The term

$$P\left(\frac{\partial V}{\partial T}\right)_P$$

represents the additional atmospheric work that the system does as it undergoes thermal expansion at constant pressure, and the second term involving

$$\left(\frac{\partial U}{\partial V}\right)_T$$

represents the internal work that must be done to pull the system apart against the forces of attraction between the molecules of the substance (internal stickiness). Because there is no internal stickiness for an ideal gas, this term is zero, and, from the ideal gas law, the remaining partial derivative is

$$P\left(\frac{\partial V}{\partial T}\right)_P = nR \tag{36}$$

With these substitutions the equation for C_P becomes simply

$$C_P = C_V + nR \tag{37}$$

or

$$c_P = c_V + R \tag{38}$$

for the molar specific heats. For example, for a monatomic ideal gas (such as helium), $c_V = 3R/2$ and $c_P = 5R/2$ to a good approximation. $c_V T$ represents the amount of translational kinetic energy possessed by the atoms of an ideal gas as they bounce around randomly inside their container. Diatomic molecules (such as oxygen) and polyatomic molecules (such as water) have additional rotational motions that also store thermal energy in their kinetic energy of rotation. Each additional degree of freedom contributes an additional amount R to c_V. Because diatomic molecules can rotate about two axes and polyatomic molecules can rotate about three axes, the values of c_V increase to $5R/2$ and $3R$ respectively, and c_p correspondingly increases to $7R/2$ and $4R$. (c_V and c_p increase still further at high temperatures because of vibrational degrees of freedom.) For a real gas such as water vapour, these values are only approximate, but they give the correct order of magnitude. For example, the correct values are c_p = 37.468 joules per K (i.e., $4.5R$) and c_p - c_V = 9.443 joules per K (i.e., $1.14R$) for water vapour at 100 °C and 1 atmosphere pressure.

ENTROPY AS AN EXACT DIFFERENTIAL

Because the quantity $dS = d'Q_{max}/T$ is an exact differential, many other important relationships connecting the thermodynamic properties of substances can be derived. For example, with the substitutions $d'Q = T\,dS$ and $d'W = P\,dV$, the differential form ($dU = d'Q - d'W$) of the first law of thermodynamics becomes (for a single pure substance)

$$dU = T\,dS - P\,dV. \qquad (39)$$

The advantage gained by the above formula is that dU is now expressed entirely in terms of state functions in place of the path-dependent quantities $d'Q$ and $d'W$. This change has the very important mathematical implication that the appropriate independent variables are S and V in place of T and V, respectively, for internal energy.

This replacement of T by S as the most appropriate independent variable for the internal energy of substances is the single most valuable insight provided by the combined first and second laws of thermodynamics. With U regarded as a function $U(S, V)$, its differential dU is

$$dU = \left(\frac{\partial U}{\partial S}\right)_V dS + \left(\frac{\partial U}{\partial V}\right)_S dV. \tag{40}$$

A comparison with the preceding equation shows immediately that the partial derivatives are

$$\left(\frac{\partial U}{\partial S}\right)_V = T \text{ and } \left(\frac{\partial U}{\partial V}\right)_S = -P. \tag{41}$$

Furthermore, the cross partial derivatives,

$$\left(\frac{\partial^2 U}{\partial V \partial S}\right) = \left(\frac{\partial T}{\partial V}\right)_S \text{ and } \left(\frac{\partial^2 U}{\partial S \partial V}\right) = -\left(\frac{\partial P}{\partial S}\right)_V. \tag{42}$$

must be equal because the order of differentiation in calculating the second derivatives of U does not matter. Equating the right-hand sides of the above pair of equations then yields

$$\left(\frac{\partial T}{\partial V}\right)_S = -\left(\frac{\partial P}{\partial S}\right)_V. \tag{43}$$

This is one of four Maxwell relations (the others will follow shortly). They are all extremely useful in that the quantity on the right-hand side is virtually impossible to measure directly, while the quantity on the left-hand side is easily measured in the laboratory. For the present case one simply measures the adiabatic variation of temperature with volume in an insulated cylinder so that there is no heat flow (constant S).

The other three Maxwell relations follow by similarly considering the differential expressions for the thermodynamic potentials $F(T, V)$, $H(S, P)$, and $G(T, P)$, with independent variables as indicated. The results are

$$\left(\frac{\partial P}{\partial T}\right)_V = \left(\frac{\partial S}{\partial V}\right)_T, \left(\frac{\partial V}{\partial S}\right)_P = \left(\frac{\partial T}{\partial P}\right)_S, \text{ and } \left(\frac{\partial V}{\partial T}\right)_P = -\left(\frac{\partial S}{\partial P}\right)_T. \quad (44)$$

As an example of the use of these equations, equation (35) for $C_P - C_V$ contains the partial derivative

$$\left(\frac{\partial U}{\partial V}\right)_T$$

which vanishes for an ideal gas and is difficult to evaluate directly from experimental data for real substances. The general properties of partial derivatives can first be used to write it in the form

$$\left(\frac{\partial U}{\partial V}\right)_T = \left(\frac{\partial U}{\partial V}\right)_S + \left(\frac{\partial U}{\partial S}\right)_V\left(\frac{\partial S}{\partial V}\right)_T. \quad (45)$$

Combining this with equation (41) for the partial derivatives together with the first of the Maxwell equations from equation (44) then yields the desired result

$$\left(\frac{\partial U}{\partial V}\right)_T = -P + T\left(\frac{\partial P}{\partial T}\right)_V. \quad (46)$$

The quantity

$$\left(\frac{\partial P}{\partial T}\right)_V$$

comes directly from differentiating the equation of state. For an ideal gas

$$\left(\frac{\partial P}{\partial T}\right)_V = \frac{nR}{V} = \frac{P}{T},\qquad (47)$$

and so

$$\left(\frac{\partial U}{\partial V}\right)_T$$

is zero as expected. The departure of

$$\left(\frac{\partial U}{\partial V}\right)_T$$

from zero reveals directly the effects of internal forces between the molecules of the substance and the work that must be done against them as the substance expands at constant temperature.

THE CLAUSIUS-CLAPEYRON EQUATION

Phase changes, such as the conversion of liquid water to steam, provide an important example of a system in which there is a large change in internal energy with volume at constant temperature. Suppose that the cylinder contains both water and steam in equilibrium with each other at pressure P, and the cylinder is held at constant temperature T. The pressure remains equal to the vapour pressure P_{vap} as the piston moves up, as long as both phases remain present. All that happens is that more water turns to steam, and the heat reservoir must supply the latent heat of vaporization, $\lambda = 40.65$ kilojoules per mole, in order to keep the temperature constant.

The results of the preceding section can be applied now to find the variation of the boiling point of water with pressure. Suppose that as the piston moves up, 1 mole of water turns to steam. The change in volume inside the cylinder is then $\Delta V = V_{gas} - V_{liquid}$, where $V_{gas} = 30.143$ litres is the volume of 1 mole of steam at 100 °C, and $V_{liquid} = 0.0188$ litre is the volume of 1 mole of water. By the first law of thermodynamics, the change in internal energy ΔU for the finite process at constant P and T is $\Delta U = \lambda - P\Delta V$.

The variation of U with volume at constant T for the complete system of water plus steam is thus

$$\left(\frac{\partial U}{\partial V}\right)_T = \frac{\Delta U}{\Delta V} = \frac{\lambda}{\Delta V} - P. \tag{48}$$

A comparison with equation (46) then yields the equation

$$\left(\frac{\partial P}{\partial T}\right)_V = \frac{\lambda}{\Delta V}. \tag{49}$$

However, for the present problem, P is the vapour pressure P_{vapour}, which depends only on T and is independent of V. The partial derivative is then identical to the total derivative

$$\frac{dP_{vapour}}{dT}, \tag{50}$$

giving the Clausius-Clapeyron equation

$$\left(\frac{\partial P}{\partial T}\right)_V = \frac{\lambda}{\Delta V}. \tag{51}$$

This equation is very useful because it gives the variation with temperature of the pressure at which water and steam are in equilibrium—i.e., the boiling temperature. An approximate but even more useful version of it can be obtained by neglecting V_{liquid} in comparison with V_{gas} and using

$$V_{gas} = \frac{RT}{P_{vapour}} \tag{52}$$

from the ideal gas law. The resulting differential equation can be integrated to give

$$\frac{1}{T} = \frac{1}{T_0} + \frac{R}{\lambda} \ln \frac{P_0}{P}. \tag{53}$$

For example, at the top of Mount Everest, atmospheric pressure is about 30 percent of its value at sea level. Using the values $R = 8.3145$ joules per K and $\lambda = 40.65$ kilojoules per mole, the above equation gives $T = 342$ K (69 °C) for the boiling temperature of water, which is barely enough to make tea.

CHAPTER 3
THE LAWS OF
FORCE AND MOTION

Mechanics is the science concerned with the motion of bodies under the action of forces, including the special case in which a body remains at rest. Of first concern in the problem of motion are the forces that bodies exert on one another. This leads to the study of such topics as gravitation, electricity, and magnetism, according to the nature of the forces involved. Given the forces, one can seek the manner in which bodies move under the action of forces; this is the subject matter of mechanics proper.

Historically, mechanics was among the first of the exact sciences to be developed. Its internal beauty as a mathematical discipline and its early remarkable success in accounting in quantitative detail for the motions of the Moon, Earth, and other planetary bodies had enormous influence on philosophical thought and provided impetus for the systematic development of science into the 20th century.

Mechanics may be divided into three branches: statics, which deals with forces acting on and in a body at rest; kinematics, which describes the possible motions of a body or system of bodies; and kinetics, which attempts to explain or predict the motion that will occur in a given situation. Alternatively, mechanics may be divided according to the kind of system studied. The simplest mechanical system is the particle, defined as a body so small that its shape and internal structure are of no consequence in the given problem. More complicated is the motion of a system of two or more particles that exert forces on one another and possibly undergo forces exerted by bodies outside of the system.

Classical mechanics deals with the motion of bodies under the influence of forces or with the equilibrium of bodies when all forces are balanced. The subject may be thought of as the elaboration and application of basic postulates first enunciated by Isaac Newton in his *Philosophiae Naturalis Principia Mathematica* (1687), commonly known as the *Principia*. These postulates, called Newton's laws of motion, are set forth below. They may be used to predict with great precision a wide variety of phenomena ranging from the motion of individual particles to the interactions of highly complex systems.

In the framework of modern physics, classical mechanics can be understood to be an approximation arising out of the more profound laws of quantum mechanics and the theory of relativity. However, that view of the subject's place greatly undervalues its importance in forming the context, language, and intuition of modern science and scientists. Our present-day view of the world and man's place in it is firmly rooted in classical mechanics. Moreover, many ideas and results of classical mechanics survive and play an important part in the new physics.

The central concepts in classical mechanics are force, mass, and motion. Neither force nor mass is very clearly defined by Newton, and both have been the subject of much philosophical speculation since Newton. Both of them are best known by their effects. Mass is a measure of the tendency of a body to resist changes in its state of motion. Forces, on the other hand, accelerate bodies, which is to say, they change the state of motion of bodies to which they are applied. The interplay of these effects is the principal theme of classical mechanics.

Although Newton's laws focus attention on force and mass, three other quantities take on special importance because their total amount never changes. These three quantities are energy, (linear) momentum, and angular momentum. Any one of these can be shifted from one body or system of bodies to another. In addition, energy may change form while associated with a single system, appearing as kinetic energy, the energy of motion; potential energy, the energy of position; heat, or internal energy, associated with the random motions of the atoms or molecules composing any real body; or any combination of the three. Nevertheless, the total energy, momentum, and angular momentum in the universe never changes. This fact is expressed in physics by saying that energy, momentum, and angular momentum are conserved. These three conservation laws arise out of Newton's laws, but Newton himself did not express them. They had to be discovered later.

It is a remarkable fact that, although Newton's laws are no longer considered to be fundamental, nor even exactly correct, the three conservation laws derived from his laws—the conservation of energy, momentum, and angular momentum—remain exactly true even in quantum mechanics and relativity. In fact, in modern physics, force is no longer a central concept, and mass is only one of a number of attributes of matter. Energy, momentum, and angular momentum, however, still firmly hold centre stage. The continuing importance of these ideas inherited from classical mechanics may help to explain why this subject retains such great importance in science today.

ORIGINS AND FOUNDATIONS

The discovery of classical mechanics was made necessary by the publication, in 1543, of the book *De revolutionibus orbium coelestium libri VI* ("Six Books Concerning the Revolutions of the Heavenly Orbs") by the Polish astronomer Nicolaus Copernicus. The book was about revolutions, real ones in the heavens, and it sparked the metaphorically named scientific revolution that culminated in Newton's *Principia* about 150 years later. The scientific revolution would change forever how people think about the universe.

In his book, Copernicus pointed out that the calculations needed to predict the positions of the planets in the night sky would be somewhat simplified if the Sun, rather than Earth, were taken to be the centre of the universe (by which he meant what is now called the solar system). Among the many problems posed by Copernicus's book was an important and legitimate scientific question: if Earth is hurtling through space and spinning on its axis as Copernicus's model prescribed, why is the motion not apparent?

To the casual observer, Earth certainly seems to be solidly at rest. Scholarly thought about the universe in the centuries before Copernicus was largely dominated by the philosophy of Plato and Aristotle. According to Aristotelian science, the Earth was the centre of the universe. The four elements—earth, water, air, and fire— were naturally disposed in concentric spheres, with earth at the centre, surrounded respectively by water, air, and fire. Outside these were the crystal spheres on which the heavenly bodies rotated. Heavy, earthy objects fell because they sought their natural place. Smoke would rise through air, and bubbles through water for the same reason. These were natural motions. All other kinds of motion were violent motion and required a proximate cause. For example, an oxcart would not move without the help of an ox.

When Copernicus displaced Earth from the centre of the universe, he tore the heart out of Aristotelian mechanics, but he did not suggest how it might be replaced. Thus, for those who wished to promote Copernicus's ideas, the question of why the motion of Earth is not noticed took on a special urgency. Without suitable explanation,

Copernicanism was a violation not only of Aristotelian philosophy but also of plain common sense.

The solution to the problem was discovered by the Italian mathematician and scientist Galileo Galilei. Inventing experimental physics as he went along, Galileo studied the motion of balls rolling on inclined planes. He noticed that, if a ball rolled down one plane and up another, it would seek to regain its initial height above the ground, regardless of the inclines of the two planes. That meant, he reasoned, that, if the second plane were not inclined at all but were horizontal instead, the ball, unable to regain its original height, would keep rolling forever. From this observation he deduced that bodies do not need a proximate cause to stay in motion. Instead, a body moving in the horizontal direction would tend to stay in motion unless something interfered with it. This is the reason that Earth's motion is not apparent; the surface of Earth and everything on and around it are always in motion together and therefore only seem to be at rest.

This observation, which was improved upon by the French philosopher and scientist René Descartes, who altered the concept to apply to motion in a straight line, would ultimately become Newton's first law, or the law of inertia. However, Galileo's experiments took him far beyond even this fundamental discovery. Timing the rate of descent of the balls (by means of precision water clocks and other ingenious contrivances) and imagining what would happen if experiments could be carried out in the absence of air resistance, he deduced that freely falling bodies would be uniformly accelerated at a rate independent of their mass. Moreover, he understood that the motion of any projectile was the consequence of simultaneous and independent inertial motion in the horizontal direction and falling motion in the vertical direction. In his book *Dialogues Concerning the Two New Sciences* (1638), Galileo wrote,

> *It has been observed that missiles and projectiles describe a curved path of some sort; however, no one has pointed out the fact that this path is a parabola. But this and other facts, not few in number or less worth knowing, I have succeeded in proving . . .*

Just as Galileo boasted, his studies would encompass many aspects of what is now known as classical mechanics, including not only discussions of the law of falling bodies and projectile motion but also an analysis of the pendulum, an example of harmonic motion. His studies fall into the branch of classical mechanics known as kinematics, or the description of motion. Although Galileo and others tried to formulate explanations of the causes of motion, the focus of the field termed dynamics, none would succeed before Newton.

Galileo's fame during his own lifetime rested not so much on his discoveries in mechanics as on his observations of the heavens, which he made with the newly invented telescope about 1610. What he saw there, particularly the moons of Jupiter, either prompted or confirmed his embrace of the Copernican system. At the time, Copernicus had few other followers in Europe. Among those few, however, was the brilliant German astronomer and mathematician Johannes Kepler.

Kepler devoted much of his scientific career to elucidating the Copernican system. Although Copernicus had put the Sun at the centre of the solar system, his astronomy was still rooted in the Platonic ideal of circular motion. Before Copernicus, astronomers had tried to account for the observed motions of heavenly bodies by imagining that they rotated on crystal spheres centred on Earth. This picture worked well enough for the stars but not for the planets. To "save the appearances" (fit the observations) an elaborate system emerged of circular orbits, called epicycles, on top of circular orbits. This system of astronomy culminated with the *Almagest* of Ptolemy, who worked in Alexandria in the 2nd century CE. The Copernican innovation simplified the system somewhat, but Copernicus's astronomical tables were still based on circular orbits and epicycles. Kepler set out to find further simplifications that would help to establish the validity of the Copernican system.

In the course of his investigations, Kepler discovered the three laws of planetary motion that are still named for him. Kepler's first law says that the orbits of the planets are ellipses, with the Sun at one focus. This observation swept epicycles out of astronomy. His second law stated that, as the planet moved through its orbit, a line joining it to the Sun would sweep out equal areas in equal times. For Kepler, this law was merely a rule that helped him make precise calculations for his astronomical tables. Later, however, it would be understood to be a direct consequence of the law of conservation of angular momentum. Kepler's third law stated that the period of a planet's orbit depended only on its distance from the Sun. In particular, the square of the period is proportional to the cube of the semimajor axis of its elliptical orbit. This observation would suggest to Newton the inverse-square law of universal gravitational attraction.

By the middle of the 17th century, the work of Galileo, Kepler, Descartes, and others had set the stage for Newton's grand synthesis. Newton is thought to have made many of his great discoveries at the age of 23, when in 1665–66 he retreated from the University of Cambridge to his Lincolnshire home to escape from the bubonic plague. However, he chose not to publish his results until the *Principia* emerged 20 years later. In the *Principia*, Newton set out his basic postulates concerning force, mass, and motion. In addition to these, he introduced the universal force of gravity, which, acting instantaneously through space, attracted every bit of matter in the universe to every other bit of matter, with a strength proportional to their masses and inversely proportional to the square of the distance between them. These principles, taken together, accounted not only for Kepler's three laws and Galileo's falling bodies and projectile motions but also for other phenomena, including the precession of the equinoxes, the oscillations of the pendulum, the speed of sound in air, and much more. The effect of Newton's *Principia* was to replace the by-then discredited Aristotelian worldview with a new, coherent view of the universe and how it worked. The way it worked is what is now referred to as classical mechanics.

UNITS AND DIMENSIONS

Quantities have both dimensions, which are an expression of their fundamental nature, and units, which are chosen by convention to express magnitude or size. For example, a series of events have a certain duration in time. Time is the dimension of the duration. The duration might be expressed as 30 minutes or as half an hour. Minutes and hours are among the units in which time may be expressed. One can compare quantities of the same dimensions, even if they are expressed in different units (an hour is longer than a minute). Quantities of different dimensions cannot be compared with one another.

The fundamental dimensions used in mechanics are time, mass, and length. Symbolically, these are written as t, m, and l, respectively. The study of electromagnetism adds an additional fundamental dimension, electric charge, or q. Other quantities have dimensions compounded of these. For example, speed has the dimensions distance divided by time, which can be written as l/t, and volume has the dimensions distance cubed, or l^3. Some quantities, such as temperature, have units but are not compounded of fundamental dimensions.

There are also important dimensionless numbers in nature, such as the number $\pi = 3.14159$ .... Dimensionless numbers may be constructed as ratios of quantities having the same dimension. Thus, the number π is the ratio of the circumference of a circle (a length) to its diameter (another length). Dimensionless numbers have the advantage that they are always the same, regardless of what set of units is being used.

Governments have traditionally been responsible for establishing and enforcing standard units for the sake of orderly commerce, navigation, science, and, of course, taxation. Today all such units are established by international treaty and revised every few years in light of scientific findings. The units used for most scientific measurements are those designated the International System of Units (Système International d'Unités), or SI for short. They are based on the metric system, first adopted officially by France in 1795. Other units, such as those of the British engineering system, are still in use in some places, but these are now defined in terms of the SI units.

The fundamental unit of length is the metre. A metre used to be defined as the distance between two scratch marks on a metal bar kept in Paris, but it is now much more precisely defined as the distance that light travels in a certain time interval (1/299,792,458 of a second). By contrast, in the British system, units of length have a clear human bias: the foot, the inch (the first joint of the thumb), the yard (distance from nose to outstretched fingertip), and the mile (one thousand standard paces of a Roman legion). Each of these is today defined as some fraction or multiple of a metre (one yard is nearly equal to one metre). In the

SI or the metric system, lengths are expressed as decimal fractions or multiples of a metre (a millimetre = one-thousandth of a metre; one centimetre = one-hundredth of a metre; one kilometre = one thousand metres).

Times longer than one second are expressed in the units seconds, minutes, hours, days, weeks, and years. Times shorter than one second are expressed as decimal fractions (a millisecond = one-thousandth of a second, a microsecond = one-millionth of a second, and so on). The fundamental unit of time (i.e., the definition of one second) is today based on the intrinsic properties of certain kinds of atoms (an excitation frequency of the isotope cesium-133).

Units of mass are also defined in a way that is technically sound, but in common usage they are the subject of some confusion because they are easily confused with units of weight, which is a different physical quantity. The weight of an object is the consequence of Earth's gravity operating on its mass. Thus, the mass of a given object is the same everywhere, but its weight varies slightly if it is moved about the surface of Earth, and it would change a great deal if it were moved to the surface of another planet. Also, weight and mass do not have the same dimensions (weight has the dimensions ml/t^2). The Constitution of the United States, which calls on the government to establish uniform "weights and measures," is oblivious to this distinction, as are merchants the world over, who measure the weight of bread or produce but sell it in units of kilograms, the SI unit of mass. (The kilogram is equal to 1,000 grams; 1 gram is the mass of 1 cubic centimetre of water—under appropriate conditions of temperature and pressure.)

VECTORS

The equations of mechanics are typically written in terms of Cartesian coordinates. At a certain time t, the position of a particle may be specified by giving its coordinates $x(t)$, $y(t)$, and $z(t)$ in a particular Cartesian frame of reference. However, a different observer of the same particle might choose a differently oriented set of mutually perpendicular axes, say, x', y', and z'. The motion of the particle is then described by the first observer in terms of the rate of change of $x(t)$, $y(t)$, and $z(t)$, while the second observer would discuss the rates of change of $x'(t)$, $y'(t)$, and $z'(t)$. That is, both observers see the same particle executing the same motion and obeying the same laws, but they describe the situation with different equations. This awkward situation may be avoided by means of a mathematical construction called a vector. Although vectors are mathematically simple and extremely useful in discussing mechanics, they were not developed in their modern form until late in the 19th century, when J. Willard Gibbs and Oliver Heaviside (of the United States and Britain, respectively) each applied vector analysis in order to help express the new laws of electromagnetism proposed by James Clerk Maxwell.

A vector is a quantity that has both magnitude and direction. It is typically represented symbolically by an arrow in the proper direction, whose length is proportional to the magnitude of the vector. Although a vector has magnitude and direction, it does not have position. A vector is not altered if it is displaced parallel to itself as long as its length is not changed.

By contrast to a vector, an ordinary quantity having magnitude but not direction is known as a scalar. In printed works vectors are often represented by boldface letters such as A or X, and scalars are represented by lightface letters, A or X. The magnitude of a vector, denoted $|A|$, is itself a scalar—i.e., $|A| = A$.

Because vectors are different from ordinary (i.e., scalar) quantities, all mathematical operations involving vectors must be carefully defined. Addition, subtraction, three kinds of multiplication, and differentiation will be discussed here. There is no mathematical operation that corresponds to division by a vector.

If vector A is added to vector B, the result is another vector, C, written $A + B = C$. The operation is performed by displacing B so that it begins where A ends. C is then the vector that starts where A begins and ends where B ends.

Vector addition is defined to have the (nontrivial) property $A + B = B + A$. There do exist quantities having magnitude and direction that do not obey this requirement. An example is finite rotations in space. Two finite rotations of a body about different axes do not necessarily result in the same orientation if performed in the opposite order.

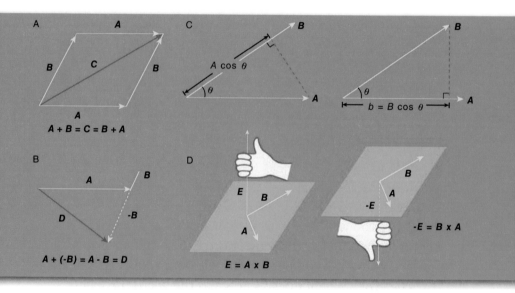

(A) The vector sum **C** = **A** + **B** = **B** + **A**. (B) The vector difference **A** + (-**B**) = **A** - **B** = **D**. (C, left) A cos θ is the component of **A** along **B** and (right) B cos θ is the component of **B** along **A**. (D, left) The right-hand rule used to find the direction of **E** = **A** × **B** and (right) the right-hand rule used to find the direction of -**E** = **B** × **A**. Copyright Encyclopædia Britannica; rendering for this edition by Rosen Educational Services

Vector subtraction is defined by $A - B = A + (-B)$, where the vector $-B$ has the same magnitude as B but the opposite direction.

A vector may be multiplied by a scalar. Thus, for example, the vector $2A$ has the same direction as A but is twice as long. If the scalar has dimensions, the resulting vector still has the same direction as the original one, but the two cannot be compared in magnitude. For example, a particle moving with constant velocity v suffers a displacement s in time t given by $s = vt$. The vector v has been multiplied by the scalar t to give a new vector, s, which has the same direction as v but cannot be compared to v in magnitude (a displacement of one metre is neither bigger nor smaller than a velocity of one metre per second). This is a typical example of a phenomenon that might be represented by different equations in differently oriented Cartesian coordinate systems but that has a single vector equation (for all observers not moving with respect to one another).

The dot product (also known as the scalar product, or sometimes the inner product) is an operation that combines two vectors to form a scalar. The operation is written $A \cdot B$. If θ is the (smaller) angle between A and B, then the result of the operation is $A \cdot B = AB \cos \theta$. The dot product measures the extent to which two vectors are parallel. It may be thought of as multiplying the magnitude of one vector (either one) by the projection of the other upon it. If the two vectors are perpendicular, the dot product is zero.

The cross product (also known as the vector product) combines two vectors to form another vector, perpendicular to the plane of the original vectors. The operation is written $A \times B$. If θ is the (smaller) angle between A and B, then $|A \times B| = AB \sin \theta$. The direction of $A \times B$ is given by the right-hand rule: if the fingers of the right hand are made to rotate from A through θ to B, the thumb points in the direction of $A \times B$. The cross product is zero if the two vectors are parallel, and it is maximum in magnitude if they are perpendicular.

The derivative, or rate of change, of a vector is defined in perfect analogy to the derivative of a scalar: if the vector A changes with time t, then

$$\frac{dA}{dt} = \lim_{\Delta t \to 0} \frac{A(t + \Delta t) - A(t)}{\Delta t}. \qquad (1)$$

Before going to the limit on the right-hand side of equation (1), the operations described are vector subtraction $[A(t + \Delta t) - A(t)]$ and scalar multiplication (by $1/\Delta t$). The result, dA/dt, is therefore itself a vector. Notice that the difference between two vectors, in this case $A(t + \Delta t) - A(t)$, may be in quite a different direction than either of the vectors from which it is formed, here $A(t + \Delta t)$ and $A(t)$. As a result, dA/dt may be in a different direction than $A(t)$.

NEWTON'S LAWS OF MOTION AND EQUILIBRIUM

In his *Principia*, Newton reduced the basic principles of mechanics to three laws:

- Every body continues in its state of rest or of uniform motion in a straight line, unless it is compelled to change that state by forces impressed upon it.
- The change of motion of an object is proportional to the force impressed and is made in the direction of the straight line in which the force is impressed.

- To every action there is always opposed an equal reaction; or, the mutual actions of two bodies upon each other are always equal and directed to contrary parts.

Newton's first law is a restatement of the principle of inertia, proposed earlier by Galileo and perfected by Descartes.

The second law is the most important of the three; it may be understood very nearly to summarize all of classical mechanics. Newton used the word "motion" to mean what is today called momentum—that is, the product of mass and velocity, or $p = mv$, where p is the momentum, m the mass, and v the velocity of a body. The second law may then be written in the form of the equation $F = dp/dt$, where F is the force, the time derivative expresses Newton's "change of motion," and the vector form of the equation assures that the change is in the same direction as the force, as the second law requires.

For a body whose mass does not change,

$$\frac{d\boldsymbol{p}}{dt} = m\frac{d\boldsymbol{v}}{dt} = m\boldsymbol{a},$$

where $\boldsymbol{a}$ is the acceleration. Thus, Newton's second law may be put in the following form:

$$F = ma \qquad\qquad (2)$$

It is probably fair to say that equation (2) is the most famous equation in all of physics.

Newton's third law assures that when two bodies interact, regardless of the nature of the interaction, they do not produce a net force acting on the two-body system as a whole. Instead, there is an action and reaction pair of equal and opposite forces, each acting on a different body (action and reaction forces never act on the same body). The third law applies whether the bodies in question are at rest, in uniform motion, or in accelerated motion.

If a body has a net force acting on it, it undergoes accelerated motion in accordance with the second law. If there is no net force acting on a body, either because there are no forces at all or because all forces are precisely balanced by contrary forces, the body does not accelerate and may be said to be in equilibrium. Conversely, a body that is observed not to be accelerated may be deduced to have no net force acting on it.

Consider, for example, a massive object resting on a table. The object is known to be acted on by the gravitational force of Earth; if the table were removed, the object would fall. It follows therefore from the fact that the object does not fall that the table exerts an upward force on the object, equal and opposite to the downward force of gravity. This upward force is not a mere physicist's bookkeeping device but rather a real physical force. The table's surface is slightly deformed by the weight of the object, causing the surface to exert a force analogous to that exerted by a coiled spring.

It is useful to recall the following distinction: the massive object exerts a downward force on the table that is equal and opposite to the upward force exerted by the table (owing to its deformation) on the object. These two forces are an action and reaction pair operating on different bodies (one on the table, the other on the object) as required by Newton's third law. On the other hand, the upward force exerted on the object by the table is balanced by a downward force exerted on the object by Earth's gravity. These two equal and opposite forces, acting on the same body, are not related to or by Newton's third law, but they do produce the equilibrium immobile state of the body.

CHAPTER 4

THE LAWS OF
PARTICLE MOTION

The applications of Newton's laws are wide-ranging. They can explain the motion of a pebble falling to the ground, a pendulum swinging in a grandfather clock, or a planet orbiting a distant star.

MOTION OF A PARTICLE
IN ONE DIMENSION

The simplest problems in mechanics involve a particle moving in one dimension—in other words, on a line. Such problems include those of falling bodies and masses oscillating back and forth.

UNIFORM MOTION

According to Newton's first law (also known as the principle of inertia), a body with no net force acting on it will either remain at rest or continue to move with uniform speed in a straight line, according to its initial condition of motion. In fact, in classical Newtonian mechanics, there is no important distinction between rest and uniform motion in a straight line; they may be regarded as the same state of motion seen by different observers, one moving at the same velocity as the particle, the other moving at constant velocity with respect to the particle.

Although the principle of inertia is the starting point and the fundamental assumption of classical mechanics, it is less than intuitively obvious to the untrained eye. In Aristotelian mechanics, and in ordinary experience, objects that are not being pushed tend to come to rest. The law of inertia was deduced by Galileo from his experiments with balls rolling down inclined planes.

For Galileo, the principle of inertia was fundamental to his central scientific task: he had to explain how it is possible that if Earth is really spinning on its axis and orbiting the Sun we do not sense that motion. The principle of inertia helps to provide the answer: Since we are in motion together with Earth, and our natural tendency is to retain that motion, Earth appears to us to be at rest. Thus, the principle of inertia, far from being a statement of the obvious, was once a central issue of scientific contention. By the time Newton had sorted out all the details, it was possible to account accurately for the small deviations from this picture caused by the fact that the motion of Earth's surface is not uniform motion in a straight line. In the Newtonian formulation, the common observation that bodies that are not pushed tend to come to rest is attributed to the fact that they have unbalanced forces acting on them, such as friction and air resistance.

As has already been stated, a body in motion may be said to have momentum equal to the product of its mass and its velocity. It also has a kind of energy that is due entirely to its motion, called kinetic energy. The kinetic energy of a body of mass m in motion with velocity v is given by

$$K = \frac{1}{2}mv^2. \tag{3}$$

FALLING BODIES AND UNIFORMLY ACCELERATED MOTION

During the 14th century, the French scholar Nicole Oresme studied the mathematical properties of uniformly accelerated motion. He had little interest in whether that kind of motion could be observed in the realm of actual human existence, but he did discover that, if a particle is uniformly accelerated, its speed increases in direct proportion to time, and the distance it traverses is proportional to the square of the time spent accelerating. Two centuries later, Galileo repeated these same mathematical discoveries (perhaps independently) and, just as important, determined that this kind of motion is actually executed by balls rolling down inclined planes. As the incline of the plane increases, the acceleration increases, but the motion continues to be uniformly accelerated. From this observation, Galileo deduced that a body falling freely in the vertical direction would also have uniform acceleration. Even more remarkably, he demonstrated that, in the absence of air resistance, all bodies would fall with the same constant acceleration regardless of their mass. If the constant acceleration of any body dropped near the surface of Earth is expressed as g, the behaviour of a body dropped from rest at height z_0 and time $t = 0$ may be summarized by the following equations:

$$z = z_0 - \frac{1}{2} g t^2,$$ (4)

$$v = g t,$$ (5)

$$a = g,$$ (6)

where z is the height of the body above the surface, v is its speed, and a is its acceleration. These equations of motion hold true until the body actually strikes the surface. The value of g is approximately 9.8 metres per second squared (m/s²).

A body of mass m at a height z_0 above the surface may be said to possess a kind of energy purely by virtue of its position. This kind of energy (energy of position) is called potential energy. The gravitational potential energy is given by

$$U = m g z_0.$$ (7)

Technically, it is more correct to say that this potential energy is a property of the Earth-body system rather than a property of the body itself, but this pedantic distinction can be ignored.

As the body falls to height z less than z_0, its potential energy U converts to kinetic energy $K = \frac{1}{2}mv^2$. Thus, the speed v of the body at any height z is given by solving the equation

$$\frac{1}{2}mv^2 + mgz = mgz_0. \tag{8}$$

Equation (8) is an expression of the law of conservation of energy. It says that the sum of kinetic energy, $\frac{1}{2}mv^2$, and potential energy, mgz, at any point during the fall, is equal to the total initial energy, mgz_0, before the fall began. Exactly the same dependence of speed on height could be deduced from the kinematic equations (4), (5), and (6) above.

In order to reach the initial height z_0, the body had to be given its initial potential energy by some external agency, such as a person lifting it. The process by which a body or a system obtains mechanical energy from outside of itself is called work. The increase of the energy of the body is equal to the work done on it. Work is equal to force times distance.

The force exerted by Earth's gravity on a body of mass m may be deduced from the observation that the body, if released, will fall with acceleration g. Since force is equal to mass times acceleration, the force of gravity is given by $F = mg$. To lift the body to height z_0, an equal and opposite (i.e., upward) force must be exerted through a distance z_0. Thus, the work done is

$$W = Fz_0 = mgz_0, \tag{9}$$

which is equal to the potential energy that results.

If work is done by applying a force to a body that is not being acted upon by an opposing force, the body is accelerated. In this case, the work endows the body with kinetic energy rather than potential energy. The energy that the body gains is equal to the work done on it in either case. It should be noted that work, potential energy, and kinetic energy, all being aspects of the same quantity, must all have the dimensions ml^2/t^2.

SIMPLE HARMONIC OSCILLATIONS

Consider a mass m held in an equilibrium position by springs. The mass may be perturbed by displacing it to the right or left. If x is the displacement of the mass from equilibrium, the springs exert a force F proportional to x, such that

$$F = -kx, \qquad (10)$$

where k is a constant that depends on the stiffness of the springs. Equation (10) is called Hooke's law, and the force

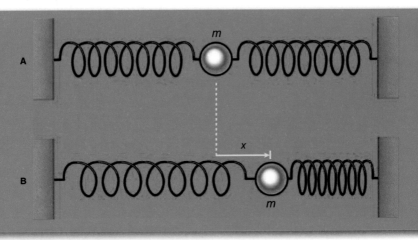

(A) A mass m held in equilibrium by springs. (B) A mass m displaced a distance x. Copyright Encyclopædia Britannica; rendering for this edition by Rosen Educational Services

is called the spring force. If x is positive (displacement to the right), the resulting force is negative (to the left), and vice versa. In other words, the spring force always acts so as to restore mass back toward its equilibrium position. Moreover, the force will produce an acceleration along the x direction given by $a = d^2x/dt^2$. Thus, Newton's second law, $F = ma$, is applied to this case by substituting $-kx$ for F and d^2x/dt^2 for a, giving $-kx = m(d^2x/dt^2)$. Transposing and dividing by m yields the equation

$$a = \frac{d^2x}{dt^2} = -\frac{k}{m}x. \tag{11}$$

Equation (11) gives the derivative—in this case the second derivative—of a quantity x in terms of the quantity itself. Such an equation is called a differential equation, meaning an equation containing derivatives. Much of the ordinary, day-to-day work of theoretical physics consists of solving differential equations. The question is, given equation (11), how does x depend on time?

The answer is suggested by experience. If the mass is displaced and released, it will oscillate back and forth about its equilibrium position. That is, x should be an oscillating function of t, such as a sine wave or a cosine wave. For example, x might obey a behaviour such as

$$x = A \cos \omega t. \tag{12}$$

The mass is initially displaced a distance $x = A$ and released at time $t = 0$. As time goes on, the mass oscillates from A to $-A$ and back to A again in the time it takes ωt to advance by 2π. This time is called T, the period of oscillation, so that $\omega T = 2\pi$, or $T = 2\pi/\omega$. The reciprocal of the period, or the frequency f, in oscillations

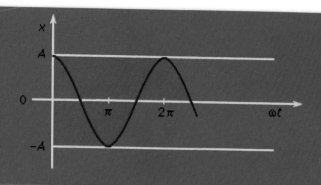

The function x = A *cos* ωt. Copyright Encyclopædia Britannica; rendering for this edition by Rosen Educational Services

per second, is given by $f = 1/T = \omega/2\pi$. The quantity ω is called the angular frequency and is expressed in radians per second.

The choice of equation (12) as a possible kind of behaviour satisfying the differential equation (11) can be tested by substituting it into equation (11). The first derivative of x with respect to t is

$$\frac{dx}{dt} = \frac{d}{dt}(A\cos \omega t)$$
$$= -\omega A \sin \omega t. \tag{13}$$

Differentiating a second time gives

$$\frac{d^2 x}{dt^2} = \frac{d}{dt}\left(\frac{dx}{dt}\right)$$
$$= \frac{d}{dt}(-\omega A \sin \omega t) \tag{14}$$
$$= -\omega^2 A \cos \omega t$$
$$= -\omega^2 x.$$

Equation (14) is the same as equation (11) if

$$\omega^2 = \frac{k}{m}. \tag{15}$$

Thus, subject to this condition, equation (12) is a correct solution to the differential equation. There are other possible correct guesses (e.g., $x = A \sin \omega t$) that differ from this one only in whether the mass is at rest or in motion at the instant $t = 0$.

The mass, as has been shown, oscillates from A to $-A$ and back again. The speed, given by dx/dt, equation (13), is zero at A and $-A$, but has its maximum magnitude, equal to ωA, when x is equal to zero. Physically, after the mass is displaced from equilibrium a distance A to the right, the restoring force F pushes the mass back toward its equilibrium position, causing it to accelerate to the left. When it reaches equilibrium, there is no force acting on it at that instant, but it is moving at speed ωA, and its inertia takes it past the equilibrium position. Before it is stopped it reaches position $-A$, and by this time there is a force acting on it again, pushing it back toward equilibrium.

The whole process, known as simple harmonic motion, repeats itself endlessly with a frequency given by equation (15). Equation (15) means that the stiffer the springs (i.e., the larger k), the higher the frequency (the faster the oscillations). Making the mass greater has exactly the opposite effect, slowing things down.

One of the most important features of harmonic motion is the fact that the frequency of the motion, ω (or f), depends only on the mass and the stiffness of the spring. It does not depend on the amplitude A of the motion. If the amplitude is increased, the mass moves faster, but the time required for a complete round trip remains the same. This fact has profound consequences, governing the nature of music and the principle of accurate timekeeping.

The potential energy of a harmonic oscillator, equal to the work an outside agent must do to push the mass from zero to x, is $U = \frac{1}{2}kx^2$. Thus, the total initial energy in the situation described above is $\frac{1}{2}kA^2$; and since the kinetic energy is always $\frac{1}{2}mv^2$, when the mass is at any point x in the oscillation,

$$\frac{1}{2}mv^2 + \frac{1}{2}kx^2 = \frac{1}{2}kA^2. \tag{16}$$

Equation (16) plays exactly the role for harmonic oscillators that equation (8) does for falling bodies.

It is quite generally true that harmonic oscillations result from disturbing any body or structure from a state of stable mechanical equilibrium. To understand this point, a brief discussion of stability is useful.

Consider a bowl with a marble resting inside, then consider a second, inverted bowl with a marble balanced on top. In both cases, the net force on the marble is zero. The marbles are thus in mechanical equilibrium. However, a small disturbance in the position of the marble balanced on top of the inverted bowl will cause it to roll away and not return. In such a case, the equilibrium is said to be unstable. Conversely, if the marble inside the first bowl is disturbed, gravity acts to push it back toward the bottom of the bowl. The marble inside the bowl is an example of a body in stable equilibrium. If it is disturbed slightly, it executes harmonic oscillations around the bottom of the bowl rather than rolling away.

This argument may be generalized by a simple mathematical argument. Consider a body or structure in mechanical equilibrium, which, when disturbed by a small amount x, finds a force acting on it that is a function of x, $F(x)$. For small x, such a function may be written generally as a power series in x; i.e.,

$$F(x) = F(0) + ax + bx^2 + \cdots, \qquad (17)$$

where $F(0)$ is the value of $F(x)$ when $x = (0)$, and a and b are constants, independent of x, determined by the nature of the system. The statement that the body is in mechanical equilibrium means that $F(0) = 0$, so that no force is acting on the body when it is undisturbed. Since x is small, x^2 is much smaller; thus the term bx^2 and all higher powers may be disregarded. This leaves $F(x) = ax$. Now, if a is positive, a disturbance produces a force in the same direction as the disturbance. This was the case when the marble was balanced on top of the inverted bowl. It describes unstable equilibrium. For the system to be stable, a must be negative. Thus, if $a = -k$, where k is some positive constant, equation (17) becomes $F(x) = -kx$, which is simply Hooke's law, equation (10). As has been described above, any system obeying Hooke's law is a harmonic oscillator.

The generality of this argument accounts for the fact that harmonic oscillators are abundantly observed in common experience. For example, any rigid structure will oscillate at many different harmonic frequencies corresponding to different possible distortions of its equilibrium shape. In addition, music may be produced either by disturbing the equilibrium of a stretched wire or fibre (as in the piano and violin), a stretched membrane (e.g., drums), or a rigid bar (the triangle and the xylophone) or by disturbing the density of an enclosed column of air (as in the trumpet and organ). While a fluid such as air is not rigid, its density is an example of a stable system that obeys Hooke's law and may therefore be set into harmonic oscillations.

All music would be quite different from what it is were it not for the general property of harmonic oscillators that the frequency is independent of the amplitude. Thus, instruments yield the same note (frequency) regardless of how loudly they are played (amplitude), and, equally important, the same note persists as the vibrations die away. This same property of harmonic oscillators is the underlying principle of all accurate timekeeping.

The first precise timekeeping mechanism, whose principles of motion were discovered by Galileo, was the simple pendulum. The accuracy of modern timekeeping has been improved dramatically by the introduction of tiny quartz crystals, whose harmonic oscillations generate electrical signals that may be incorporated into miniaturized circuits in clocks and wristwatches. All harmonic oscillators are natural timekeeping devices because they oscillate at intrinsic natural frequencies independent of amplitude. A given number of complete cycles always corresponds to the same elapsed time. Quartz crystal oscillators make more accurate clocks than pendulums do principally because they oscillate many more times per second.

DAMPED AND FORCED OSCILLATIONS

The simple harmonic oscillations discussed earlier continue forever, at constant amplitude, oscillating between A and $-A$. Common experience indicates that real oscillators behave somewhat differently, however. Harmonic oscillations tend to die away as time goes on. This behaviour, called damping of the oscillations, is produced by forces such as friction and viscosity. These forces are known collectively as dissipative forces because they tend to dissipate the potential and kinetic energies of macroscopic bodies into the energy of the chaotic motion of atoms and molecules known as heat.

Friction and viscosity are complicated phenomena whose effects cannot be represented accurately by a general equation. However, for slowly moving bodies, the dissipative forces may be represented by

$$F_d = -\gamma v, \tag{18}$$

where v is the speed of the body and γ is a constant coefficient, independent of dynamic quantities such as speed or displacement. Equation (18) is most easily understood by an argument analogous to that applied to equation (17) above. F_d is written as a sum of powers of v, or $F_d(v) = F_d(0) + av + bv^2 + \cdots$. When the body is at rest ($v = 0$), no dissipative force is expected because, if there were one, it might set the body into motion. Thus, $F_d(0) = 0$. The next term must be negative since dissipative forces always resist the motion. Thus, $a = -\gamma$ where γ is positive. Since v^2 has the same sign regardless of the direction of the motion, b must equal 0 lest it sometimes contribute a dissipative force in the same direction as the motion. The next term is proportional to v^3, and it and all subsequent terms may be neglected if v is sufficiently small. So, as in equation (17) the power series is reduced to a single term, in this case $F_d = -\gamma v$.

To find the effect of a dissipative force on a harmonic oscillator, a new differential equation must be solved. The net force, or mass times acceleration, written as md^2x/dt^2, is set equal to the sum of the Hooke's law force, $-kx$, and the dissipative force, $-\gamma v = -\gamma dx/dt$. Dividing by m yields

$$\frac{d^2x}{dt^2} = -\frac{k}{m}x - \frac{\gamma}{m}\frac{dx}{dt}. \tag{19}$$

The general solution to equation (19) is given in the form $x = Ce^{-\gamma t/2m}\cos(\omega t + \theta_o)$, where C and θ_o are arbitrary

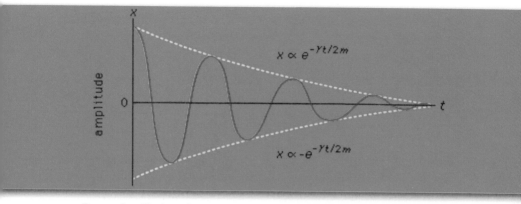

Damped oscillations. Copyright Encyclopædia Britannica; rendering for this edition by Rosen Educational Services

constants determined by the initial conditions. For the case in which $\theta_0 = 0$, the harmonic oscillations die out with time. The amplitude of the oscillations is bounded by an exponentially decreasing function of time (the dashed curves). The characteristic decay time (after which the oscillations are smaller by $1/e$, where e is the base of the natural logarithms $e = 2.718\ldots$) is equal to $2m/\gamma$. The frequency of the oscillations is given by

$$\omega^2 = \frac{k}{m} - \frac{\gamma^2}{4m^2}.\qquad(20)$$

Importantly, this frequency does not change as the oscillations decay.

Equation (20) shows that it is possible, by proper choice of γ, to turn a harmonic oscillator into a system that does not oscillate at all—that is, a system whose natural frequency is $\omega = 0$. Such a system is said to be critically damped. For example, the springs that suspend the body of an automobile cause it to be a natural harmonic oscillator. The shock absorbers of the auto are devices that seek to add just enough dissipative force to make the assembly critically damped. In this way, the passengers need not go through numerous oscillations after each bump in the road.

A simple disturbance can set a harmonic oscillator into motion. Repeated disturbances can increase the amplitude of the oscillations if they are applied in synchrony with the natural frequency. Even a very small disturbance, repeated periodically at just the right frequency, can cause a very large amplitude motion to build up. This phenomenon is known as resonance.

Periodically forced oscillations may be represented mathematically by adding a term of the form $a_0 \sin \omega t$ to the right-hand side of equation (19). This term describes a force applied at frequency ω, with amplitude ma_0. The result of applying such a force is to create a kind of motion that does not need to decay with time, since the energy lost to dissipative processes is replaced, over the course of each cycle, by the driving force. The amplitude of the motion depends on how close the driving frequency ω is to the natural frequency ω_0 of the oscillator. Interestingly, even though dissipation is present, ω_0 is not given by equation (20) but rather by equation (15): $\omega^2_0 = k/m$. In a graph of the amplitude of the steady state motion (i.e., long after the driving force has begun to be applied), the maximum amplitude occurs as expected at $\omega = \omega_0$. The height and width of the resonance curve are governed by the damping coefficient γ. If there were no damping, the maximum amplitude would be infinite. Because small disturbances at every possible frequency are always present in the natural world, every rigid structure would shake itself to pieces if not for the presence of internal damping.

Resonances are not uncommon in the world of familiar experience. For example, cars often rattle at certain engine speeds, and windows sometimes rattle when an airplane flies by. Resonance is particularly important in music. For example, the sound box of a violin does its job well if it has a natural frequency of oscillation that responds resonantly to each musical note. Very strong resonances to certain notes — called "wolf notes" by musicians — occur in cheap violins and are much to be avoided. Sometimes, a glass may be broken by a singer as a result of its resonant response to a particular musical note.

MOTION OF A PARTICLE IN TWO OR MORE DIMENSIONS

More complex problems in mechanics involve a particle moving in two or more dimensions. Such problems include those of the pendulum and the circular orbit.

PROJECTILE MOTION

Galileo pointed out with some detectable pride that none before him had realized that the curved path followed by a missile or projectile is a parabola. He had arrived at his conclusion by realizing that a body undergoing ballistic motion executes, quite independently, the motion of a freely falling body in the vertical direction and inertial motion in the horizontal direction. These considerations, and terms such as ballistic and projectile, apply to a body that, once launched, is acted upon by no force other than Earth's gravity.

Projectile motion may be thought of as an example of motion in space — that is to say, of three-dimensional motion rather than motion along a line, or one-dimensional motion. In a suitably defined system of Cartesian coordinates, the position of the projectile at any instant may be specified by giving the values of its three coordinates, $x(t)$, $y(t)$, and $z(t)$. By generally accepted convention, $z(t)$ is used to describe the vertical direction. To a very good approximation, the motion is confined to a single vertical plane, so that for any single projectile it is possible to choose a coordinate system such that the motion is two-dimensional [say, $x(t)$ and $z(t)$] rather than three-dimensional [$x(t)$, $y(t)$, and $z(t)$]. It is assumed throughout this section that the range of the motion is sufficiently limited that the curvature of Earth's surface may be ignored.

Consider a body whose vertical motion obeys equation (4), Galileo's law of falling bodies, which states $z = z_0 - \frac{1}{2}gt^2$, while, at the same time, moving horizontally at a constant speed v_x in accordance with Galileo's law of inertia. The body's horizontal motion is thus described by $x(t) = v_x t$, which may be written in the form $t = x/v_x$. Using this result to eliminate t from equation (4) gives $z = z_0 - \frac{1}{2}g(1/v_x)^2 x^2$. This latter is the equation of the trajectory of a projectile in the z–x plane, fired horizontally from an initial height z_0. It has the general form

$$z = a + bx^2, \tag{21}$$

where a and b are constants. Equation (21) may be recognized to describe a parabola, just as Galileo claimed. The

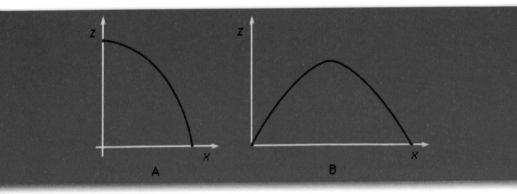

(A) The parabolic path of a projectile. (B) The parabolic path of a projectile with an initial upward component of velocity. Copyright Encyclopædia Britannica; rendering for this edition by Rosen Educational Services

parabolic shape of the trajectory is preserved even if the motion has an initial component of velocity in the vertical direction.

Energy is conserved in projectile motion. The potential energy $U(z)$ of the projectile is given by $U(z) = mgz$. The kinetic energy K is given by $K = \frac{1}{2}mv^2$, where v^2 is equal to the sum of the squares of the vertical and horizontal components of velocity, or $v^2 = v^2_x + v^2_z$.

In all of this discussion, the effects of air resistance (to say nothing of wind and other more complicated phenomena) have been neglected. These effects are seldom actually negligible. They are most nearly so for bodies that are heavy and slow-moving. This discussion, therefore, is of great value for understanding the underlying principles of projectile motion but of little utility for predicting the actual trajectory of, say, a cannonball once fired or even a well-hit baseball.

MOTION OF A PENDULUM

According to legend, Galileo discovered the principle of the pendulum while attending mass at the Duomo (cathedral) located in the Piazza del Duomo of Pisa, Italy. A lamp hung from the ceiling by a cable and, having just been lit, was swaying back and forth. Galileo realized that each complete cycle of the lamp took the same amount of time, compared to his own pulse, even though the amplitude of each swing was smaller than the last. As has already been shown, this property is common to all harmonic oscillators, and, indeed, Galileo's discovery led directly to the invention of the first accurate mechanical clocks. Galileo was also able to show that the period of oscillation of a simple pendulum is proportional to the square root of its length and does not depend on its mass.

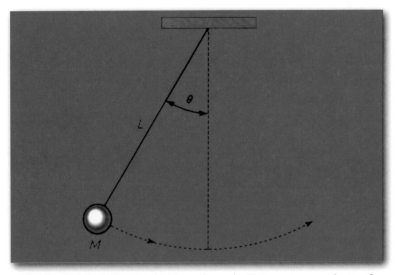

A simple pendulum. Copyright Encyclopædia Britannica; rendering for this edition by Rosen Educational Services

Consider a simple pendulum with a bob of mass M suspended by a massless cable or bar of length L from a point about which it pivots freely. The angle between the cable and the vertical is called θ. The force of gravity acting on the mass M, always equal to $-Mg$ in the vertical direction, is a vector that may be resolved into two components, one that acts ineffectually along the cable and another, perpendicular to the cable, that tends to restore the bob to its equilibrium position directly below the point of suspension. This latter component is given by

$$F = -Mg \sin \theta. \qquad (22)$$

The bob is constrained by the cable to swing through an arc that is actually a segment of a circle of radius L. If the cable is displaced through an angle θ, the bob moves a distance $L\theta$ along its arc (θ must be expressed in radians for this form to be correct). Thus, Newton's second law may be written

$$F = Ma = M\frac{d^2(L\theta)}{dt^2}. \tag{23}$$

Equating equation (22) to equation (23), one sees immediately that the mass M will drop out of the resulting equation. The simple pendulum is an example of a falling body, and its dynamics do not depend on its mass for exactly the same reason that the acceleration of a falling body does not depend on its mass: both the force of gravity and the inertia of the body are proportional to the same mass, and the effects cancel one another. The equation that results (after extracting the constant L from the derivative and dividing both sides by L) is

$$\frac{d^2\theta}{dt^2} = -\frac{g}{L}\sin\theta. \tag{24}$$

If the angle θ is sufficiently small, equation (24) may be rewritten in a form that is both more familiar and more amenable to solution. Consider a segment of a circle of radius L. A radius vector at angle θ locates a point on the circle displaced a distance $L\theta$ along the arc. It is clear from the geometry that $L\sin\theta$ and $L\theta$ are very nearly equal for small θ. It follows then that $\sin\theta$ and θ are

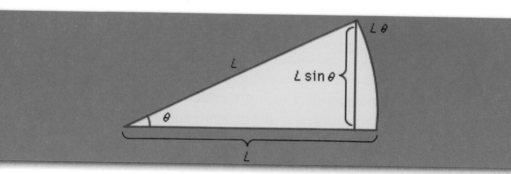

A segment of a circle of radius L. Copyright Encyclopædia Britannica; rendering for this edition by Rosen Educational Services

also very nearly equal for small θ. Thus, if the analysis is restricted to small angles, then sin θ may be replaced by θ in equation (24) to obtain

$$\frac{d^2\theta}{dt^2} = -\frac{g}{L}\theta. \qquad (25)$$

Equation (25) should be compared with equation (11): $d^2x/dt^2 = -(k/m)x$. In the first case, the dynamic variable (meaning the quantity that changes with time) is θ, in the second case it is x. In both cases, the second derivative of the dynamic variable with respect to time is equal to the variable itself multiplied by a negative constant. The equations are therefore mathematically identical and have the same solution—i.e., equation (12), or $\theta = A \cos \omega t$. In the case of the pendulum, the frequency of the oscillations is given by the constant in equation (25), or $\omega^2 = g/L$. The period of oscillation, $T = 2\pi/\omega$, is therefore

$$T = 2\pi\sqrt{\frac{L}{g}}.$$

Just as Galileo concluded, the period is independent of the mass and proportional to the square root of the length.

As with most problems in physics, this discussion of the pendulum has involved a number of simplifications and approximations. Most obviously, sin θ was replaced by θ to obtain equation (25). This approximation is surprisingly accurate. For example, at a not-very-small angle of 17.2°, corresponding to 0.300 radian, sin θ is equal to 0.296, an error of less than 2 percent. For smaller angles, of course, the error is appreciably smaller.

The problem was also treated as if all the mass of the pendulum were concentrated at a point at the end of the cable. This approximation assumes that the mass of the bob at the end of the cable is much larger than that of the cable and that the physical size of the bob is small compared with the length of the cable. When these approximations are not sufficient, one must take into account the way in which mass is distributed in the cable and bob. This is called the physical pendulum, as opposed to the idealized model of the simple pendulum. Significantly, the period of a physical pendulum does not depend on its total mass either.

The effects of friction, air resistance, and the like have also been ignored. These dissipative forces have the same effects on the pendulum as they do on any other kind of harmonic oscillator. They cause the amplitude of a freely swinging pendulum to grow smaller on successive swings. Conversely, in order to keep a pendulum clock going, a mechanism is needed to restore the energy lost to dissipative forces.

CIRCULAR MOTION

Consider a particle moving along the perimeter of a circle at a uniform rate, such that it makes one complete revolution every hour. To describe the motion mathematically, a vector is constructed from the centre of the circle to the particle. The vector then makes one complete revolution every hour. In other words, the vector behaves exactly like the large hand on a wristwatch, an arrow of fixed length that makes one complete revolution every hour. The motion of the point of the vector is an example of uniform circular motion, and the period T of the motion is equal to one hour ($T = 1$ h). The arrow sweeps out an angle of 2π radians (one complete circle) per hour. This rate is called the angular frequency and is written $\omega = 2\pi h^{-1}$. Quite generally, for uniform circular motion at any rate,

$$T = \frac{2\pi}{\omega}. \tag{26}$$

These definitions and relations are the same as they are for harmonic motion.

Consider a coordinate system with the circle centred at the origin. At any instant of time, the position of the particle may be specified by giving the radius r of the circle and the angle θ between the position vector and the x-axis. Although r is constant, θ increases uniformly with time t, such that $\theta = \omega t$, or $d\theta/dt = \omega$, where ω is the angular frequency in equation (26). Contrary to the case of

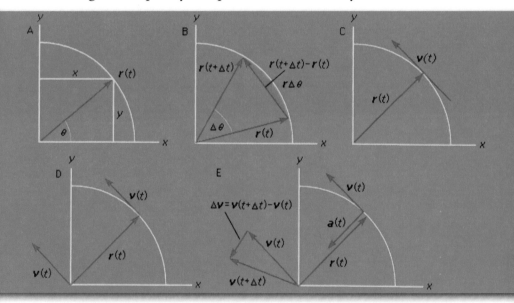

(A) A coordinate system to describe uniform circular motion.(B) The distance traveled in time Δt by a particle undergoing uniform circular motion. (C) The instantaneous velocity of the particle. (D) The velocity vector v undergoes uniform circular motion at the same angular frequency as the particle. (E) The acceleration vector of the particle. Copyright Encyclopædia Britannica; rendering for this edition by Rosen Educational Services

the wristwatch, however, ω is positive by convention when the rotation is in the counterclockwise sense. The vector r has x and y components given by

$$x = r \cos \theta = r \cos \omega t, \tag{27}$$

$$y = r \sin \theta = r \sin \omega t. \tag{28}$$

One meaning of equations (27) and (28) is that, when a particle undergoes uniform circular motion, its x and y components each undergo simple harmonic motion. They are, however, not in phase with one another: at the instant when x has its maximum amplitude (say, at θ = 0), y has zero amplitude, and vice versa.

In a short time, Δt, the particle moves $r\Delta\theta$ along the circumference of the circle. The average speed of the particle is thus given by

$$\bar{v} = r \frac{\Delta\theta}{\Delta t}. \tag{29}$$

The average velocity of the particle is a vector given by

$$\bar{v} = \frac{r(t + \Delta t) - r(t)}{\Delta t}. \tag{30}$$

This operation of vector subtraction yields a vector that is nearly perpendicular to $r(t)$ and $r(t + \Delta t)$. Indeed, the instantaneous velocity, found by allowing Δt to shrink to zero, is a vector v that is perpendicular to r at every instant and whose magnitude is

$$|v| = r \frac{d\theta}{dt} = r\omega. \tag{31}$$

The relationship between r and v means that the particle's instantaneous velocity is always tangent to the circle.

Notice that, just as the position vector r may be described in terms of the components x and y given by equations (27) and (28), the velocity vector v may be described in terms of its projections on the x and y axes, given by

$$v_x = \frac{dx}{dt} = -r\omega \sin \omega t, \tag{32}$$

$$v_y = \frac{dy}{dt} = r\omega \cos \omega t. \tag{33}$$

Imagine a new coordinate system, in which a vector of length ωr extends from the origin and points at all times in the same direction as v. Each time the particle sweeps out a complete circle, this vector also sweeps out a complete circle. In fact, its point is executing uniform circular motion at the same angular frequency as the particle itself. Because vectors have magnitude and direction, but not position in space, the vector that has been constructed is the velocity v. The velocity of the particle is itself undergoing uniform circular motion at angular frequency ω.

Although the speed of the particle is constant, the particle is nevertheless accelerated, because its velocity is constantly changing direction. The acceleration a is given by

$$a = \frac{dv}{dt}. \tag{34}$$

Since v is a vector of length $r\omega$ undergoing uniform circular motion, equations (29) and (30) may be repeated, giving

$$\bar{a} = r\omega \frac{\Delta \theta}{\Delta t} \tag{35}$$

$$\bar{a} = \frac{v(t + \Delta t) - v(t)}{\Delta t}. \qquad (36)$$

Thus, one may conclude that the instantaneous acceleration is always perpendicular to v and its magnitude is

$$|a| = r\omega \frac{d\theta}{dt} = r\omega^2. \qquad (37)$$

Since v is perpendicular to r, and a is perpendicular to v, the vector a is rotated 180° with respect to r. In other words, the acceleration is parallel to r but in the opposite direction. The same conclusion may be reached by realizing that a has x and y components given by

$$a_x = \frac{dv_x}{dt} = -r\omega^2 \cos \omega t, \qquad (38)$$

$$a_y = \frac{dv_y}{dt} = -r\omega^2 \sin \omega t, \qquad (39)$$

similar to equations (32) and (33). When equations (38) and (39) are compared with equations (27) and (28) for x and y, it is clear that the components of a are just those of r multiplied by $-\omega^2$, so that $a = -\omega^2 r$. This acceleration is called the centripetal acceleration, meaning that it is inward, pointing along the radius vector toward the centre of the circle. It is sometimes useful to express the centripetal acceleration in terms of the speed v. Using $v = \omega r$, one can write

$$a = -\frac{v^2}{r}. \qquad (40)$$

CIRCULAR ORBITS

The detailed behaviour of real orbits is the concern of celestial mechanics. This section treats only the idealized, uniform circular orbit of a planet such as Earth about a central body such as the Sun. In fact, Earth's orbit about the Sun is not quite exactly uniformly circular, but it is a close enough approximation for the purposes of this discussion.

A body in uniform circular motion undergoes at all times a centripetal acceleration given by equation (40). According to Newton's second law, a force is required to produce this acceleration. In the case of an orbiting planet, the force is gravity. The gravitational attraction of the Sun is an inward (centripetal) force acting on Earth. This force produces the centripetal acceleration of the orbital motion.

Before these ideas are expressed quantitatively, an understanding of why a force is needed to maintain a body in an orbit of constant speed is useful. The reason is that, at each instant, the velocity of the planet is tangent to the orbit. In the absence of gravity, the planet would obey the law of inertia (Newton's first law) and fly off in a straight line in the direction of the velocity at constant speed. The force of gravity serves to overcome the inertial tendency of the planet, thereby keeping it in orbit.

The gravitational force between two bodies such as the Sun and Earth is given by

$$F = -G \frac{M_S M_E}{r^2}, \tag{41}$$

where M_S and M_E are the masses of the Sun and Earth, respectively, r is the distance between their centres, and

G is a universal constant equal to 6.672×10^{-11} Nm²/kg² (Newton metres squared per kilogram squared). The force acts along the direction connecting the two bodies (i.e., along the radius vector of the uniform circular motion), and the minus sign signifies that the force is attractive, acting to pull Earth toward the Sun.

To an observer on the surface of Earth, the planet appears to be at rest at (approximately) a constant distance from the Sun. It would appear to the observer, therefore, that any force (such as the Sun's gravity) acting on Earth must be balanced by an equal and opposite force that keeps Earth in equilibrium. In other words, if gravity is trying to pull Earth into the Sun, some opposing force must be present to prevent that from happening. In reality, no such force exists. Earth is in freely accelerated motion caused by an unbalanced force. The apparent force, known in mechanics as a pseudoforce, is due to the fact that the observer is actually in accelerated motion. In the case of orbital motion, the outward pseudoforce that balances gravity is called the centrifugal force.

For a uniform circular orbit, gravity produces an inward acceleration given by equation (40), $a = -v^2/r$. The pseudoforce f needed to balance this acceleration is just equal to the mass of Earth times an equal and opposite acceleration, or $f = M_E v^2/r$. The earthbound observer then believes that there is no net force acting on the planet—i.e., that $F + f = 0$, where F is the force of gravity given by equation (41). Combining these equations yields a relation between the speed v of a planet and its distance r from the Sun:

$$v^2 = G \frac{M_S}{r}. \tag{42}$$

It should be noted that the speed does not depend on the mass of the planet. This occurs for exactly the same reason that all bodies fall toward Earth with the same acceleration and that the period of a pendulum is independent of its mass. An orbiting planet is in fact a freely falling body.

Equation (42) is a special case (for circular orbits) of Kepler's third law. Using the fact that $v = 2\pi r/T$, where $2\pi r$ is the circumference of the orbit and T is the time to make a complete orbit (i.e., T is one year in the life of the planet), it is easy to show that $T^2 = (4\pi^2/GM_S)r^3$. This relation also may be applied to satellites in circular orbit around Earth (in which case, M_E must be substituted for M_S) or in orbit around any other central body.

ANGULAR MOMENTUM AND TORQUE

A particle of mass m and velocity v has linear momentum $p = mv$. The particle may also have angular momentum L with respect to a given point in space. If r is the vector from the point to the particle, then

$$L = r \times p. \qquad (43)$$

Notice that angular momentum is always a vector perpendicular to the plane defined by the vectors r and p (or v). For example, if the particle (or a planet) is in a circular orbit, its angular momentum with respect to the centre of the circle is perpendicular to the plane of the orbit and in the direction given by the vector cross product right-hand rule. Moreover, since in the case of a circular orbit, r is perpendicular to p (or v), the magnitude of L is simply

$$L = rp = mvr. \qquad (44)$$

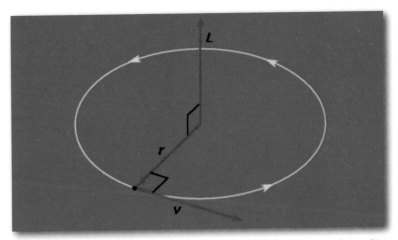

The angular momentum L *of a particle traveling in a circular orbit.* Copyright Encyclopædia Britannica; rendering for this edition by Rosen Educational Services

The significance of angular momentum arises from its derivative with respect to time,

$$\frac{d\mathbf{L}}{dt} = \frac{d}{dt}(\mathbf{r} \times \mathbf{p}) = m\frac{d}{dt}(\mathbf{r} \times \mathbf{v}), \qquad (45)$$

where $\mathbf{p}$ has been replaced by $m\mathbf{v}$ and the constant m has been factored out. Using the product rule of differential calculus,

$$\frac{d}{dt}(\mathbf{r} \times \mathbf{v}) = \frac{d\mathbf{r}}{dt} \times \mathbf{v} + \mathbf{r} \times \frac{d\mathbf{v}}{dt}. \qquad (46)$$

In the first term on the right-hand side of equation (46), $d\mathbf{r}/dt$ is simply the velocity $\mathbf{v}$, leaving $\mathbf{v} \times \mathbf{v}$. Since the cross product of any vector with itself is always zero, that term drops out, leaving

$$\frac{d}{dt}(\mathbf{r} \times \mathbf{v}) = \mathbf{r} \times \frac{d\mathbf{v}}{dt}. \qquad (47)$$

Here, dv/dt is the acceleration a of the particle. Thus, if equation (47) is multiplied by m, the left-hand side becomes dL/dt, as in equation (45), and the right-hand side may be written $r \times ma$. Since, according to Newton's second law, ma is equal to F, the net force acting on the particle, the result is

$$\frac{dL}{dt} = r \times F. \qquad (48)$$

Equation (48) means that any change in the angular momentum of a particle must be produced by a force that is not acting along the same direction as r. One particularly important application is the solar system. Each planet is held in its orbit by its gravitational attraction to the Sun, a force that acts along the vector from the Sun to the planet. Thus the force of gravity cannot change the angular momentum of any planet with respect to the Sun. Therefore, each planet has constant angular momentum with respect to the Sun. This conclusion is correct even though the real orbits of the planets are not circles but ellipses.

The quantity $r \times F$ is called the torque τ. Torque may be thought of as a kind of twisting force, the kind needed to tighten a bolt or to set a body into rotation. Using this definition, equation (48) may be rewritten

$$\tau = r \times F = \frac{dL}{dt}. \qquad (49)$$

Equation (49) means that if there is no torque acting on a particle, its angular momentum is constant, or conserved. Suppose, however, that some agent applies a force F_a to the particle resulting in a torque equal to $r \times F_a$.

According to Newton's third law, the particle must apply a force $-F_a$ to the agent. Thus there is a torque equal to $-r \times F_a$ acting on the agent. The torque on the particle causes its angular momentum to change at a rate given by $dL/dt = r \times F_a$. However, the angular momentum L_a of the agent is changing at the rate $dL_a/dt = -r \times F_a$. Therefore, $dL/dt + dL_a/dt = 0$, meaning that the total angular momentum of particle plus agent is constant, or conserved. This principle may be generalized to include all interactions between bodies of any kind, acting by way of forces of any kind. Total angular momentum is always conserved. The law of conservation of angular momentum is one of the most important principles in all of physics.

MOTION OF A GROUP OF PARTICLES

The word "particle" has been used in this article to signify an object whose entire mass is concentrated at a point in space. In the real world, however, there are no particles of this kind. All real bodies have sizes and shapes. Furthermore, as Newton believed and is now known, all bodies are in fact compounded of smaller bodies called atoms. Therefore, the science of mechanics must deal not only with particles but also with more complex bodies that may be thought of as collections of particles.

CENTRE OF MASS

To take a specific example, the orbit of a planet around the Sun was discussed earlier as if the planet and the Sun were each concentrated at a point in space. In reality, of course, each is a substantial body. However, because each is nearly spherical in shape, it turns out to be permissible, for the purposes of this problem, to treat each body as if its mass were concentrated at its centre. This is an example of an idea that is often useful in discussing bodies of all kinds: the centre of mass. The centre of mass of a uniform sphere is located at the centre of the sphere. For many purposes the sphere may be treated as if all its mass were concentrated at its centre of mass.

To extend the idea further, consider the Earth and the Sun not as two separate bodies but as a single system of two bodies interacting with one another by means of the force of gravity. In the previous discussion of circular orbits, the Sun was assumed to be at rest at the centre of the orbit, but, according to Newton's third law, it must actually be accelerated by a force due to Earth that is equal and opposite to the force that the Sun exerts on Earth. In other words, considering only the Sun and Earth (ignoring, for example, all the other planets), if M_S and M_E are, respectively, the masses of the Sun and Earth, and if a_S and a_E are their respective accelerations, then combining Newton's second and third laws results in the equation $M_S a_S = -M_E a_E$. Writing each a as dv/dt, this equation is easily manipulated to give

$$\frac{d}{dt}(M_S v_S + M_E v_E) = 0, \tag{50}$$

$$M_S v_S + M_E v_E = \text{constant}. \tag{51}$$

This remarkable result means that, as Earth orbits the Sun and the Sun moves in response to Earth's gravitational attraction, the entire two-body system has constant linear momentum, moving in a straight line at constant speed. Without any loss of generality, one can imagine observing the system from a frame of reference moving along with that same speed and direction. This is sometimes called the centre-of-mass frame. In this frame, the momentum of the two-body system—i.e., the constant in equation (51)—is equal to zero. Writing each of the v's as the corresponding dr/dt, equation (51) may be expressed in the form

$$\frac{d}{dt}(M_S r_S + M_E r_E) = 0. \tag{52}$$

Thus, $M_S r_S$ and $M_E r_E$ are two vectors whose vector sum does not change with time. The sum is defined to be the constant vector MR, where M is the total mass of the system and equals $M_S + M_E$. Thus,

$$MR = M_S r_S + M_E r_E. \tag{53}$$

This procedure defines a constant vector R, from any arbitrarily chosen point in space. The fact that R is constant (although r_S and r_E are not constant) means that, rather than Earth orbiting the Sun, Earth and Sun are both orbiting an imaginary point fixed in space. This point is known as the centre of mass of the two-body system.

Knowing the masses of the two bodies ($M_S = 1.99 \times 10^{30}$ kilograms, $M_E = 5.98 \times 10^{24}$ kilograms), it is easy to find

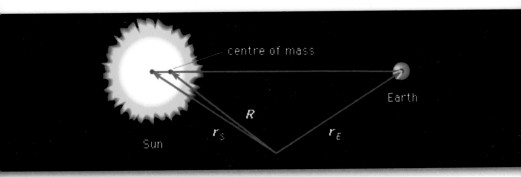

The centre of mass of the two-body Earth-Sun system. Copyright Encyclopædia Britannica; rendering for this edition by Rosen Educational Services

the position of the centre of mass. The origin of the coordinate system may be chosen to be located at the centre of mass merely by defining $R = 0$. Then $r_S = (M_E/M_S)\, r_E \approx$ 450 kilometres, when r_E is rounded to 1.5×10^8 km. A few hundred kilometres is so small compared to r_E that, for all practical purposes, no appreciable error occurs when r_S is ignored and the Sun is assumed to be stationary at the centre of the orbit.

With this example as a guide, it is now possible to define the centre of mass of any collection of bodies. Assume that there are N bodies altogether, each labeled with numbers ranging from 1 to N, and that the vector from an arbitrary origin to the ith body—where i is some number between 1 and N—is r_i. Let the mass of the ith body be m_i. Then the total mass of the N-body system is

$$m = \sum_{i=1}^{N} m_i , \qquad (54)$$

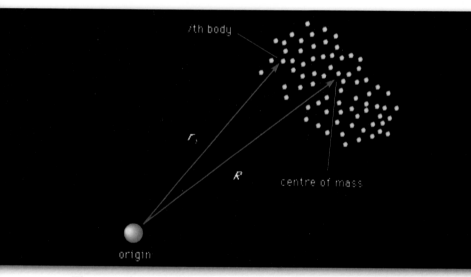

The centre of mass of an N-body system. Copyright Encyclopædia Britannica; rendering for this edition by Rosen Educational Services

and the centre of mass of the system is found at the end of a vector R given by

$$mR = \sum_{i=1}^{N} m_i r_i,\qquad(55)$$

where this definition applies regardless of whether the N bodies making up the system are the stars in a galaxy, the atoms in a rigid body, larger and arbitrarily chosen segments of a rigid body, or any other system of masses. According to equation (55), the vector to the centre of mass of any system is a kind of weighted average of the vectors to all the components of the system.

As will be demonstrated in the sections that follow, the statics and dynamics of many complicated bodies or systems may often be understood by simply applying Newton's laws as if the system's mass were concentrated at the centre of mass.

CONSERVATION OF MOMENTUM

Newton's second law, in its most general form, says that the rate of a change of a particle's momentum p is given by the force acting on the particle; i.e., $F = dp/dt$. If there is no force acting on the particle, then, since $dp/dt = 0$, p must be constant, or conserved. This observation is merely a restatement of Newton's first law, the principle of inertia: if there is no force acting on a body, it moves at constant speed in a straight line.

Now suppose that an external agent applies a force F_a to the particle so that p changes according to

$$\frac{dp}{dt} = F_a.\qquad(56)$$

According to Newton's third law, the particle must apply an equal and opposite force $-F_a$ to the external agent. The momentum p_a of the external agent therefore changes according to

$$\frac{dp_a}{dt} = -F_a.$$

(57)

Adding together equations (56) and (57) results in the equation

$$\frac{d}{dt}(p + p_a) = 0.$$

(58)

The force applied by the external agent changes the momentum of the particle, but at the same time the momentum of the external agent must also change in such a way that the total momentum of both together is constant, or conserved. This idea may be generalized to give the law of conservation of momentum: in all the interactions between all the bodies in the universe, total momentum is always conserved.

It is useful in this light to examine the behaviour of a complicated system of many parts. The centre of mass of the system may be found using equation (55). Differentiating with respect to time gives

$$mv = \sum_{i=1}^{N} m_i v_i,$$

(59)

where $v = dR/dt$ and $v_i = dr_i/dt$. Note that $m_i v_i$ is the momentum of the ith part of the system, and mv is the momentum that the system would have if all its mass (i.e., m) were concentrated at its centre of mass, the point whose velocity is v. Thus, the momentum associated with the centre of mass is the sum of the momenta of the parts.

Suppose now that there is no external agent applying a force to the entire system. Then the only forces acting on the system are those exerted by the parts on one another. These forces may accelerate the individual parts. Differentiating equation (59) with respect to time gives

$$m\frac{dv}{dt} = \sum_{i=1}^{N} m_i \frac{dv_i}{dt} = \sum_{i=1}^{N} F_i, \tag{60}$$

where F_i is the net force, or the sum of the forces, exerted by all the other parts of the body on the ith part. F_i is defined mathematically by the equation

$$F_i = \sum_{j=1}^{N} F_{ij}, \tag{61}$$

where F_{ij} represents the force on body i due to body j (the force on body i due to itself, F_{ii}, is zero). The motion of the centre of mass is then given by the complicated-looking formula

$$m\frac{dv}{dt} = \sum_{i=1}^{N} \left(\sum_{j=1}^{N} F_{ij} \right). \tag{62}$$

This complicated formula may be greatly simplified, however, by noting that Newton's third law requires that for every force F_{ij} exerted by the jth body on the ith body, there is an equal and opposite force $-F_{ij}$ exerted by the ith body on the jth body. In other words, every term in the double sum has an equal and opposite term. The double summation on the right-hand side of equation (61) always adds up to zero. This result is true regardless of the complexity of the system, the nature of the forces acting between the parts, or the motions of the parts. In short, in the absence of external forces acting on the system as a whole, mdv/dt = 0, which means that the momentum of the centre of mass of the system is always conserved. Having determined that momentum is conserved whether or not there is an external force acting, one may conclude that the total momentum of the universe is always conserved.

COLLISIONS

A collision is an encounter between two bodies that alters at least one of their courses. Altering the course of a body requires that a force be applied to it. Thus, each body exerts a force on the other. These forces of interaction may operate at some distance, as do the gravitational and electromagnetic forces, or the bodies may appear to make physical contact. However, even apparent contact between two bodies is only a macroscopic manifestation of microscopic forces that act between atoms some distance apart. There is no fundamental distinction between physical contact and interaction at a distance.

The importance of understanding the mechanics of collisions is obvious to anyone who has ever driven an automobile. In modern physics, however, collisions are important for a different reason. The current understanding of the subatomic particles of which atoms are composed is derived entirely from studying the results of collisions among them. Thus, in modern physics, the description of collisions is a significant part of the understanding of matter. These descriptions are quantum mechanical rather than classical, but they are nevertheless closely based on principles that arise out of classical mechanics.

It is possible in principle to predict the result of a collision using Newton's second law directly. Suppose that two bodies are going to collide and that F, the force of interaction between them, is known to be a function of r, the distance between them. Then, if it is known that, say, one particle has incident momentum p, the problem is solved if the final momentum $p + \Delta p$ can be determined. Inverting Newton's second law, $F = dp/dt$, the change in momentum is given by

$$\Delta p = \int_{-\infty}^{\infty} F\,dt. \tag{63}$$

This integral is known as the impulse imparted to the particle. In order to perform the integral, it is necessary to know r at all times so that F may be known at all times. More realistically, Δp is the sum of a series of small steps, such that

$$\delta p = F \delta t, \tag{64}$$

where F depends on the instantaneous distance between the particles. Because $p = mv = mdr/dt$, the change in r in this step is

$$\delta r = \frac{p}{m} \delta t. \tag{65}$$

At the next step, there is a new distance, $r + \delta r$, giving a new value of the force in equation (64) and a new momentum, $p + \delta p$, in equation (65). This method of analyzing collisions is used in numerical calculations on digital computers.

To predict the result of a collision analytically (rather than numerically) it is often most useful to apply conservation laws. In any collision (as in any other phenomenon), energy, momentum, and angular momentum are always conserved. Judicious application of these laws may be extremely useful because they do not depend in any way on the detailed nature of the interaction (i.e., the force as a function of distance).

This point can be illustrated by the following example. A collision is to take place between two bodies of the same mass m. One of the bodies is initially at rest (its momentum is zero). The other has initial momentum p_0. After the collision, the body previously at rest has momentum p_1, and the body initially in motion has momentum p_2. Since momentum is conserved, the total momentum after the collision, $p_1 + p_2$, must be equal to the total momentum before the collision, p_0; that is,

$$P_0 = P_1 + P_2. \qquad (66)$$

Equation (66) is the equation of a vector triangle. However, p_1 and p_2 are not determined by this condition; they are only constrained by it.

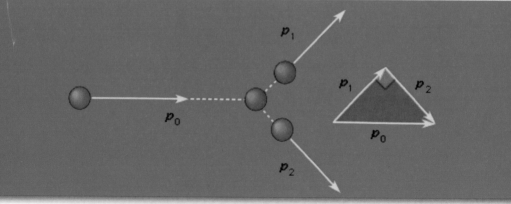

Collision between two particles of equal mass. Copyright Encyclopædia Britannica; rendering for this edition by Rosen Educational Services

Although energy is always conserved, the kinetic energy of the incident body is not always converted entirely into the kinetic energy of the two bodies after the collision. For example, if the bodies are microscopic (say, two identical atoms), the collision may cause one or both to be excited into a state of higher internal energy than it started with. Such an event would leave correspondingly less kinetic energy for the outgoing atoms. In fact, it is precisely by studying the trajectories of outgoing projectiles in collisions like these that physicists are able to determine the possible excited states of microscopic particles.

In a collision between macroscopic objects, some of the kinetic energy is always converted to heat. Heat is the energy of random vibrations of the atoms and molecules that constitute the bodies. However, if the amount of heat is negligible compared to the initial kinetic energy, it may be ignored. Such a collision is said to be elastic.

Suppose the collision just described between two bodies, each of mass m, is between billiard balls, and suppose it is elastic (a reasonably good approximation of real billiard balls). The kinetic energy of the incident ball is then equal to the sum of the kinetic energies of the outgoing balls. According to equation (3), the kinetic energy of a moving object is given by $K = \frac{1}{2}mv^2$, where v is the speed of the ball (technically, the energy associated with the fact that the ball is rolling as well as translating is ignored here). Equation (3) may be written in a particularly useful form by recognizing that since $p = mv$

$$K = \frac{1}{2}mv^2 = \frac{p^2}{2m}. \qquad (67)$$

Then the conservation of kinetic energy may be written

$$\frac{p_0^2}{2m} = \frac{p_1^2}{2m} + \frac{p_2^2}{2m}, \qquad (68)$$

or, canceling the factors $2m$,

$$p_0^2 = p_1^2 + p_2^2. \qquad (69)$$

Comparing this result with equation (66) shows that the vector triangle is pythagorean; p_1 and p_2 are perpendicular. This result is well known to all experienced pool players. Notice that it was possible to arrive at this result without any knowledge of the forces that act when billiard balls collide.

RELATIVE MOTION

A collision between two bodies can always be described in a frame of reference in which the total momentum is zero. This is the centre-of-mass (or centre-of-momentum) frame mentioned earlier. Then, for example, in the collision between two bodies of the same mass, the two bodies always have equal and opposite velocities. It should be noted that, in this frame of reference, the outgoing momenta are antiparallel and not perpendicular.

Any collection of bodies may similarly be described in a frame of reference in which the total momentum is zero. This frame is simply the one in which the centre of mass is at rest. This fact is easily seen by differentiating equation (55) with respect to time, giving

$$m\frac{dR}{dt} = \sum_{i=1}^{N} m_i \frac{dr_i}{dt}. \qquad (70)$$

The right-hand side is the sum of the momenta of all the bodies. It is equal to zero if the velocity of the centre of mass, dR/dt, is equal to zero.

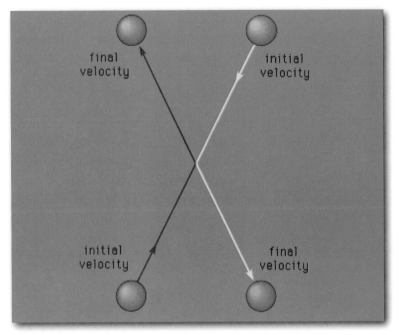

Collision between two particles of equal mass as seen from the centre-of-mass frame of reference. Copyright Encyclopædia Britannica; rendering for this edition by Rosen Educational Services

If Newton's second law is correct in any frame of reference, it will also appear to be correct to an observer moving with any constant velocity with respect to that frame. This principle, called the principle of Galilean relativity, is true because, to the moving observer, the same constant velocity seems to have been added to the velocity of every particle in the system. This change does not affect the accelerations of the particles (since the added velocity is constant, not accelerated) and therefore does not change the apparent force (mass times acceleration) acting on each particle. That is why it is permissible to describe a problem from the centre-of-momentum frame (provided that the centre of mass is not accelerated) or from any other frame moving at constant velocity with respect to it.

If this principle is strictly correct, the fundamental forces of physics should not contain any particular speed. This must be true because the speed of any object will be different to observers in different but equally good frames of reference, but the force should always be the same. It turns out, according to the theory of James Clerk Maxwell, that there is an intrinsic speed in the force laws of electricity and magnetism: the speed of light appears in the forces between electric charges and between magnetic poles. This discrepancy was ultimately resolved by Albert Einstein's special theory of relativity. According to the special theory of relativity, Newtonian mechanics breaks down when the relative speed between particles approaches the speed of light.

COUPLED OSCILLATORS

In the section on simple harmonic oscillators, the motion of a single particle held in place by springs was considered. In this section, the motion of a group of particles bound by springs to one another is discussed. The solutions of this seemingly academic problem have far-reaching implications in many fields of physics. For example, a system of particles held together by springs turns out to be a useful model of the behaviour of atoms mutually bound in a crystalline solid.

To begin with a simple case, consider two particles in a line. Each particle has mass m, each spring has spring constant k, and motion is restricted to the horizontal, or x, direction. Even this elementary system is capable of surprising behaviour, however. For instance, if one particle is held in place while the other is displaced, and then both are released, the displaced particle immediately begins to execute simple harmonic motion. This motion, by stretching

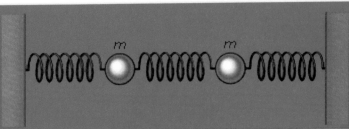

Coupled oscillators. Copyright Encyclopædia Britannica; rendering for this edition by Rosen Educational Services

the spring between the particles, starts to excite the second particle into motion. Gradually the energy of motion passes from the first particle to the second until a point is reached at which the first particle is at rest and only the second is oscillating. Then the process starts all over again, the energy passing in the opposite direction.

To analyze the possible motions of the system, one writes equations similar to equation (11), giving the acceleration of each particle owing to the forces acting on it. There is one equation for each particle (two equations in this case). The force on each particle depends not only on its displacement from its equilibrium position but also on its distance from the other particle, since the spring between them stretches or compresses according to that distance. For this reason the motions are coupled, the solution of each equation (the motion of each particle) depending on the solution of the other (the motion of the other).

Analyzing the system yields the fact that there are two special states of motion in which both particles are always in oscillation with the same frequency. In one state, the two particles oscillate in opposite directions with equal and opposite displacements from equilibrium at all times. In the other state, both particles move together, so that the spring between them is never stretched or compressed. The first of these motions has higher frequency than the second because the centre spring contributes an increase in the restoring force.

These two collective motions, at different, definite frequencies, are known as the normal modes of the system.

If a third particle is inserted into the system together with another spring, there will be three equations to solve, and the result will be three normal modes. A large number N of particles in a line will have N normal modes. Each normal mode has a definite frequency at which all the particles oscillate. In the highest frequency mode each particle moves in the direction opposite to both of its neighbours. In the lowest frequency mode, neighbours move almost together, barely disturbing the springs between them. Starting from one end, the amplitude of the motion gradually builds up, each particle moving a bit more than the one before, reaching a maximum at the centre, and then decreasing again. A plot of the amplitudes

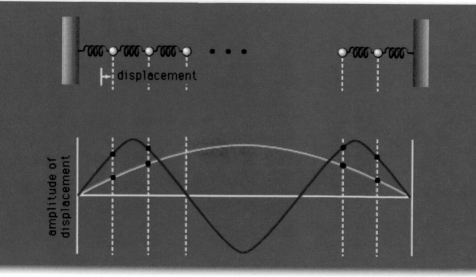

Normal modes. Copyright Encyclopædia Britannica; rendering for this edition by Rosen Educational Services

basically describes one-half of a sine wave from one end of the system to the other. The next mode is a full sine wave, then $\frac{3}{2}$ of a sine wave, and so on to the highest frequency mode, which may be visualized as $\frac{N}{2}$ sine waves. If the vibrations were up and down rather than side to side, these modes would be identical to the fundamental and harmonic vibrations excited by plucking a guitar string.

The atoms of a crystal are held in place by mutual forces of interaction that oppose any disturbance from equilibrium positions, just as the spring forces in the example. For small displacements of the atoms, they behave mathematically just like spring forces—i.e., they obey Hooke's law, equation (10). Each atom is free to move in three dimensions rather than one, however; therefore each atom added to a crystal adds three normal modes. In a typical crystal at ordinary temperature, all these modes are always excited by random thermal energy. The lower-frequency, longer-wavelength modes may also be excited mechanically. These are called sound waves.

CHAPTER 5

RIGID BODIES

The previous chapter discussed mechanics in terms of particles. However, many objects are not particles but what physicists call rigid bodies. A body is formally regarded as rigid if the distance between any set of two points in it is always constant. In reality no body is perfectly rigid. When equal and opposite forces are applied to a body, it is always deformed slightly. The body's own tendency to restore the deformation has the effect of applying counterforces to whatever is applying the forces, thus obeying Newton's third law. Calling a body rigid means that the changes in the dimensions of the body are small enough to be neglected, even though the force produced by the deformation may not be neglected.

STATICS

Statics is the study of bodies and structures that are in equilibrium. For a body to be in equilibrium, there must be no net force acting on it. In addition, there must be no net torque acting on it.

When a body has a net force and a net torque acting on it owing to a combination of forces, all the forces acting on the body may be replaced by a single (imaginary) force called the resultant, which acts at a single point on the body, producing the same net force and the same net torque. The body can be brought into equilibrium by applying to it a real force at the same point, equal and opposite to the resultant. This force is called the equilibrant.

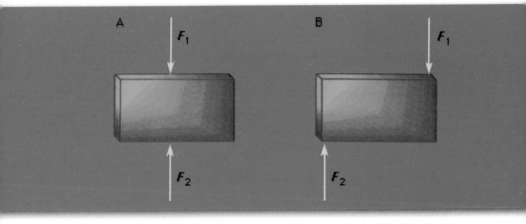

(A) A body in equilibrium under equal and opposite forces. (B) A body not in equilibrium under equal and opposite forces. Copyright Encyclopædia Britannica; rendering for this edition by Rosen Educational Services

The torque on a body due to a given force depends on the reference point chosen, since the torque τ by definition equals $r \times F$, where r is a vector from some chosen reference point to the point of application of the force. Thus, for a body to be at equilibrium, not only must the net force on it be equal to zero but the net torque with respect to any point must also be zero. Fortunately, it is

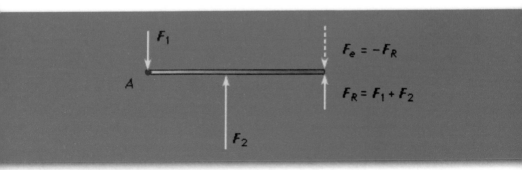

The resultant force (F_R) *produces the same net force and the same net torque about point A as* $F_1 + F_2$*; the body can be brought into equilibrium by applying the equilibrant force* F_e. Copyright Encyclopædia Britannica; rendering for this edition by Rosen Educational Services

easily shown for a rigid body that, if the net force is zero and the net torque is zero with respect to any one point, then the net torque is also zero with respect to any other point in the frame of reference.

Equal and opposite forces acting on a rigid body may act so as to compress the body or to stretch it. The bodies are then said to be under compression or under tension, respectively. Strings, chains, and cables are rigid under tension but may collapse under compression. On the other hand, certain building materials, such as brick and mortar, stone, or concrete, tend to be strong under compression but very weak under tension.

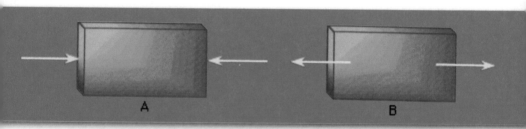

(A) Compression produced by equal and opposite forces. (B) Tension produced by equal and opposite forces. Copyright Encyclopædia Britannica; rendering for this edition by Rosen Educational Services

The most important application of statics is to study the stability of structures, such as edifices and bridges. In these cases, gravity applies a force to each component of the structure as well as to any bodies the structure may need to support. The force of gravity acts on each bit of mass of which each component is made, but for each rigid component it may be thought of as acting at a single point, the centre of gravity, which is in these cases the same as the centre of mass.

To give a simple but important example of the application of statics, consider two situations in which a mass *m* is supported by two symmetric members, each making an

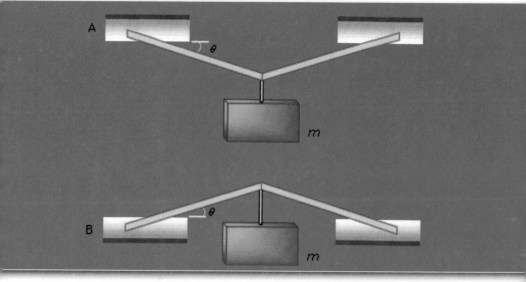

(A) A body supported by two rigid members under tension. (B) A body supported by two rigid members under compression. Copyright Encyclopædia Britannica; rendering for this edition by Rosen Educational Services

angle θ with respect to the horizontal. When the members are below the horizontal, the members are under tension; when they are above the horizontal, they are under compression. In either case, the force acting along each of the members is shown to be

$$F = \frac{mg}{2 \sin \theta}.$$ (71)

The force in either case thus becomes intolerably large if the angle θ is allowed to be very small. In other words, the mass cannot be hung from thin horizontal members only capable of carrying either the compression or the tension forces of the mass.

The ancient Greeks built magnificent stone temples; however, the horizontal stone slabs that constituted the roofs of the temples could not support even their own weight over more than a very small span. For this reason, one characteristic that identifies a Greek temple is the many closely spaced pillars needed to hold up the flat roof. The problem posed by equation (71) was solved by the ancient Romans, who incorporated into their architecture the arch, a structure that supports its weight by compression.

A suspension bridge illustrates the use of tension. The weight of the span and any traffic on it is supported by cables, which are placed under tension by the weight. The cables are not stretched to be horizontal, but rather they are always hung so as to have substantial curvature.

It should be mentioned in passing that equilibrium under static forces is not sufficient to guarantee the stability of a structure. It must also be stable against perturbations such as the additional forces that might be imposed, for example, by winds or by earthquakes. Analysis of the stability of structures under such perturbations is an important part of the job of an engineer or architect.

ROTATION ABOUT A FIXED AXIS

Consider a rigid body that is free to rotate about an axis fixed in space. Because of the body's inertia, it resists being set into rotational motion, and equally important, once rotating, it resists being brought to rest. Exactly how that inertial resistance depends on the mass and geometry of the body is discussed here.

Take the axis of rotation to be the z-axis. A vector in the x-y plane from the axis to a bit of mass fixed in the body makes an angle θ with respect to the x-axis. If the body is rotating, θ changes with time, and the body's angular frequency is

$$\omega = \frac{d\theta}{dt};$$

(72)

ω is also known as the angular velocity. If ω is changing in time, there is also an angular acceleration a, such that

$$\alpha = \frac{d\omega}{dt}. \tag{73}$$

Because linear momentum p is related to linear speed v by $p = mv$, where m is the mass, and because force F is related to acceleration a by $F = ma$, it is reasonable to assume that there exists a quantity I that expresses the rotational inertia of the rigid body in analogy to the way m expresses the inertial resistance to changes in linear motion. One would expect to find that the angular momentum is given by

$$L = I\omega \tag{74}$$

and that the torque (twisting force) is given by

$$\tau = I\alpha. \tag{75}$$

One can imagine dividing the rigid body into bits of mass labeled m_1, m_2, m_3, and so on. Let the bit of mass at the tip of the vector be called m_i. If the length of the vector from the axis to this bit of mass is R_i, then m_i's linear velocity v_i equals ωR_i (see equation [31]), and its angular momentum L_i equals $m_i v_i R_i$ (see equation [44]), or $m_i R_i^2 \omega$. The angular momentum of the rigid body is found by summing all the contributions from all the bits of mass labeled $i = 1, 2, 3 \ldots$:

$$L = \left(\sum_i m_i R_i^2 \right) \omega. \tag{76}$$

In a rigid body, the quantity in parentheses in equation (76) is always constant (each bit of mass m_i always remains

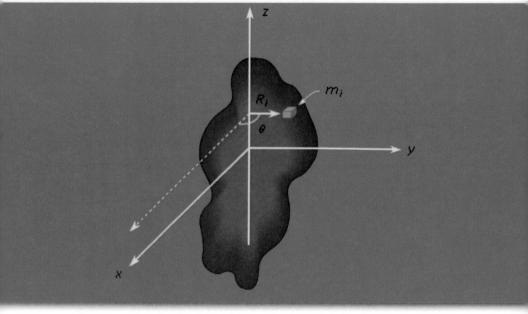

Rotation around a fixed axis. Copyright Encyclopædia Britannica; rendering for this edition by Rosen Educational Services

the same distance R_i from the axis). Thus if the motion is accelerated, then

$$\frac{dL}{dt} = \left(\sum_i m_i R_i^2 \right) \frac{d\omega}{dt}. \tag{77}$$

Recalling that $\tau = dL/dt$, one may write

$$\tau = \left(\sum_i m_i R_i^2 \right) \alpha. \tag{78}$$

(These equations may be written in scalar form, since L and τ are always directed along the axis of rotation in this discussion.) Comparing equations (76) and (78) with (74) and (75), one finds that

$$I = \sum_i m_i R_i^2.$$

(79)

The quantity I is called the moment of inertia.

According to equation (79), the effect of a bit of mass on the moment of inertia depends on its distance from the axis. Because of the factor R_i^2, mass far from the axis makes a bigger contribution than mass close to the axis. It is important to note that R_i is the distance from the axis, not from a point. Thus, if x_i and y_i are the x and y coordinates of the mass m_i, then $R_i^2 = x_i^2 + y_i^2$, regardless of the value of the z coordinate.

The moment of inertia of any body depends on the axis of rotation. Depending on the symmetry of the body, there may be as many as three different moments of inertia about mutually perpendicular axes passing through the centre of mass. If the axis does not pass through the centre of mass, the moment of inertia may be related to that about a parallel axis that does so. Let I_c be the moment of inertia about the parallel axis through the centre of mass, r the distance between the two axes, and M the total mass of the body. Then

$$I = I_c + Mr^2.$$

(80)

In other words, the moment of inertia about an axis that does not pass through the centre of mass is equal to the moment of inertia for rotation about an axis through the centre of mass (I_c) plus a contribution that acts as if the mass were concentrated at the centre of mass, which then rotates about the axis of rotation.

The dynamics of rigid bodies rotating about fixed axes may be summarized in three equations. The angular momentum is $L = I\omega$, the torque is $\tau = I a$, and the kinetic energy is $K = \frac{1}{2} I \omega^2$.

ROTATION ABOUT A MOVING AXIS

The general motion of a rigid body tumbling through space may be described as a combination of translation of the body's centre of mass and rotation about an axis through the centre of mass. The linear momentum of the body of mass M is given by

$$p = Mv_c,\qquad(81)$$

where v_c is the velocity of the centre of mass. Any change in the momentum is governed by Newton's second law, which states that

$$F = \frac{dp}{dt},\qquad(82)$$

where F is the net force acting on the body. The angular momentum of the body with respect to any reference point may be written as

$$L = L_c + r \times p,\qquad(83)$$

where L_c is the angular momentum of rotation about an axis through the centre of mass, r is a vector from the reference point to the centre of mass, and $r \times p$ is therefore the angular momentum associated with motion of the centre of mass, acting as if all the body's mass were concentrated at that point. The quantity L_c in equation (83) is sometimes called the body's spin, and $r \times p$ is called the orbital angular momentum. Any change in the angular momentum of the body is given by the torque equation,

$$\tau = \frac{dL}{dt}.\qquad(84)$$

An example of a body that undergoes both translational and rotational motion is the Earth, which rotates about an axis through its centre once per day while executing an orbit around the Sun once per year. Because the Sun exerts no torque on Earth with respect to its own centre, the orbital angular momentum of Earth is constant in time. However, the Sun does exert a small torque on Earth with respect to the planet's centre, owing to the fact that Earth is not perfectly spherical. The result is a slow shifting of Earth's axis of rotation, known as the precession of the equinoxes.

The kinetic energy of a body that is both translating and rotating is given by

$$K = \frac{1}{2} M v_c^2 + \frac{1}{2} I \omega^2, \tag{85}$$

where I is the moment of inertia and ω is the angular velocity of rotation about the axis through the centre of mass.

A common example of combined rotation and translation is rolling motion, as exhibited by a billiard ball rolling on a table, or a ball or cylinder rolling down an inclined plane. Consider the latter example. Motion is impelled by the force of gravity, which may be resolved into two components, F_N, which is normal to the plane, and F_p, which is parallel to it. In addition to gravity, friction plays an essential role. The force of friction, written as f, acts parallel to the plane, in opposition to the direction of motion, at the point of contact between the plane and the rolling body. If f is very small, the body will slide without rolling. If f is very large, it will prevent motion from occurring. The magnitude of f depends on the smoothness and composition of the body and the plane, and it is proportional to F_N, the normal component of the force.

Consider a case in which f is just large enough to cause the body (sphere or cylinder) to roll without slipping. The

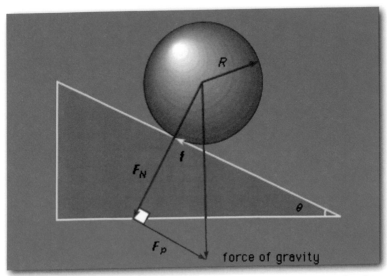

Rolling motion. Copyright Encyclopædia Britannica; rendering for this edition by Rosen Educational Services

motion may be analyzed from the point of view of an axis passing through the point of contact between the rolling body and the plane. Remarkably, the point of contact may always be regarded to be instantaneously at rest. To understand why, suppose that the rolling body has radius R and angular velocity ω about its centre-of-mass axis. Then, with respect to its own axis, each point on the circular cross section moves with instantaneous tangential linear speed $v_c = R\omega$. In particular, the point of contact is moving backward with this speed relative to the centre of mass. But with respect to the inclined plane, the centre of mass is moving forward with exactly this same speed. The net effect of the two equal and opposite speeds is that the point of contact is always instantaneously at rest. Therefore, although friction acts at that point, no work is done by friction, so mechanical energy (potential plus kinetic) may be regarded as conserved.

With respect to the axis through the point of contact, the torque is equal to RF_p, giving rise to an angular acceleration a given by $I_p a = RF_p$, where I_p is the moment of inertia about the point-of-contact axis and can be determined by applying equation (80) relating moments of inertia about parallel axes ($I_p = I + MR^2$). Thus,

$$\alpha = \frac{RF_p}{I + MR^2}. \qquad (86)$$

From this result, the motion of the body is easily obtained using the fact that the velocity of the centre of mass is $v_c = R\omega$ and hence the linear acceleration of the centre of mass is $a_c = Ra$.

Notice that, although without friction no angular acceleration would occur, the force of friction does not affect the magnitude of a. Because friction does no work, this same result may be obtained by applying energy conservation. The situation also may be analyzed entirely from the point of view of the centre of mass. In that case, the torque is $-fR$, but f also provides a linear force on the body. The f may then be eliminated by using Newton's second law and the fact that the torque equals the moment of inertia times the angular acceleration, once again leading to the same result.

One more interesting fact is hidden in the form of equation (86). The parallel component of the force of gravity is given by

$$F_p = Mg \sin \theta, \qquad (87)$$

where θ is the angle of inclination of the plane. The moment of inertia about the centre of mass of any body of mass M may be written

$$I = Mk^2, \qquad (88)$$

where k is a distance called the radius of gyration. Comparison to equation (79) shows that k is a measure of how far from the centre of mass the mass of the body is concentrated. Using equations (87) and (88) in equation (86), one finds that

$$\alpha = \frac{Rg \sin \theta}{k^2 + R^2}. \tag{89}$$

Thus, the angular acceleration of a body rolling down a plane does not depend on its total mass, although it does depend on its shape and distribution of mass. The same may be said of a_c, the linear acceleration of the centre of mass. The acceleration of a rolling ball, like the acceleration of a freely falling object, is independent of its mass. This observation helps to explain why Galileo was able to discover many of the basic laws of dynamics in gravity by studying the behaviour of balls rolling down inclined planes.

CENTRIFUGAL FORCE

According to the principle of Galilean relativity, if Newton's laws are true in any reference frame, they are also true in any other frame moving at constant velocity with respect to the first one. Conversely, they do not appear to be true in any frame accelerated with respect to the first. Instead, in an accelerated frame, objects appear to have forces acting on them that are not in fact present. These are called pseudoforces. Since rotational motion is always accelerated motion, pseudoforces may always be observed in rotating frames of reference.

As one example, a frame of reference in which Earth is at rest must rotate once per year about the Sun. In this reference frame, the gravitational force attracting Earth toward the Sun appears to be balanced by an equal and opposite outward force that keeps Earth in stationary equilibrium. This outward pseudoforce is the centrifugal force.

The rotation of Earth about its own axis also causes pseudoforces for observers at rest on Earth's surface. There is a centrifugal force, but it is much smaller than the force of gravity. Its effect is that, at the Equator, where it is largest, the gravitational acceleration g is about 0.5 percent smaller than at the poles, where there is no centrifugal force. This same centrifugal force is responsible for the fact that Earth is slightly nonspherical, bulging just a bit at the Equator.

Pseudoforces can have real consequences. The oceanic tides on Earth, for example, are a consequence of centrifugal forces in the Earth-Moon and Earth-Sun systems. The Moon appears to be orbiting Earth, but in reality both the Moon and Earth orbit their common centre of mass. The centre of mass of the Earth-Moon system is located inside Earth nearly three-fourths of the distance from the centre to the surface, or roughly 4,700 kilometres from the centre of Earth. Earth rotates about this point approximately once a month. The gravitational attraction of the Moon and the centrifugal force of this rotation are exactly balanced at the centre of Earth. At the surface of Earth closest to the Moon, the Moon's gravity is stronger than the centrifugal force. The ocean's waters, which are free to move in response to this unbalanced force, tend to build up a small bulge at that point. On the surface of Earth exactly opposite the Moon, the centrifugal force is stronger than the Moon's gravity, and a small bulge of water tends to build up there as well. The water is correspondingly depleted at the points 90° on either side of these. Each day Earth rotates beneath these bulges and troughs, which remain stationary with respect to the Earth-Moon system. The result is two high tides and two low tides every day every place on Earth. The Sun has a similar effect, but of only about half the size; it increases or decreases the size of the tides depending on its relative alignment with Earth and Moon.

CORIOLIS FORCE

The Coriolis force is a pseudoforce that operates in all rotating frames. One way to envision it is to imagine a rotating platform (such as a merry-go-round or a phonograph turntable) with a perfectly smooth surface and a smooth block sliding inertially across it. The block, having no (real) forces acting on it, moves in a straight line at constant speed in inertial space. However, the platform rotates under it, so that to an observer on the platform, the block appears to follow a curved trajectory, bending in the opposite direction to the motion of the platform. Since the motion is curved, and hence accelerated, there appears, to the observer, to be a force operating. That pseudoforce is called the Coriolis force.

The Coriolis force also may be observed on the surface of Earth. For example, many science museums have a pendulum, called a Foucault pendulum, suspended from a long cable with markers to show that its plane of motion rotates slowly. The rotation of the plane of motion is caused by the Coriolis force. The effect is most easily imagined by picturing the pendulum swinging directly above the North Pole. The plane of its motion remains stationary in inertial space, while Earth rotates once a day beneath it.

At lower latitudes, the effect is a bit more subtle, but it is still present. Imagine that, somewhere in the Northern Hemisphere, a projectile is fired due south. As viewed from inertial space, the projectile initially has an eastward component of velocity as well as a southward component because the gun that fired it, which is stationary on the surface of Earth, was moving eastward with Earth's rotation at the instant it was fired. However, since it was fired to the south, it lands at a slightly lower latitude, closer to the Equator. As one moves south, toward the Equator, the tangential speed of Earth's surface due to its rotation increases because the surface is farther from the axis of rotation. Thus, although the projectile has an eastward component of velocity (in inertial space), it lands at a place where the surface of Earth has a larger eastward component of velocity. Thus, to the observer on Earth, the projectile seems to curve slightly to the west. That westward curve is attributed to the Coriolis force. If the projectile were fired to the north, it would seem to curve eastward.

The same analysis applied to a Foucault pendulum explains why its plane of motion tends to rotate in the clockwise direction anywhere in the Northern Hemisphere and in the counterclockwise direction in the Southern Hemisphere. Storms, known as cyclones, tend to rotate in the opposite direction in each hemisphere, also due to the Coriolis force. Air moves in all directions toward a low-pressure centre. In the Northern Hemisphere, air moving up from the south is deflected eastward, while air moving down from the north is deflected westward. This effect tends to give cyclones a counterclockwise circulation in the Northern Hemisphere. In the Southern Hemisphere, cyclones tend to circulate in the clockwise direction.

SPINNING TOPS AND GYROSCOPES

Consider a wheel that is weighted in its rim to maximize its moment of inertia I and that is spinning with angular frequency ω on a horizontal axle supported at both ends. The wheel has an angular momentum L along the x direction equal to $I\omega$. Now suppose the support at point P is removed, leaving the axle supported only at one end. Gravity, acting on the mass of the wheel as if it were concentrated at the centre of mass, applies a downward force on the wheel. The wheel, however, does not fall. Instead, the axle remains (nearly) horizontal but rotates in the counterclockwise direction as seen from above. This motion is called gyroscopic precession.

Horizontal precession occurs in this case because the gravitational force results in a torque with respect to the point of suspension, such that $\tau = r \times F$ and is directed, initially, in the positive y direction. The torque causes the angular momentum L to move toward that direction according to $\tau = dL/dt$. Because τ is perpendicular to L, it does not change the magnitude of the angular momentum, only its direction. As precession proceeds, the torque remains horizontal, and the angular momentum vector, continually redirected by the torque, executes uniform circular motion in the horizontal plane at a frequency Ω, the frequency of precession.

In reality, the motion is a bit more complicated than uniform precession in the horizontal plane. When the support at P is released, the centre of mass of the wheel initially drops slightly below the horizontal plane. This drop reduces the gravitational potential energy of the system, releasing kinetic energy for the orbital motion of the centre of mass as it precesses. It also provides a small component of L in the negative z direction, which balances the angular momentum in the positive z direction that results from the orbital motion of the centre of mass. There can be no net angular momentum in the vertical direction because there is no component of torque in that direction.

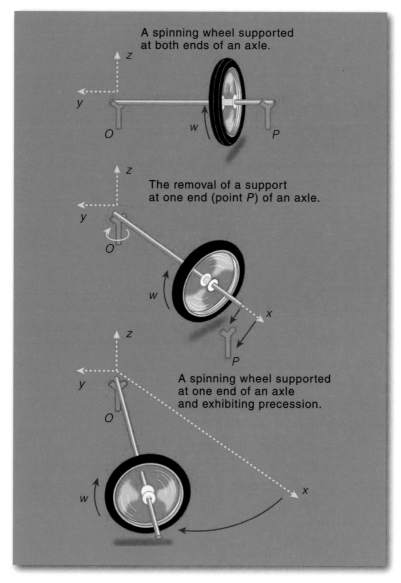

Gyroscopic precession. Copyright Encyclopædia Britannica; rendering for this edition by Rosen Educational Services

One more complication: the initial drop of the centre of mass carries it too far for a stable plane of precession, and it tends to bounce back up after overshooting. This produces an up-and-down oscillation during precession, called nutation ("nodding"). In most cases, nutation is quickly damped by friction in the bearings, leaving uniform precession.

If a top is initially set spinning with a vertical axis, there will be virtually no torque, and conservation of angular momentum will keep the axis vertical for a long time. Eventually, however, friction at the point of contact will require the centre of mass to lower itself, which can only happen if the axis tilts. The spinning will also slow down, making the tilting process easier. Once the top tilts, gravity produces a horizontal torque that leads to precession of the spin axis. The subsequent motion depends on whether the point of contact is fixed or free to slip on the horizontal plane. Vast tomes have been written on the motions of tops.

A gyroscope is a device that is designed to resist changes in the direction of its axis of spin. That purpose is generally accomplished by maximizing its moment of inertia about the spin axis and by spinning it at the maximum practical frequency. Each of these considerations has the effect of maximizing the magnitude of the angular momentum, thus requiring a larger torque to change its direction. It is quite generally true that the torque τ, the angular momentum L, and the precession frequency Ω (defined as a vector along the precession axis in the direction given by the right-hand rule) are related by

$$\tau = \Omega \times L. \tag{90}$$

Equation (90) is called the gyroscope equation.

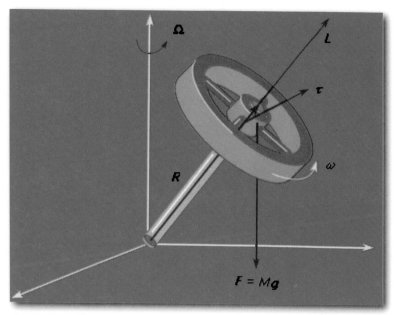

A gyroscope. Copyright Encyclopædia Britannica; rendering for this edition by Rosen Educational Services

Gyroscopes are used for a variety of purposes, including navigation. Use of gyroscopes for this purpose is called inertial guidance. The gyroscope is suspended as nearly as possible at its centre of mass, so that gravity does not apply a torque that causes it to precess. The gyroscope tends therefore to point in a constant direction in space, allowing the orientation of the vehicle to be accurately maintained.

One further application of the gyroscope principle may be seen in the precession of the equinoxes. Earth is a kind of gyroscope, spinning on its axis once each day. The Sun would apply no torque to Earth if Earth were perfectly spherical, but it is not. Earth bulges slightly at the Equator. The effect of the Sun's gravity on the near bulge (larger than it is on the far bulge) results in a net torque about the centre of Earth. When Earth is on the other side of

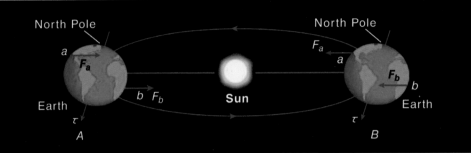

Forces acting on equatorial bulges in (A) the summer and (B) the winter cause the axis of the Earth to precess. Copyright Encyclopædia Britannica; rendering for this edition by Rosen Educational Services

the Sun, the net torque remains in the same direction. The torque is small but persistent. It causes the axis of Earth to precess, about one revolution every 25,800 years.

As seen from Earth, the Sun passes through the plane of the Equator twice each year. These points are called the equinoxes, and on the days of the equinoxes the hours of daylight and night are equal. From antiquity it has been known that the point in the sky where the Sun intersects the plane of the Equator is not the same each year but rather drifts very slowly to the west. This ancient observation, first explained by Newton, is due to the precession of Earth's axis. It is called the precession of the equinoxes.

ANALYTIC APPROACHES

Classical mechanics can, in essence, be reduced to Newton's laws, starting with the second law, in the form

$$F = \frac{d\boldsymbol{p}}{dt}. \tag{91}$$

If the net force acting on a particle is F, knowledge of F permits the momentum p to be found; and knowledge of p permits the position r to be found, by solving the equation

$$\frac{dr}{dt} = \frac{p}{m}.\tag{92}$$

These solutions give the components of p—that is, p_x, p_y, and p_z—and the components of r—x, y, and z—each as a function of time. To complete the solution, the value of each quantity—p_x, p_y, p_z, x, y, and z—must be known at some definite time, say, $t = 0$. If there is more than one particle, an equation in the form of equation (91) must be written for each particle, and the solution will involve finding the six variables x, y, z, p_x, p_y, and p_z, for each particle as a function of time, each once again subject to some initial condition. The equations may not be independent, however. For example, if the particles interact with one another, the forces will be related by Newton's third law. In this case (and others), the forces may also depend on time.

If the problem involves more than a very few particles, this method of solution quickly becomes intractable. Furthermore, in many cases it is not useful to express the problem purely in terms of particles and forces. Consider, for example, the problem of a sphere or cylinder rolling without slipping on a plane surface. Rolling without slipping is produced by friction due to forces acting between atoms in the rolling body and atoms in the plane, but the interactions are very complex; they probably are not fully understood even today, and one would like to be able to formulate and solve the problem without introducing them or needing to understand them. For all these reasons, methods that go beyond solving equations (91) and (92) have had to be introduced into classical mechanics.

The methods that have been introduced do not involve new physics. In fact, they are deduced directly from Newton's laws. They do, however, involve new concepts, new language to describe those concepts, and the adoption of powerful mathematical techniques. Some of those methods are briefly surveyed here.

CONFIGURATION SPACE

The position of a single particle is specified by giving its three coordinates, x, y, and z. To specify the positions of two particles, six coordinates are needed, x_1, y_1, z_1, x_2, y_2, z_2. If there are N particles, $3N$ coordinates will be needed. Imagine a system of $3N$ mutually orthogonal coordinates in a $3N$-dimensional space (a space of more than three dimensions is a purely mathematical construction, sometimes known as a hyperspace). To specify the exact position of one single point in this space, $3N$ coordinates are needed. However, one single point can represent the entire configuration of all N particles in the problem. Furthermore, the path of that single point as a function of time is the complete solution of the problem. This $3N$-dimensional space is called configuration space.

Configuration space is particularly useful for describing what is known as constraints on a problem. Constraints are generally ways of describing the effects of forces that are best not explicitly introduced into the problem. For example, consider the simple case of a falling body near the surface of Earth. The equations of motion—equations (4), (5), and (6)—are valid only until the body hits the ground. Physically, this restriction is due to forces between atoms in the falling body and atoms in the ground, but, as a practical matter, it is preferable to say that the solutions are valid only for $z > 0$ (where $z = 0$ is ground level). This constraint, in the form of an inequality, is very difficult to incorporate directly into the equations of the problem. In the language of configuration space, however, one merely needs to specify that the problem is being solved only in the region of configuration space for which $z > 0$.

Notice that the constraint, rolling without sliding on a plane, cannot easily be described in configuration space, since it is basically a condition on relative velocities of rotation and translation; but another constraint, that the body is restricted to motion along the plane, is easily described in configuration space.

Another type of constraint specifies that a body is rigid. Then, even though the body is composed of a very large number of atoms, it is not necessary to find separately the x, y, and z coordinate of each atom because these are related to those of the other atoms by the condition of rigidity. A careful analysis yields that, rather than needing $3N$ coordinates (where N may be, for example, 10^{24} atoms), only 6 are needed: 3 to specify the position of the centre of mass and 3 to give the orientation of the body. Thus, in this case, the constraint has reduced the number of independent coordinates from $3N$ to 6. Rather than restricting the behaviour of the system to a portion of the original $3N$-dimensional configuration space, it is possible to describe the system in a much simpler 6-dimensional configuration space. It should be noted, however, that the six coordinates are not necessarily all distances. In fact, the most convenient coordinates are three distances (the x, y, and z coordinates of the centre of mass of the body) and three angles, which specify the orientation of a set of axes fixed in the body relative to a set of axes fixed in space. This is an example of the use of constraints to reduce the number of dynamic variables in a problem (the x, y, and z coordinates of each particle) to a smaller number of generalized dynamic variables, which need not even have the same dimensions as the original ones.

The Principle of Virtual Work

A special class of problems in mechanics involves systems in equilibrium. The problem is to find the configuration of the system, subject to whatever constraints there may be, when all forces are balanced. The body or system will be at rest (in the inertial rest frame of its centre of mass), meaning that it occupies one point in configuration space for all time. The problem is to find that point. One criterion for finding that point, which makes use of the calculus of variations, is called the principle of virtual work.

According to the principle of virtual work, any infinitesimal virtual displacement in configuration space, consistent with the constraints, requires no work. A virtual displacement means an instantaneous change in coordinates (a real displacement would require finite time during which particles might move and forces might change). To express the principle, label the generalized coordinates r_1, $r_2, \ldots, r_i, \ldots$. Then if F_i is the net component of generalized force acting along the coordinate r_i,

$$\sum_i F_i \, dr_i = 0. \qquad (93)$$

Here, $F_i dr_i$ is the work done when the generalized coordinate is changed by the infinitesimal amount dr_i. If r_i is a real coordinate (say, the x coordinate of a particle), then F_i is a real force. If r_i is a generalized coordinate (say, an angular displacement of a rigid body), then F_i is the generalized force such that $F_i dr_i$ is the work done (for an angular displacement, F_i is a component of torque).

Take two simple examples to illustrate the principle. First consider two particles that are restricted to motion in the x direction and are constrained by a taut string connecting them. If their x coordinates are called x_1 and x_2, then $F_1 dx_1 + F_2 dx_2 = 0$ according to the principle of virtual work. But the taut string requires that the particles be displaced the same amount, so that $dx_1 = dx_2$, with the result that $F_1 + F_2 = 0$. The particles might be in equilibrium, for example, under equal and opposite forces, but F_1 and F_2 do not need individually to be zero. This is generally true of the F_i in equation (93). As a second example, consider a rigid body in space. Here, the constraint of rigidity has already been expressed by reducing the coordinate space to that of six generalized coordinates. These six coordinates (x, y, z, and three angles) can change quite independently of one another. In other words, in equation (93), the six dr_i are arbitrary. Thus, the only way equation (93) can be satisfied is if all six F_i are zero. This means that the rigid body can have no net component of force and no net component of torque acting on it. Of course, this same conclusion was reached earlier by less abstract arguments.

LAGRANGE'S AND HAMILTON'S EQUATIONS

Elegant and powerful methods have also been devised for solving dynamic problems with constraints. One of the best known is called Lagrange's equations. The Lagrangian L is defined as $L = T - V$, where T is the kinetic energy and V the potential energy of the system in question. Generally speaking, the potential energy of a system depends on the coordinates of all its particles; this may be written as $V = V(x_1, y_1, z_1, x_2, y_2, z_2, \ldots)$. The kinetic energy generally depends on the velocities, which, using the notation $v_x = dx/dt = \dot{x}$, may be written $T = T(\dot{x}_1, \dot{y}_1, \dot{z}_1, \dot{x}_2, \dot{y}_2, \dot{z}_2, \ldots)$. Thus, a dynamic problem has six dynamic variables for each particle—that is, x, y, z and $\dot{x}, \dot{y}, \dot{z}$—and the Lagrangian depends on all $6N$ variables if there are N particles.

In many problems, however, the constraints of the problem permit equations to be written relating at least some of these variables. In these cases, the $6N$ related dynamic variables may be reduced to a smaller number of independent generalized coordinates (written symbolically as $q_1, q_2, \ldots q_i, \ldots$) and generalized velocities (written as $\dot{q}_1, \dot{q}_2, \ldots \dot{q}_i, \ldots$), just as, for the rigid body, $3N$ coordinates were reduced to six independent generalized coordinates (each of which has an associated velocity). The Lagrangian, then, may be expressed as a function of all the q_i and $\dot{q}_i$. It is possible, starting from Newton's laws only, to derive Lagrange's equations

$$\frac{d}{dt}\frac{\partial L}{\partial \dot{q}_i} - \frac{\partial L}{\partial q_i} = 0, \tag{94}$$

where the notation $\partial L/\partial q_i$ means differentiate L with respect to q_i only, holding all other variables constant. There is one equation of the form (94) for each of the generalized coordinates q_i (e.g., six equations for a rigid body), and their solutions yield the complete dynamics of the system. The use of generalized coordinates allows many coupled equations of the form (91) to be reduced to fewer, independent equations of the form (94).

There is an even more powerful method called Hamilton's equations. It begins by defining a generalized momentum p_i, which is related to the Lagrangian and the generalized velocity $\dot{q}_i$ by $p_i = \partial L/\partial \dot{q}_i$. A new function, the Hamiltonian, is then defined by $H = \Sigma i \dot{q}_i p_i - L$. From this point it is not difficult to derive

$$\dot{q}_i = \frac{\partial H}{\partial p_i} \qquad (95)$$

and

$$-\dot{p}_i = \frac{\partial H}{\partial q_i}. \qquad (96)$$

There are two Hamilton equations for each generalized coordinate. They may be used in place of Lagrange's equations, with the advantage that only first derivatives — not second derivatives — are involved.

The Hamiltonian method is particularly important because of its utility in formulating quantum mechanics. However, it is also significant in classical mechanics. If the constraints in the problem do not depend explicitly on time, then it may be shown that $H = T + V$, where T is the kinetic energy and V is the potential energy of the system — i.e., the Hamiltonian is equal to the total energy of the system. Furthermore, if the problem is isotropic (H does not depend on direction in space) and homogeneous (H does not change with uniform translation in space), then Hamilton's equations immediately yield the laws of conservation of angular momentum and linear momentum, respectively.

I n the previous chapter, the motion of a rigid body as a whole was discussed. For a body to be rigid, the distance between any set of two points in it is always constant. This does not happen in reality. But what does? To answer this question, we have to consider what, then, is a solid. Any material, fluid or solid, can support normal forces. These are forces directed perpendicular, or normal, to a material plane across which they act. The force per unit of area of that plane is called the normal stress. Water at the base of a pond, air in an automobile tire, the stones of a Roman arch, rocks at the base of a mountain, the skin of a pressurized airplane cabin, a stretched rubber band, and the bones of a runner all support force in that way (some only when the force is compressive).

A material is called solid rather than fluid if it can also support a substantial shearing force over the time scale of some natural process or technological application of interest. Shearing forces are directed parallel, rather than perpendicular, to the material surface on which they act; the force per unit of area is called shear stress. For example, consider a vertical metal rod that is fixed to a support at its upper end and has a weight attached at its lower end. If one considers a horizontal surface through the material of the rod, it will be evident that the rod supports normal stress. But it also supports shear stress, and this becomes evident when one considers the forces carried across a plane that is neither horizontal nor vertical through the rod. Thus, while water and air provide no long-term support of shear stress, granite, steel, and rubber normally do so and are therefore called solids. Materials with tightly bound atoms or molecules, such as the crystals formed below melting temperature by most substances or simple compounds and the amorphous structures formed in glass and many polymer substances at sufficiently low temperature, are usually considered solids.

The distinction between solids and fluids is not precise and in many cases will depend on the time scale. Consider the hot rocks of the Earth's mantle. When a large earthquake occurs, an associated deformation disturbance called a seismic wave propagates through the adjacent rock, and the entire Earth is set into vibrations which, following a sufficiently large earthquake, may remain detectable with precise instruments for several weeks. The rocks of the mantle are then described as solid—as they would also be on the time scale of, say, tens to thousands of years, over which stresses rebuild enough in the source region to cause one or a few repetitions of the earthquake. But on a significantly longer time scale, say, on the order of a million years, the hot rocks of the mantle are unable to support shearing stresses and flow as a fluid. The substance called Silly Putty (trademark), a polymerized silicone gel familiar to many children, is another example. If a ball of it is left to sit on a table at room temperature, it flows and flattens on a time scale of a few minutes to an hour. But if picked up and tossed as a ball against a wall, so that large forces act only over the short time of the impact, the Silly Putty bounces back and retains its shape like a highly elastic solid.

Several types of solids can be distinguished according to their mechanical behaviour. In the simple but common case when a solid material is loaded at a sufficiently low temperature or short time scale, and with sufficiently limited stress magnitude, its deformation is fully recovered upon unloading. The material is then said to be elastic. But substances can also deform permanently, so that not all the deformation is recovered. For example, if one bends a metal coat hanger substantially and then releases the loading, it springs back only partially toward its initial shape; it does not fully recover but remains bent. The metal of the coat hanger has been permanently deformed, and in this case, for which the permanent deformation is not so much a consequence of longtime loading at sufficiently high temperature but more a consequence of subjecting the material to large stresses (above the yield stress), the permanent deformation is described as a plastic deformation and the material is called elastic-plastic. Permanent deformation of a sort that depends mainly on time of exposure to a stress—and that tends to increase significantly with time of exposure—is called viscous, or creep, deformation, and materials that exhibit those characteristics, as well as tendencies for elastic response, are called viscoelastic solids (or sometimes viscoplastic solids, when the permanent strain is emphasized rather than the tendency for partial recovery of strain upon unloading).

Solid mechanics has many applications. All those who seek to understand natural phenomena involving the stressing, deformation, flow, and fracture of solids, as well as all those who would have knowledge of such phenomena to improve living conditions and accomplish human objectives, have use for solid mechanics. The latter activities are, of course, the domain of engineering, and many important modern subfields of solid mechanics have been actively developed by engineering scientists concerned, for example, with mechanical, structural, materials, civil, or aerospace engineering. Natural phenomena involving solid mechanics are studied in geology, seismology, and tectonophysics, in materials science and the physics of condensed matter, and in some branches of biology and physiology. Furthermore, because solid mechanics poses challenging mathematical and computational problems, it (as well as fluid mechanics) has long been an important topic for applied mathematicians concerned, for example, with partial differential equations and with numerical techniques for digital computer formulations of physical problems.

Here is a sampling of some of the issues addressed using solid mechanics concepts: How do flows develop in Earth's mantle and cause continents to move and ocean floors to subduct (i.e., be thrust) slowly beneath them? How do mountains form? What processes take place along a fault during an earthquake, and how do the resulting disturbances propagate through Earth as seismic waves, shaking, and perhaps collapsing, buildings and bridges? How do landslides occur? How does a structure on a clay soil settle with time, and what is the maximum bearing pressure that the footing of a building can exert on a soil or rock foundation without rupturing it? What materials should be chosen, and how should their proportion, shape, and loading be controlled, to make safe, reliable, durable, and economical structures—whether airframes, bridges, ships, buildings, chairs, artificial heart valves, or computer chips—and to make machinery such as jet engines, pumps, and bicycles? How do vehicles (cars, planes, ships) respond by vibration to the irregularity of surfaces or mediums along which they move, and how are vibrations controlled for comfort, noise reduction, and safety against fatigue failure? How rapidly does a crack grow in a cyclically loaded structure, whether a bridge, engine, or airplane wing or fuselage, and when will it propagate catastrophically? How can the deformability of structures during impact be controlled so as to design crashworthiness into vehicles? How are the materials and products of a technological civilization formed—e.g., by extruding metals or polymers through dies, rolling material into sheets, punching out complex shapes, and so on? By what microscopic processes do plastic and creep strains occur in polycrystals? How can different materials, such as fibre-reinforced composites, be fashioned together to achieve combinations of stiffness and strength needed in specific applications? What is the combination of material properties and overall response needed in downhill skis or in a tennis racket? How does the human skull respond to impact in an accident? How do heart muscles control the pumping of blood in the human body, and what goes wrong when an aneurysm develops?

HISTORY

Solid mechanics developed in the outpouring of mathematical and physical studies following the great achievement of Newton in stating the laws of motion, although it has earlier roots. The need to understand and control the fracture of solids seems to have been a first motivation. Leonardo da Vinci sketched in his notebooks a possible test of the tensile strength of a wire. Galileo, who died in the year of Newton's birth (1642), investigated the breaking loads of rods under tension and concluded that the load was independent of length and proportional to the cross section area, this being a first step toward a concept of stress. He also investigated the breaking loads on beams that were suspended horizontally from a wall into which they were built.

CONCEPTS OF STRESS, STRAIN, AND ELASTICITY

The English scientist Robert Hooke discovered in 1660, but published only in 1678, that for many materials the displacement under a load was proportional to force, thus establishing the notion of (linear) elasticity but not yet in a way that was expressible in terms of stress and strain.

Edme Mariotte in France published similar discoveries in 1680 and, in addition, reached an understanding of how beams like those studied by Galileo resist transverse loadings—or, more precisely, resist the torques caused by those transverse loadings—by developing extensional and compressional deformations, respectively, in material fibres along their upper and lower portions. It was for the Swiss mathematician and mechanician Jakob Bernoulli to observe, in the final paper of his life, in 1705, that the proper way of describing deformation was to give force per unit area, or stress, as a function of the elongation per unit length, or strain, of a material fibre under tension. The Swiss mathematician and mechanician Leonhard Euler, who was taught mathematics by Jakob's brother Johann Bernoulli, proposed, among many contributions, a linear relation between stress σ and strain ε, in 1727, of the form $\sigma = E\varepsilon$, where the coefficient E is now generally called Young's modulus after the British naturalist Thomas Young, who developed a related idea in 1807.

The notion that there is an internal tension acting across surfaces in a deformed solid was expressed by the German mathematician and physicist Gottfried Wilhelm Leibniz in 1684 and Jakob Bernoulli in 1691. Also, Jakob Bernoulli and Euler introduced the idea that at a given section along the length of a beam there were internal tensions amounting to a net force and a net torque. Euler introduced the idea of compressive normal stress as the pressure in a fluid in 1752. The French engineer and physicist Charles-Augustin Coulomb was apparently the first to relate the theory of a beam as a bent elastic line to stress and strain in an actual beam, in a way never quite achieved by Bernoulli and, although possibly recognized, never published by Euler. He developed the famous expression $\sigma = My/I$ for the stress due to the pure bending of a homogenous linear elastic beam; here M is the torque, or bending moment, y is the distance of a point from an axis that passes through the section centroid, parallel to the torque axis, and I is the integral of y^2 over the section area. The French mathematician Antoine Parent introduced the concept of shear stress in 1713, but Coulomb was the one who extensively developed the idea, first in connection with beams and with the stressing and failure of soil in 1773 and then in studies of frictional slip in 1779.

It was the great French mathematician Augustin-Louis Cauchy, originally educated as an engineer, who in 1822 formalized the concept of stress in the context of a generalized three-dimensional theory, showed its properties

Augustin-Louis Cauchy. SSPL via Getty Images

as consisting of a 3 × 3 symmetric array of numbers that transform as a tensor, derived the equations of motion for a continuum in terms of the components of stress, and developed the theory of linear elastic response for isotropic solids. As part of his work in this area, Cauchy also introduced the equations that express the six components of strain (three extensional and three shear) in terms of derivatives of displacements for the case in which all those derivatives are much smaller than unity; similar expressions had been given earlier by Euler in expressing rates of straining in terms of the derivatives of the velocity field in a fluid.

BEAMS, COLUMNS, PLATES, AND SHELLS

The 1700s and early 1800s were a productive period during which the mechanics of simple elastic structural elements were developed—well before the beginnings in the 1820s of the general three-dimensional theory. The development of beam theory by Euler, who generally modeled beams as elastic lines that resist bending, as well as by several members of the Bernoulli family and by Coulomb, remains among the most immediately useful aspects of solid mechanics, in part for its simplicity and in part because of the pervasiveness of beams and columns in structural technology. Jakob Bernoulli proposed in his final paper of 1705 that the curvature of a beam was proportional to its bending moment. Euler in 1744 and Johann's son, Daniel Bernoulli, in 1751 used the theory to address the transverse vibrations of beams, and in 1757 Euler gave his famous analysis of the buckling of an initially straight beam subjected to a compressive loading; such a beam is commonly called a column. Following a suggestion of Daniel Bernoulli in 1742, Euler in 1744 introduced the concept of strain energy per unit length for a beam and showed that it is proportional to the square of the beam's curvature. Euler regarded the total strain energy as the quantity analogous to the potential energy of a discrete mechanical system. By adopting procedures that were becoming familiar in analytical mechanics and following from the principle of virtual work as introduced in 1717 by Johann Bernoulli for such discrete systems as pin-connected rigid bodies, Euler rendered the energy stationary and in this way developed the calculus of variations as an approach to the equations of equilibrium and motion of elastic structures.

That same variational approach played a major role in the development by French mathematicians in the early 1800s of a theory of small transverse displacements and vibrations of elastic plates. This theory was developed in preliminary form by Sophie Germain and was also worked on by Siméon-Denis Poisson in the early 1810s; they considered a flat plate as an elastic plane that resists curvature. Claude-Louis-Marie Navier gave a definitive development of the correct energy expression and governing differential equation a few years later. An uncertainty of some duration arose in the theory from the fact that the final partial differential equation for the transverse displacement is such that it is impossible to prescribe, simultaneously, along an unsupported edge of the plate, both the twisting moment per unit length of middle surface and the transverse shear force per unit length. This was finally resolved in 1850 by the Prussian physicist Gustav Robert Kirchhoff, who applied virtual work and variational calculus procedures in the framework of simplifying kinematic assumptions that fibres initially perpendicular to the plate's middle surface remain so after deformation of that surface.

The first steps in the theory of thin shells were taken by Euler in the 1770s; he addressed the deformation of an initially curved beam as an elastic line and provided a simplified analysis of the vibration of an elastic bell as an array of annular beams. Johann's grandson, Jakob Bernoulli "the Younger," further developed this model in the last year of his life as a two-dimensional network of elastic lines, but he could not develop an acceptable treatment. Shell theory did not attract attention again until a century after Euler's work. The first consideration of shells from a three-dimensional elastic viewpoint was advanced by Hermann Aron in 1873. Acceptable thin-shell theories for general situations, appropriate for cases of small deformation, were then developed by the British mathematician, mechanician, and geophysicist Augustus Edward Hough Love in 1888 and by the British mathematician and physicist Horace Lamb in 1890 (there is no uniquely correct theory, as the Dutch applied mechanician and engineer W.T. Koiter and the Soviet mechanician V.V. Novozhilov clarified in the 1950s; the difference between predictions of acceptable theories is small when the ratio of shell thickness to a typical length scale is small). Shell theory remained of immense interest well beyond the mid-1900s, in part because so many problems lay beyond the linear theory (rather small transverse displacements often dramatically alter the way that a shell supports load by a combination of bending and membrane action) and in part because of the interest in such lightweight structural forms for aeronautical technology.

THE GENERAL THEORY OF ELASTICITY

Linear elasticity as a general three-dimensional theory began to be developed in the early 1820s based on Cauchy's work. Simultaneously, Navier had developed an elasticity theory based on a simple corpuscular, or particle, model of matter in which particles interacted with their neighbours by a central force attraction between particle pairs. As was gradually realized, following work by Navier, Cauchy, and Poisson in the 1820s and '30s, the particle model is too simple and makes predictions concerning relations among elastic moduli that are not met by experiment. Most of the subsequent development of this subject was in terms of the continuum theory. Controversies concerning the maximum possible number of independent elastic moduli in the most general anisotropic solid were settled by the British mathematician George Green in 1837. Green pointed out that the existence of an elastic strain energy required that of the 36 elastic constants relating the 6 stress components to the 6 strains, at most 21 could be independent. The Scottish physicist Lord Kelvin put this consideration on sounder ground in 1855 as part of his development of macroscopic thermodynamics, showing that a strain energy function must exist for reversible isothermal or adiabatic (isentropic) response and working out such results as the (very modest) temperature changes associated with isentropic elastic deformation.

The middle and late 1800s were a period in which many basic elastic solutions were derived and applied to technology and to the explanation of natural phenomena. The French mathematician Adhémar-Jean-Claude Barré de Saint-Venant derived in the 1850s solutions for the torsion of noncircular cylinders, which explained the necessity of warping displacement of the cross section in the direction parallel to the axis of twisting, and for the flexure of beams due to transverse loadings; the latter allowed understanding of approximations inherent in the simple beam theory of Jakob Bernoulli, Euler, and Coulomb. The German physicist Heinrich Rudolf Hertz developed solutions for the deformation of elastic solids as they are brought into contact and applied these to model details of impact collisions. Solutions for stress and displacement due to concentrated forces acting at an interior point of a full space were derived by Kelvin, and those on the surface of a half space by the French mathematician Joseph Valentin Boussinesq and the Italian mathematician Valentino Cerruti. The Prussian mathematician Leo August Pochhammer analyzed the vibrations of an elastic cylinder, and Lamb and the Prussian physicist Paul Jaerisch derived the equations of general vibration of an elastic sphere in the 1880s, an effort that was continued by many seismologists in the 1900s to describe the vibrations of Earth. In 1863 Kelvin had derived the basic form of the solution of the static elasticity equations for a spherical solid, and these were applied in following years to such problems as calculating the deformation of Earth due to rotation and tidal forcing and measuring the effects of elastic deformability on the motions of Earth's rotation axis.

The classical development of elasticity never fully confronted the problem of finite elastic straining, in which material fibres change their lengths by other than very small amounts. Possibly this was because the common materials of construction would remain elastic only for very small strains before exhibiting either plastic straining or brittle failure. However, natural polymeric materials show elasticity over a far wider range (usually also with enough time or rate effects that they would more accurately be characterized as viscoelastic), and the widespread use of natural rubber and similar materials motivated the development of finite elasticity. While many roots of the subject were laid in the classical theory, especially in the work of Green, Gabrio Piola, and Kirchhoff in the mid-1800s, the development of a viable theory with forms of stress-strain relations for specific rubbery elastic materials, as well as an understanding of the physical effects of the nonlinearity in simple problems such as torsion and bending, was mainly the achievement of the British-born engineer and applied mathematician Ronald S. Rivlin in the 1940s and '50s.

WAVES

Poisson, Cauchy, and George G. Stokes showed that the equations of the general theory of elasticity predicted the existence of two types of elastic deformation waves which could propagate through isotropic elastic solids. These are called body waves. In the faster type, called longitudinal, dilational, or irrotational waves, the particle motion is in the same direction as that of wave propagation; in the slower type, called transverse, shear, or rotational waves, it is perpendicular to the propagation direction. No analogue of the shear wave exists for propagation through a fluid medium, and that fact led seismologists in the early 1900s to understand that Earth has a liquid core (at the centre of which there is a solid inner core).

Lord Rayleigh showed in 1885 that there is a wave type that could propagate along surfaces, such that the motion associated with the wave decayed exponentially with distance into the material from the surface. This type of surface wave, now called a Rayleigh wave, propagates typically at slightly more than 90 percent of the shear wave speed and involves an elliptical path of particle motion that lies in planes parallel to that defined by the normal to the surface and the propagation direction. Another type of surface wave, with motion transverse to the propagation direction and parallel to the surface, was found by Love for solids in which a surface layer of material sits atop an elastically stiffer bulk solid; this defines the situation for Earth's crust. The shaking in an earthquake is communicated first to distant places by body waves, but these spread out in three dimensions and to conserve the energy propagated by the wave field must diminish in their displacement amplitudes as r^{-1}, where r is the distance from the source. The surface waves spread out in only two dimensions and must, for the same reason, diminish only as fast as $r^{-1/2}$. Thus, the shaking effect of the surface waves from a crustal earthquake is normally felt more strongly, and is potentially more damaging, at moderate to large distances. Indeed, well before the theory of waves in solids was in hand, Thomas Young had suggested in his 1807 lectures on natural philosophy that the shaking of an earthquake "is probably propagated through the earth in the same manner as noise is conveyed through air." (It had been suggested by the American mathematician and astronomer John Winthrop, following his experience of the Boston-area earthquake of 1755, that the ground shaking was due to a disturbance propagated like sound through the air.)

With the development of ultrasonic transducers operated on piezoelectric principles, the measurement of the reflection and scattering of elastic waves has developed into an effective engineering technique for the nondestructive evaluation of materials for detection of such potentially dangerous defects as cracks. Also, very strong impacts, whether from meteorite collision, weaponry, or blasting and the like in technological endeavours, induce waves in which material response can be well outside the range of linear elasticity, involving any or all of finite elastic strain, plastic or viscoplastic response, and phase transformation. These are called shock waves; they can propagate much beyond the speed of linear elastic waves and are accompanied by significant heating.

STRESS CONCENTRATIONS AND FRACTURE

In 1898 G. Kirsch derived the solution for the stress distribution around a circular hole in a much larger plate under remotely uniform tensile stress. The same solution can be adapted to the tunnel-like cylindrical cavity of a circular section in a bulk solid. Kirsch's solution showed a significant concentration of stress at the boundary, by a factor of three when the remote stress was uniaxial tension. Then in 1907 the Russian mathematician Gury Vasilyevich Kolosov, and independently in 1914 the British engineer Charles Edward Inglis, derived the analogous solution for stresses around an elliptical hole. Their solution showed that the concentration of stress could become far greater, as the radius of curvature at an end of the hole becomes small compared with the overall length of the hole. These results provided the insight to sensitize engineers to the possibility of dangerous stress concentrations at sharp reentrant corners, notches, cutouts, keyways, screw threads, and similar openings in structures for which the nominal stresses were at otherwise safe levels. Such stress concentration sites are places from which a crack can nucleate.

The elliptical hole of Kolosov and Inglis defines a crack in the limit when one semimajor axis goes to zero, and the Inglis solution was adopted by the British aeronautical engineer A.A. Griffith in 1921 to describe a crack in a brittle solid. In that work Griffith made his famous proposition that a spontaneous crack growth would occur when the energy released from the elastic field just balanced the work required to separate surfaces in the solid. Following a hesitant beginning, in which Griffith's work was initially regarded as important only for very brittle solids such as glass, there developed, largely under the impetus of the American engineer and physicist George R. Irwin, a major body of work on the mechanics of crack growth and fracture, including fracture by fatigue and stress corrosion cracking, starting in the late 1940s and continuing into the 1990s. This was driven initially by the cracking of a number of American Liberty ships during World War II, by the failures of the British Comet airplane, and by a host of reliability and safety issues arising in aerospace and nuclear reactor technology. The new complexion of the subject extended beyond the Griffith energy theory and, in its simplest and most widely employed version in engineering practice, used Irwin's stress intensity factor as the basis for predicting crack growth response under service loadings in terms of laboratory data that is correlated in terms of that factor. That stress intensity factor is the coefficient of a characteristic singularity in the linear elastic solution for the stress field near a crack tip; it is recognized as providing a proper characterization of crack tip stressing in many cases, even though the linear elastic solution must be wrong in detail near the crack tip owing to nonelastic material response, large strain, and discreteness of material microstructure.

DISLOCATIONS

The Italian elastician and mathematician Vito Volterra introduced in 1905 the theory of the elastostatic stress and displacement fields created by dislocating solids. This involves making a cut in a solid, displacing its surfaces relative to one another by some fixed amount, and joining the sides of the cut back together, filling in with material as necessary. The initial status of this work was simply regarded as an interesting way of generating elastic fields, but, in the early 1930s, Geoffrey Ingram Taylor, Egon Orowan, and Michael Polanyi realized that just such a process could be going on in ductile crystals and could provide an explanation of the low plastic shear strength of typical ductile solids, much as Griffith's cracks explained low fracture strength under tension. In this case, the displacement on the dislocated surface corresponds to one atomic lattice spacing in the crystal. It quickly became clear that this concept provided the correct microscopic description of metal plasticity, and, starting with Taylor in the 1930s and continuing into the 1990s, the use of solid mechanics to explore dislocation interactions and the microscopic basis of plastic flow in crystalline materials has been a major topic, with many distinguished contributors.

The mathematical techniques advanced by Volterra are now in common use by earth scientists in explaining ground displacement and deformation induced by tectonic faulting. Also, the first elastodynamic solutions for the rapid motion of crystal dislocations, developed by South African materials scientist F.R.N. Nabarro in the early 1950s, were quickly adapted by seismologists to explain the radiation from propagating slip distributions on faults. The Japanese seismologist H. Nakano had already shown in 1923 how to represent the distant waves radiated by an earthquake as the elastodynamic response to a pair of force dipoles amounting to zero net torque. (All his manuscripts were destroyed in the fire in Tokyo associated with the great Kwanto earthquake in that same year, but copies of some had been sent to Western colleagues and the work survived.)

CONTINUUM PLASTICITY THEORY

The macroscopic theory of plastic flow has a history nearly as old as that of elasticity. While in the microscopic theory of materials, the word "plasticity" is usually interpreted as denoting deformation by dislocation processes, in macroscopic continuum mechanics it is taken to denote any type of permanent deformation of materials, especially those of a type for which time or rate of deformation effects are not the most dominant feature of the phenomenon (the terms viscoplasticity, creep, or viscoelasticity are usually used in such cases). Coulomb's work of 1773 on the frictional yielding of soils under shear and normal stress has been mentioned; yielding denotes the occurrence of large shear deformations without significant increase in applied stress. His results were used to explain the pressure of soils against retaining walls and footings in the work of the French mathematician and engineer Jean Victor Poncelet in 1840 and the Scottish engineer and physicist William John Macquorn Rankine in 1853. The inelastic deformation of soils and rocks often takes place in situations for which the deforming mass is infiltrated by groundwater, and Austrian-American civil engineer Karl Terzaghi in the 1920s developed the concept of effective stress, whereby the stresses that enter a criterion of yielding or failure are not the total stresses applied to the saturated soil or rock mass but rather the effective stresses, which are the difference between the total stresses and those of a purely hydrostatic stress state with pressure equal to that in the pore fluid. Terzaghi also introduced the concept of consolidation, in which the compression of a fluid-saturated soil can take place only as the fluid slowly flows through the pore space under pressure gradients, according to Darcy's law; this effect accounts for the time-dependent settlement of constructions over clay soils.

Apart from the earlier observation of plastic flow at large stresses in the tensile testing of bars, the theory of continuum plasticity for metallic materials begins with Henri Edouard Tresca in 1864. His experiments on the compression and indentation of metals led him to propose that this type of plasticity, in contrast to that in soils, was essentially independent of the average normal stress in the material and dependent only on shear stresses, a feature later rationalized by the dislocation mechanism. Tresca proposed a yield criterion for macroscopically isotropic metal polycrystals based on the maximum shear stress in the material, and that was used by Saint-Venant to solve an early elastic-plastic problem, that of the partly plastic cylinder in torsion, and also to solve for the stresses in a completely plastic tube under pressure.

The German applied mechanician Ludwig Prandtl developed the rudiments of the theory of plane plastic flow in 1920 and 1921, with an analysis of indentation of a ductile solid by a flat-ended rigid indenter, and the resulting theory of plastic slip lines was completed by H. Hencky in 1923 and Hilda Geiringer in 1930. Additional developments include the methods of plastic limit analysis, which allowed engineers to directly calculate upper and lower bounds to the plastic collapse loads of structures or to forces required in metal forming. Those methods developed gradually over the early 1900s on a largely intuitive basis, first for simple beam structures and later for plates, and were put on a rigorous basis within the rapidly developing mathematical theory of plasticity about 1950 by Daniel C. Drucker and William Prager in the United States and Rodney Hill in Great Britain.

The Austrian-American applied mathematician Richard von Mises proposed in 1913 that a mathematically simpler theory of plasticity than that based on the Tresca yield criterion could be based on the second tensor invariant of the deviatoric stresses (i.e., of the total stresses minus those of a hydrostatic state in which pressure is equal to the average normal stress over all planes). An equivalent yield criterion had been proposed independently by the Polish engineer Maksymilian Tytus Huber. The Mises theory incorporates a proposal by M. Levy in 1871 that components of the plastic strain increment tensor are in proportion to one another just as are the components of deviatoric stress. This criterion was generally found to provide slightly better agreement with experiment than did that of Tresca, and most work on the application of plasticity theory uses this form. Following a suggestion of Prandtl, E. Reuss completed the theory in 1930 by adding an elastic component of strain increments, related to stress increments in the same way as for linear elastic response. This formulation was soon generalized to include strain hardening, whereby the value of the second invariant for continued yielding increases with ongoing plastic deformation, and was extended to high-temperature creep response in metals or other hot solids by assuming that the second invariant of the plastic (now generally called "creep") strain rate is a function of that same invariant of the deviatoric stress, typically a power law type with Arrhenius temperature dependence.

This formulation of plastic and viscoplastic, or creep, response has been applied to all manner of problems in materials and structural technology and in flow of geologic masses. Representative problems addressed include the growth and subsequent coalescence of microscopic voids in the ductile fracture of metals, the theory of the indentation hardness test, the extrusion of metal rods and rolling of metal sheets, design against collapse of ductile steel structures, estimation of the thickness of the Greenland Ice Sheet, and modeling the geologic evolution of the Plateau of Tibet. Other types of elastic-plastic theories intended for analysis of ductile single crystals originate from the work of G.I. Taylor and Hill and base the criterion for yielding on E. Schmid's concept from the 1920s of a critical resolved shear stress along a crystal slip plane, in the direction of an allowed slip on that plane; this sort of yield condition has approximate support from the dislocation theory of plasticity.

VISCOELASTICITY

The German physicist Wilhelm Weber noticed in 1835 that a load applied to a silk thread produced not only an immediate extension but also a continuing elongation of the thread with time. This type of viscoelastic response is especially notable in polymeric solids but is present to some extent in all types of solids and often does not have a clear separation from what could be called viscoplastic, or creep, response. In general, if all of the strain is ultimately recovered when a load is removed from a body, the response is termed viscoelastic, but the term is also used in cases for which sustained loading leads to strains that are not fully recovered. The Austrian physicist Ludwig Boltzmann developed in 1874 the theory of linear viscoelastic stress-strain relations. In their most general form, these involve the notion that a step loading (a suddenly imposed stress that is subsequently maintained constant) causes an immediate strain followed by a time-dependent strain which, for different materials, either may have a finite limit at long time or may increase indefinitely with time. Within the assumption of linearity, the strain at time t in response to a general time-dependent stress history $\sigma(t)$ can then be written as the sum (or integral) of terms that involve the step-loading strain response due to a step loading $dt' d\sigma(t')/dt'$ at time t'. The theory of viscoelasticity is important for consideration of the attenuation of stress waves and the damping of vibrations.

A new class of problems arose with the mechanics of very-long-molecule polymers, which do not have significant cross-linking and exist either in solution or as a melt. These are fluids in the sense that they cannot long support shear stress, but at the same time they have remarkable properties like those of finitely deformed elastic solids. A famous demonstration is to pour one of these fluids slowly from a beaker and to cut the flowing stream suddenly with scissors; if the cut is not too far below the place of exit from the beaker, the stream of falling fluid immediately contracts elastically and returns to the beaker. The molecules are elongated during flow but tend to return to their thermodynamically preferred coiled configuration when forces are removed.

The theory of such materials came under intense development in the 1950s after the British applied mathematician James Gardner Oldroyd showed in 1950 how viscoelastic stress-strain relations of a memory type could be generalized to a flowing fluid. This requires that the constitutive relation, or rheological relation, between the stress history and the deformation history at a material "point" be properly invariant to a superposed history of rigid rotation, which should not affect the local physics determining that relation (the resulting Coriolis and centrifugal effects are quite negligible at the scale of molecular interactions). Important contributions on this issue were made by the applied mathematicians Stanisław Zaremba and Gustav Andreas Johannes Jaumann in the first decade of the 1900s; they showed how to make tensorial definitions of stress rate that were invariant to superposed spin and thus were suitable for use in constitutive relations. But it was only during the 1950s that these concepts found their way into the theory of constitutive relations for general viscoelastic materials; independently, a few years later, properly invariant stress rates were adopted in continuum formulations of elastic-plastic response.

COMPUTATIONAL MECHANICS

The digital computer revolutionized the practice of many areas of engineering and science, and solid mechanics was among the first fields to benefit from its impact. Many computational techniques have been used in this field, but the one that emerged by the end of 1970s as, by far, the most widely adopted is the finite-element method. This method was outlined by the mathematician Richard Courant in 1943 and was developed independently, and put to practical use on computers, in the mid-1950s by the aeronautical structures engineers M.J. Turner, Ray W. Clough, Harold Clifford Martin, and LeRoy J. Topp in the United States and J.H. Argyris and Sydney Kelsey in Britain. Their work grew out of earlier attempts at systematic structural analysis for complex frameworks of beam elements. The method was soon recast in a variational framework and related to earlier efforts at deriving approximate solutions of problems described by variational principles. The new technique involved substituting trial functions of unknown amplitude into the variational functional, which is then rendered stationary as an algebraic function of the amplitude coefficients. In the most common version of the finite-element method, the domain to be analyzed is divided into cells, or elements, and the displacement field within each element is interpolated in terms of displacements at a few points around the element boundary (and sometimes within it) called nodes. The interpolation is done so that the displacement field is continuous across element boundaries for any choice of the nodal displacements. The strain at every point can thus be expressed in terms of nodal displacements, and it is then required that the stresses associated with these strains, through the stress-strain relations of the material, satisfy the principle of virtual work for arbitrary variation of the nodal displacements. This generates as many simultaneous equations as there are degrees of freedom in the finite element model, and numerical techniques for solving such systems of equations are programmed for computer solution.

CHAPTER 7
STRESS AND STRAIN

I n addressing any problem in continuum or solid mechanics, three factors must be considered: (1) the Newtonian equations of motion, in the more general form recognized by Euler, expressing conservation of linear and angular momentum for finite bodies (rather than just for point particles), and the related concept of stress, as formalized by Cauchy, (2) the geometry of deformation and thus the expression of strains in terms of gradients in the displacement field, and (3) the relations between stress and strain that are characteristic of the material in question, as well as of the stress level, temperature, and time scale of the problem considered.

These three considerations suffice for most problems. They must be supplemented, however, for solids undergoing diffusion processes in which one material constituent moves relative to another (which may be the case for fluid-infiltrated soils or petroleum reservoir rocks) and in cases for which the induction of a temperature field by deformation processes and the related heat transfer cannot be neglected. These cases require that the following also be considered: (4) equations for conservation of mass of diffusing constituents, (5) the first law of thermodynamics, which introduces the concept of heat flux and relates changes in energy to work and heat supply, and (6) relations that express the diffusive fluxes and heat flow in terms of spatial gradients of appropriate chemical potentials and of temperature. In many important technological devices, electric and magnetic fields affect the stressing, deformation, and motion of matter. Examples are provided by piezoelectric

The linear momentum P and angular momentum H (relative to the coordinate origin) of the matter instantaneously occupying any volume V of space are then given by summing up the linear and angular momentum vectors of each element of material. Such summation over infinitesimal elements is represented mathematically by the integrals $P = \int_V \rho v dV$ and $H = \int_V \rho x \times v dV$. In this discussion attention is limited to situations in which relativistic effects can be ignored. Let F denote the total force and M the total torque, or moment (relative to the coordinate origin), acting instantaneously on the material occupying any arbitrary volume V. The basic laws of Newtonian mechanics are the linear and angular momentum principles that $F = dP/dt$ and $M = dH/dt$, where time derivatives of P and H are calculated following the motion of the matter that occupies V at time t. When either F or M vanishes, these equations of motion correspond to conservation of linear or angular momentum.

An important, very common, and nontrivial class of problems in solid mechanics involves determining the deformed and stressed configuration of solids or structures that are in static equilibrium; in that case the relevant basic equations are $F = 0$ and $M = 0$. The understanding of such conditions for equilibrium, at least in a rudimentary form, long predates Newton. Indeed, Archimedes of Syracuse (3rd century BCE), the great Greek mathematician and arguably the first theoretically and experimentally minded physical scientist, understood these equations at least in a nonvectorial form appropriate for systems of parallel forces. This is shown by his treatment of the hydrostatic equilibrium of a partially submerged body and by his establishment of the principle of the lever (torques about the fulcrum sum to zero) and the concept of centre of gravity.

STRESS

Assume that F and M derive from two types of forces, namely, body forces f, such as gravitational attractions — defined such that force fdV acts on volume element dV — and surface forces, which represent the mechanical effect of matter immediately adjoining that along the surface S of the volume V being considered. Cauchy formalized in 1822 a basic assumption of continuum mechanics that such surface forces could be represented as a stress vector T, defined so that TdS is an element of force acting over the area dS of the surface. Hence, the principles of linear and angular momentum take the forms

$$\int_S T\, dS + \int_V f\, dV = F = \frac{dP}{dt} = \int_V \rho a\, dV, \text{ and} \qquad (111)$$

$$\int_S x \times T\, ds + \int_V x \times f\, dV = M = \frac{dH}{dt} = \int_V \rho x \times a\, dV, \qquad (112)$$

which are now assumed to hold good for every conceivable choice of region V. In calculating the right-hand sides, which come from dP/dt and dH/dt, it has been noted that ρdV is an element of mass and is therefore time-invariant; also, $a = a(x, t) = dv/dt$ is the acceleration, where the time derivative of v is taken following the motion of a material point so that $a(x, t)dt$ corresponds to the difference between $v(x + vdt, t + dt)$ and $v(x, t)$. A more detailed analysis of this step shows that the understanding of what TdS denotes must now be adjusted to include averages, over temporal and spatial scales that are large compared to those of microscale fluctuations, of transfers of momentum across the surface S due to the microscopic fluctuations about the motion described by the macroscopic velocity v.

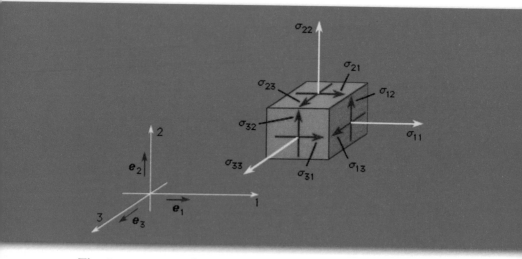

The nine components of a stress tensor. The first index denotes the direction of the normal, or perpendicular, stresses to the plane across which the contact force acts, and the second index denotes the direction of the component of force. Copyright Encyclopædia Britannica; rendering for this edition by Rosen Educational Services

The nine quantities $\sigma_{ij}(i, j = 1, 2, 3)$ are called stress components; these will vary with position and time—i.e., $\sigma_{ij} = \sigma_{ij}(\boldsymbol{x}, t)$—and have the following interpretation. Consider an element of surface dS through a point $\boldsymbol{x}$ with dS oriented so that its outer normal (pointing away from the region V, bounded by S) points in the positive x_i direction, where i is any of 1, 2, or 3. Then σ_{i1}, σ_{i2}, and σ_{i3} at $\boldsymbol{x}$ are defined as the Cartesian components of the stress vector $\boldsymbol{T}$ (called $\boldsymbol{T}^{(i)}$) acting on this dS. To use a vector notation with $\boldsymbol{e}_1$, $\boldsymbol{e}_2$, and $\boldsymbol{e}_3$ denoting unit vectors along the coordinate axes, $\boldsymbol{T}^{(i)} = \sigma_{i1}\boldsymbol{e}_1 + \sigma_{i2}\boldsymbol{e}_2 + \sigma_{i3}\boldsymbol{e}_3$. Thus, the stress σ_{ij} at $\boldsymbol{x}$ is the stress in the j direction associated with an i-oriented face through point $\boldsymbol{x}$; the physical dimension of the σ_{ij} is [force]/[length]². The components σ_{11}, σ_{22}, and σ_{33} are stresses directed perpendicular, or normal, to the face on which they act and are normal stresses; the σ_{ij} with $i \neq j$ are directed parallel to the face on which they act and are shear stresses.

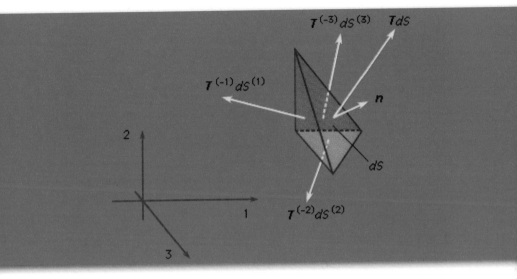

The force TdS *acting on an arbitrarily inclined face (whose outward unit normal vector is* n*). Stress vectors* $T^{(-1)}$*,* $T^{(-2)}$*, and* $T^{(-3)}$ *act on the faces perpendicular to the coordinate axes.* Copyright Encyclopædia Britannica; rendering for this edition by Rosen Educational Services

By hypothesis, the linear momentum principle applies for any volume V. Consider a small tetrahedron at x with an inclined face having an outward unit normal vector n and its other three faces oriented perpendicular to the three coordinate axes. Letting the size of the tetrahedron shrink to zero, the linear momentum principle requires that the stress vector T on a surface element with outward normal n be expressed as a linear function of the σ_{ij} at x. The relation is such that the j component of the stress vector T is $T_j = n_1\sigma_{1j} + n_2\sigma_{2j} + n_3\sigma_{3j}$ for ($j = 1, 2, 3$). This relation for T (or T_j) also demonstrates that the σ_{ij} have the mathematical property of being the components of a second-rank tensor.

Suppose that a different set of Cartesian reference axes $1'$, $2'$, and $3'$ have been chosen. Let x_1', x_2', and x_3' denote the components of the position vector of point x and let $\sigma_{kl}'(k, l = 1, 2, 3)$ denote the nine stress components relative to that coordinate system. The σ_{kl}' can be written as the 3×3 matrix $[\sigma']$, and the σ_{ij} as the matrix $[\sigma]$, where the first index is the matrix row number and the second is the column number. Then the expression for T_j implies that $[\sigma'] = [a][\sigma][a]^T$, which is the defining equation of a second-rank tensor. Here $[a]$ is the orthogonal transformation matrix, having components $a_{pq} = e_p' \cdot e_q$ for $p, q = 1, 2, 3$ and satisfying $[a]^T[a] = [a][a]^T = [I]$, where the superscript T denotes transpose (interchange rows and columns) and $[I]$ denotes the unit matrix, a 3×3 matrix with unity for every diagonal element and zero elsewhere; also, the matrix multiplications are such that if $[A] = [B][C]$, then $A_{ij} = B_{i1}C_{1j} + B_{i2}C_{2j} + B_{i3}C_{3j}$.

EQUATIONS OF MOTION

Now the linear momentum principle may be applied to an arbitrary finite body. Using the expression for T_j above and the divergence theorem of multivariable calculus, which states that integrals over the area of a closed surface S, with integrand $nf(x)$, may be rewritten as integrals over the volume V enclosed by S, with integrand $\partial f(x)/\partial x_i$; when $f(x)$ is a differentiable function, one may derive that

$$\frac{\partial \sigma_{1j}}{\partial x_1} + \frac{\partial \sigma_{2j}}{\partial x_2} + \frac{\partial \sigma_{3j}}{\partial x_3} + f_j = \rho a_j \quad (j = 1, 2, 3), \qquad (113)$$

at least when the σ_{ij} are continuous and differentiable, which is the typical case. These are the equations of motion for a continuum. Once the above consequences of the linear momentum principle are accepted, the only further result that can be derived from the angular momentum principle is that $\sigma_{ij} = \sigma_{ji}$ ($i, j = 1, 2, 3$). Thus, the stress tensor is symmetric.

PRINCIPAL STRESSES

Symmetry of the stress tensor has the important consequence that, at each point x, there exist three mutually perpendicular directions along which there are no shear stresses. These directions are called the principal stress directions, and the corresponding normal stresses are called the principal stresses. If the principal stresses are ordered algebraically as σ_I, σ_{II}, and σ_{III}, then the normal stress on any face (given as $\sigma_n = n \cdot T$) satisfies $\sigma_I \leq \sigma_n \leq \sigma_{III}$. The principal stresses are the eigenvalues (or characteristic values) s, and the principal directions the eigenvectors n, of the problem $T = sn$, or $[\sigma]\{n\} = s\{n\}$ in matrix notation with the 3-column $\{n\}$ representing n. It has solutions when $\det([\sigma] - s[I]) = -s^3 + I_1 s^2 + I_2 s + I_3 = 0$, with $I_1 = \mathrm{tr}[\sigma]$, $I_2 = -(1/2)I\,2/1 + (1/2)\mathrm{tr}([\sigma][\sigma])$, and $I_3 = \det[\sigma]$. Here "det" denotes determinant and "tr" denotes trace, or sum of diagonal elements, of a matrix. Since the principal stresses

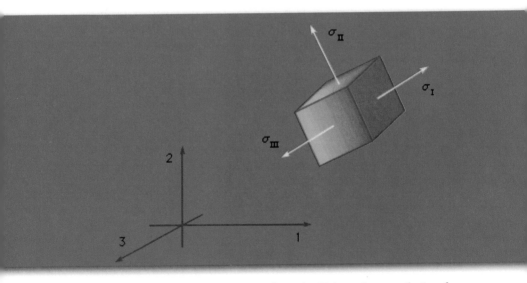

Principal stresses. Copyright Encyclopædia Britannica; rendering for this edition by Rosen Educational Services

are determined by I_1, I_2, and I_3 and can have no dependence on how one chooses the coordinate system with respect to which the components of stress are referred, I_1, I_2, and I_3 must be independent of that choice and are therefore called stress invariants. One may readily verify that they have the same values when evaluated in terms of σ_{ij}' above as in terms of σ_{ij} by using the tensor transformation law and properties noted for the orthogonal transformation matrix.

Very often, in both nature and technology, there is interest in structural elements in forms that might be identified as strings, wires, rods, bars, beams, or columns, or as membranes, plates, or shells. These are usually idealized as, respectively, one- or two-dimensional continua. One possible approach is then to develop the consequences of the linear and angular momentum principles entirely within that idealization, working in terms of net axial and shear forces and bending and twisting torques at each point along a one-dimensional continuum, or in terms of forces and torques per unit length of surface in a two-dimensional continuum.

STRAIN

The shape of a solid or structure changes with time during a deformation process. To characterize deformation, or strain, a certain reference configuration is adopted and called undeformed. Often, that reference configuration is chosen as an unstressed state, but such is neither necessary nor always convenient. If time is measured from zero at a moment when the body exists in that reference configuration, then the upper case X may be used to denote the position vectors of material points when $t = 0$. At some other time t, a material point that was at X will have moved to some spatial position x. The deformation is thus described as the mapping $x = x(X, t)$, with $x = x(X, 0) = X$. The displacement vector u is then $u = x(X, t) - X$; also, $v = \partial x(X, t)/\partial t$ and $a = \partial^2 x(X, t)/\partial t^2$.

STRAIN-DISPLACEMENT RELATIONS

It is simplest to write equations for strain in a form that, while approximate in general, is suitable for the case when any infinitesimal line element dX of the reference configuration undergoes extremely small rotations and fractional change in length, in deforming to the corresponding line element dx. These conditions are met when $|\partial u_i/\partial X_j| \ll 1$. Many solids are often sufficiently rigid, at least under the loadings typically applied to them, that these conditions are realized in practice. Linearized expressions for strain in terms of $[\partial u/\partial X]$, appropriate to this situation, are called small strain or infinitesimal strain. Expressions for strain will also be given that are valid for rotations and fractional length changes of arbitrary magnitude; such expressions are called finite strain.

Two simple types of strain are extensional strain and shear strain. Consider a rectangular parallelepiped, a brick-like block of material with mutually perpendicular planar faces, and let the edges of the block be parallel to the 1, 2, and 3 axes. If the block is deformed homogeneously, so that each planar face moves perpendicular to itself and so that the faces remain orthogonal (i.e., the parallelepiped is deformed into another rectangular parallelepiped), then the block is said to have undergone extensional strain relative to each of the 1, 2, and 3 axes but no shear strain relative to these axes. If the edge lengths of the undeformed parallelepiped are denoted as ΔX_1, ΔX_2, and ΔX_3, and those of the deformed parallelepiped as Δx_1, Δx_2,

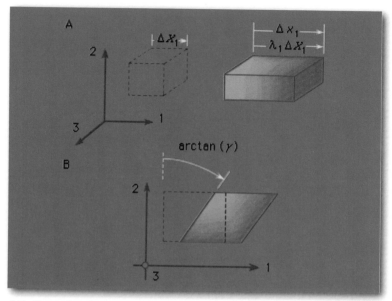

(A) Extensional strain and (B) simple shear strain, where the element drawn with dashed lines represents the reference configuration, and the element drawn with solid lines represents the deformed configuration. Copyright Encyclopædia Britannica; rendering for this edition by Rosen Educational Services

and Δx_3, then the quantities $\lambda_1 = \Delta x_1/\Delta X_1$, $\lambda_2 = \Delta x_2/\Delta X_2$, and $\lambda = \Delta x_3/\Delta X_3$ are called stretch ratios. There are various ways that extensional strain can be defined in terms of them. Note that the change in displacement in, say, the x_1 direction between points at one end of the block and those at the other is $\Delta u_1 = (\lambda_1 - 1)\Delta X_1$. For example, if E_{11} denotes the extensional strain along the x_1 direction, then the most commonly understood definition of strain is E_{11} = (change in length)/(initial length) = $(\Delta x_1 - \Delta X_1)/\Delta X_1 = \Delta u_1/\Delta X_1 = \lambda_1 - 1$. A variety of other measures of extensional strain can be defined by $E_{11} = g(\lambda_1)$, where the function $g(\lambda)$ satisfies $g(1) = 0$ and $g'(1) = 1$, so as to agree with the above definition when λ_1 is very near 1. Two such measures in common use are the strain $E\,M = (\lambda^{2}_{1} - 1)/2$, based on the change of metric tensor, and the logarithmic strain $E\,L = \ln(\lambda_1)$.

To define a simple shear strain, consider the same rectangular parallelepiped, but now deform it so that every point on a plane of type X_2 = constant moves only in the x_1 direction by an amount that increases linearly with X_2. Thus, the deformation $x_1 = \gamma X_2 + X_1, x_2 = X_2, x_3 = X_3$ defines a homogeneous simple shear strain of amount γ. Note that this strain causes no change of volume. For small strain, the shear strain γ can be identified as the reduction in angle between two initially perpendicular lines.

SMALL-STRAIN TENSOR

The small strains, or infinitesimal strains, ε_{ij} are appropriate for situations with $|\partial u_k/\partial X_l| \ll 1$ for all k and l. Consider two infinitesimal material fibres, one initially in the 1 direction and the other in the 2 direction. To first-order accuracy in components of $[\partial u/\partial X]$, the extensional strains of these fibres are $\varepsilon_{11} = \partial u_1/\partial X_1$ and $\varepsilon_{22} = \partial u_2/\partial X_2$, and the reduction of the angle between them is $\gamma_{12} = \partial u_2/\partial X_1$

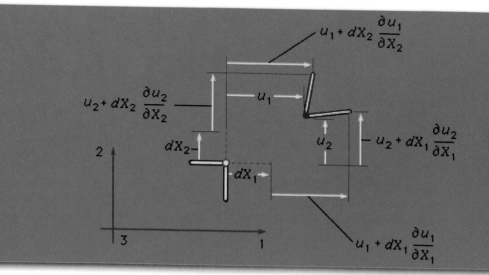

Relations of strains to gradients of displacement. Copyright Encyclopædia Britannica; rendering for this edition by Rosen Educational Services

+ $\partial u_1 / \partial X_2$. For the shear strain denoted ε_{12}, however, half of γ_{12} is used. Thus, considering all extensional and shear strains associated with infinitesimal fibres in the 1, 2, and 3 directions at a point of the material, the set of strains is given by

$$\varepsilon_{ij} = \frac{1}{2}\left(\frac{\partial u_j}{\partial X_i} + \frac{\partial u_i}{\partial X_j}\right) \quad (i, j = 1, 2, 3). \quad (114)$$

The ε_{ij} are symmetric—i.e., $\varepsilon_{ij} = \varepsilon_{ji}$—and form a second-rank tensor (that is, if Cartesian reference axes 1′, 2′, and 3′ were chosen instead and the ε_{kl}' were determined, then the ε_{kl}' are related to the ε_{ij} by the same equations that relate the stresses σ_{kl}' to the σ_{ij}). These mathematical features require that there exist principal strain directions; at every point of the continuum it is possible to identify three mutually perpendicular directions along which there is purely extensional strain, with no shear strain between these special directions. The directions are the principal strain directions, and the corresponding strains include the least and greatest extensional strains experienced by fibres through the material point considered. Invariants of the strain tensor may be defined in a way paralleling those for the stress tensor.

An important fact to note is that the strains cannot vary in an arbitrary manner from point to point in the body. This is because the six strain components are all derivable from three displacement components. Restrictions on strain resulting from such considerations are called compatibility relations; the body would not fit together after deformation unless they were satisfied. Consider, for example, a state of plane strain in the 1, 2 plane (so that $\varepsilon_{33} = \varepsilon_{23} = \varepsilon_{31} = 0$). The nonzero strains ε_{11}, ε_{22}, and ε_{12} cannot vary arbitrarily from point to point but must satisfy

$\partial^2\varepsilon_{22}/\partial X\,{}^2_1 + \partial^2\varepsilon_{11}/\partial X\,{}^2_2 = 2\partial^2\varepsilon_{12}/\partial X_1\partial X_2$, as may be verified by directly inserting the relations for strains in terms of displacements.

When the smallness of stretch and rotation of line elements allows use of the infinitesimal strain tensor, a derivative $\partial/\partial X_i$ will be very nearly identical to $\partial/\partial x_i$. Frequently, but not always, it will then be acceptable to ignore the distinction between the deformed and undeformed configurations in writing the governing equations of solid mechanics. For example, the differential equations of motion in terms of stress are rigorously correct only with derivatives relative to the deformed configuration, but, in the circumstances considered, the equations of motion can be written relative to the undeformed configuration. This is what is done in the most widely used variant of solid mechanics, in the form of the theory of linear elasticity. The procedure can be unsatisfactory and go badly wrong in some important cases, however, such as for columns that buckle under compressive loadings or for elastic-plastic materials when the slope of the stress versus strain relation is of the same order as existing stresses. Cases such as these are instead best approached through finite deformation theory.

FINITE DEFORMATION AND STRAIN TENSORS

In the theory of finite deformations, extension and rotations of line elements are unrestricted as to size. For an infinitesimal fibre that deforms from an initial point given by the vector $d\mathbf{X}$ to the vector $d\mathbf{x}$ in the time t, the deformation gradient is defined by $F_{ij} = \partial x_i(\mathbf{X}, t)/\partial X_j$; the 3×3 matrix $[F]$, with components F_{ij}, may be represented as a pure deformation, characterized by a symmetric matrix $[U]$, followed by a rigid rotation $[R]$. This result is called the polar decomposition theorem and takes the form, in matrix notation, $[F] = [R][U]$. For an arbitrary deformation, there exist three mutually orthogonal principal stretch directions at each point of the material; call these directions in the reference configuration $N^{(I)}$, $N^{(II)}$, $N^{(III)}$, and let the stretch ratios be $\lambda_I, \lambda_{II}, \lambda_{III}$. Fibres in these three principal strain directions undergo extensional strain but have no shearing between them. Those three fibres in the deformed configuration remain orthogonal but are rotated by the operation $[R]$.

As noted earlier, an extensional strain may be defined by $E = g(\lambda)$, where $g(1) = 0$ and $g'(1) = 1$, with examples for $g(\lambda)$ given above. A finite strain tensor E_{ij} may then be defined based on any particular function $g(\lambda)$ by $E_{ij} = g(\lambda_I)N_i^{(I)}N_j^{(I)} + g(\lambda_{II})N_i^{(II)}N_j^{(II)} + g(\lambda_{III})N_i^{(III)}N_j^{(III)}$. Usually, it is rather difficult to actually solve for the λ's and N's associated with any general $[F]$, so it is not easy to use this strain definition. However, for the special choice identified as $g^M(\lambda) = (\lambda^2 - 1)/2$ above, it may be shown that

$$2E_{ij}^M = \sum_{k=1}^{3} F_{ki} F_{kj} - \delta_{ij} = \partial u_i / \partial X_j + \partial u_j / \partial X_i + \sum_{k=1}^{3} (\partial u_k / \partial X_i)(\partial u_k / \partial X_j),$$

which, like the finite strain generated by any other $g(\lambda)$, reduces to ε_{ij} when linearized in $[\partial u / \partial X]$.

STRESS-STRAIN RELATIONS

In general, the stress-strain relations are to be determined by experiment. A variety of mechanical testing machines and geometric configurations of material specimens have been devised to measure them. These allow, in different cases, simple tensile, compressive, or shear stressing, and sometimes combined stressing with several different components of stress, as well as the determination of material response over a range of temperatures, strain rates, and loading histories. The testing of round bars under tensile stress, with precise measurement of their extension to obtain the strain, is common for metals and for technological ceramics and polymers. For rocks and soils, which generally carry load in compression, the most common test involves a round cylinder that is compressed along its axis, often while being subjected to confining pressure on its curved face. Frequently, a measurement interpreted by solid mechanics theory is used to determine some of the properties entering stress-strain relations. For example, measuring the speed of deformation waves or the natural frequencies of vibration of structures can be used to extract the elastic moduli of materials of known mass density, and measurement of indentation hardness of a metal can be used to estimate its plastic shear strength.

In some favourable cases, stress-strain relations can be calculated approximately by applying principles of mechanics at the microscale of the material considered. In a composite material, the microscale could be regarded as the scale of the separate materials making up the reinforcing fibres and matrix. When their individual stress-strain relations are known from experiment, continuum mechanics principles applied at the scale of the individual constituents can be used to predict the overall stress-strain relations for the composite. For rubbery polymer materials, made up of long chain molecules that randomly configure themselves into coil-like shapes, some aspects of the elastic stress-strain response can be obtained by applying principles of statistical thermodynamics to the partial uncoiling of the array of molecules by imposed strain. For a single crystallite of an element such as silicon or aluminum or for a simple compound like silicon carbide, the relevant microscale is that of the atomic spacing in the crystals; quantum mechanical principles governing atomic force laws at that scale can be used to estimate elastic constants. In the case of plastic flow processes in metals and in sufficiently hot ceramics, the relevant microscale involves the network of dislocation lines that move within crystals. These lines shift atom positions relative to one another by one atomic spacing as they move along slip planes. Important features of elastic-plastic and viscoplastic stress-strain relations can be understood by modeling the stress dependence of dislocation generation and motion and the resulting dislocation entanglement and immobilization processes that account for strain hardening.

Linear Elastic Isotropic Solid

The simplest type of stress-strain relation is that of the linear elastic solid, considered in circumstances for which $|\partial u_i/\partial X_j| << 1$ and for isotropic materials, whose mechanical response is independent of the direction of stressing. If a material point sustains a stress state $\sigma_{11} = \sigma$, with all other $\sigma_{ij} = 0$, it is subjected to uniaxial tensile stress. This can be realized in a homogeneous bar loaded by an axial force. The resulting strain may be rewritten as $\varepsilon_{11} = \sigma/E$, $\varepsilon_{22} = \varepsilon_{33} = -\nu\varepsilon_{11} = -\nu\sigma/E$, $\varepsilon_{12} = \varepsilon_{23} = \varepsilon_{31} = 0$. Two new parameters have been introduced here, E and ν. E is called Young's modulus, and it has dimensions of [force]/[length]^2 and is measured in units such as the pascal (1 Pa = 1 N/m^2), dyne/cm^2, or pounds per square inch (psi); ν, which equals the ratio of lateral strain to axial strain, is dimensionless and is called the Poisson ratio.

If the isotropic solid is subjected only to shear stress τ—i.e., $\sigma_{12} = \sigma_{21} = \tau$, with all other $\sigma_{ij} = 0$—then the response is shearing strain of the same type, $\varepsilon_{12} = \tau/2G$, $\varepsilon_{23} = \varepsilon_{31} = \varepsilon_{11} = \varepsilon_{22} = \varepsilon_{33} = 0$. Notice that because $2\varepsilon_{12} = \gamma_{12}$, this is equivalent to $\gamma_{12} = \tau/G$. The constant G introduced is called the shear modulus. (Frequently, the symbol μ is used instead of G.) The shear modulus G is not independent of E and v but is related to them by $G = E/2(1 + v)$, as follows from the tensor nature of stress and strain. The general stress-strain relations are then

$$\varepsilon_{ij} = (1 + v)\frac{\sigma_{ij}}{E} - v\delta_{ij}\frac{\sigma_{11} + \sigma_{22} + \sigma_{33}}{E}$$

(114)

$$(i, j = 1, 2, 3),$$

where δ_{ij} is defined as 1 when its indices agree and 0 otherwise.

These relations can be inverted to read $\sigma_{ij} = \lambda\delta_{ij}(\varepsilon_{11} + \varepsilon_{22} + \varepsilon_{33}) + 2\mu\varepsilon_{ij}$, where μ has been used rather than G as the notation for the shear modulus, following convention, and where $\lambda = 2v\mu/(1 - 2v)$. The elastic constants λ and μ are sometimes called the Lamé constants. Since v is typically in the range ¼ to ⅓ for hard polycrystalline solids, λ falls often in the range between μ and 2μ. (Navier's particle model with central forces leads to $\lambda = \mu$ for an isotropic solid.)

Another elastic modulus often cited is the bulk modulus K, defined for a linear solid under pressure $p(\sigma_{11} = \sigma_{22} = \sigma_{33} = -p)$ such that the fractional decrease in volume is p/K. For example, consider a small cube of side length L in the reference state. If the length along, say, the 1 direction changes to $(1 + \varepsilon_{11})L$, the fractional change of volume is $(1 + \varepsilon_{11})(1 + \varepsilon_{22})(1 + \varepsilon_{33}) - 1 = \varepsilon_{11} + \varepsilon_{22} + \varepsilon_{33}$, neglecting quadratic and cubic order terms in the εij compared to the linear, as is appropriate when using linear elasticity. Thus, $K = E/3(1 - 2v) = \lambda + 2\mu/3$.

THERMAL STRAINS

Temperature change can also cause strain. In an isotropic material the thermally induced extensional strains are equal in all directions, and there are no shear strains. In the simplest cases, these thermal strains can be treated as being linear in the temperature change $\theta - \theta_o$ (where θ_o is the temperature of the reference state), writing $\varepsilon_{ij}^{thermal} = \delta_{ij}a(\theta - \theta_o)$ for the strain produced by temperature change in the absence of stress. Here a is called the coefficient of thermal expansion. Thus, in cases of temperature change, ε_{ij} is replaced in the stress-strain relations above with $\varepsilon_{ij} - \varepsilon_{ij}^{thermal}$, with the thermal part given as a function of temperature. Typically, when temperature changes are modest, the small dependence of E and v on temperature can be neglected.

ANISOTROPY

Anisotropic solids also are common in nature and technology. Examples are single crystals; polycrystals in which the grains are not completely random in their crystallographic orientation but have a "texture," typically owing to some plastic or creep flow process that has left a preferred grain orientation; fibrous biological materials such as wood or bone; and composite materials that, on a microscale, either have the structure of reinforcing fibres in a matrix, with fibres oriented in a single direction or in multiple directions (e.g., to ensure strength along more than a single direction), or have the structure of a lamination of thin layers of separate materials. In the most general case, the application of any of the six components of stress induces all six components of strain, and there is no shortage of elastic constants. There would seem to be $6 \times 6 = 36$ in the most general case, but, as a consequence of the laws of thermodynamics, the maximum number of independent elastic constants is 21 (compared with 2 for isotropic solids). In many cases of practical interest, symmetry considerations reduce the number to far below 21.

For example, crystals of cubic symmetry, such as rock salt (NaCl); face-centred cubic metals, such as aluminum, copper, or gold; body-centred cubic metals, such as iron at low temperatures or tungsten; and such nonmetals as diamond, germanium, or silicon have only three independent elastic constants. Solids with a special direction, and with identical properties along any direction perpendicular to that direction, are called transversely isotropic; they have five independent elastic constants. Examples are provided by fibre-reinforced composite materials, with fibres that are randomly emplaced but aligned in a single direction in an isotropic or transversely isotropic matrix, and by single crystals of hexagonal close packing such as zinc.

General linear elastic stress-strain relations have the form

$$\sigma_{ij} = \sum_{k=1}^{3} \sum_{l=1}^{3} C_{ijkl}\, \varepsilon_{kl},$$

where the coefficients C_{ijkl} are known as the tensor elastic moduli. Because the ε_{kl} are symmetric, one may choose $C_{ijkl} = C_{ijlk}$, and, because the σ_{ij} are symmetric, $C_{ijkl} = C_{jikl}$. Hence the $3 \times 3 \times 3 \times 3 = 81$ components of C_{ijkl} reduce to the $6 \times 6 = 36$ mentioned. In cases of temperature change, the ε_{ij} above is replaced by $\varepsilon_{ij} - \varepsilon_{ij}^{thermal}$, where $\varepsilon_{ij}^{thermal} = a_{ij}(\theta - \theta_o)$ and a_{ij} is the set of thermal strain coefficients, with $a_{ij} = a_{ji}$. An alternative matrix notation is sometimes employed, especially in the literature on single crystals. That approach introduces 6-element columns of stress and strain $\{\sigma\}$ and $\{\varepsilon\}$, defined so that the columns, when transposed (superscript T) or laid out as rows, are $\{\sigma\}^T = (\sigma_{11}, \sigma_{22}, \sigma_{33}, \sigma_{12}, \sigma_{23}, \sigma_{31})$ and $\{\varepsilon\}^T = (\varepsilon_{11}, \varepsilon_{22}, \varepsilon_{33}, 2\varepsilon_{12}, 2\varepsilon_{23}, 2\varepsilon_{31})$. These forms assure that the scalar $\{\sigma\}^T\{d\varepsilon\} \equiv \mathrm{tr}([\sigma][d\varepsilon])$ is an increment of stress working per unit volume. The stress-strain relations are then written $\{\sigma\} = [c]\{\varepsilon\}$, where $[c]$ is the 6×6 matrix of elastic moduli. Thus, $c_{13} = C_{1133}$, $c_{15} = C_{1123}$, $c_{44} = C_{1212}$, and so on.

THERMODYNAMIC CONSIDERATIONS

In thermodynamic terminology, a state of purely elastic material response corresponds to an equilibrium state, and a process during which there is purely elastic response corresponds to a sequence of equilibrium states and hence to a reversible process. The second law of thermodynamics assures that the heat absorbed per unit mass can be written θds, where θ is the thermodynamic (absolute) temperature and s is the entropy per unit mass. Hence, writing the work per unit volume of reference configuration in a manner appropriate to cases when infinitesimal strain can be used, and letting ρ_o be the density in that configuration, from the first law of thermodynamics it can be stated that $\rho_o \theta ds + \mathrm{tr}([\sigma][d\varepsilon]) = \rho_o de$, where e is the internal energy per unit mass. This relation shows that if e is expressed as a function of entropy s and strains $[\varepsilon]$, and if e is written so as to depend identically on ε_{ij} and ε_{ji}, then $\sigma_{ij} = \rho_o \partial e([\varepsilon], s)/\partial \varepsilon_{ij}$.

Alternatively, one may introduce the Helmholtz free energy f per unit mass, where $f = e - \theta s = f([\varepsilon], \theta)$, and show that $\sigma_{ij} = \rho_o \partial f([\varepsilon], \theta)/\partial \varepsilon_{ij}$. The latter form corresponds to the variables with which the stress-strain relations were written above. Sometimes $\rho_o f$ is called the strain energy for states of isothermal (constant θ) elastic deformation; $\rho_o e$ has the same interpretation for adiabatic (s = constant) elastic deformation, achieved when the time scale is too short to allow heat transfer to or from a deforming element. Since the mixed partial derivatives must be independent of order, a consequence of the last equation is that $\partial \sigma_{ij}([\varepsilon], \theta)/\partial \varepsilon_{kl} = \partial \sigma_{kl}([\varepsilon], \theta)/\partial \varepsilon_{ij}$, which requires that $C_{ijkl} = C_{klij}$, or equivalently that the matrix $[c]$ be symmetric, $[c] = [c]^T$, reducing the maximum possible number of independent elastic constraints from 36 to 21. The strain energy $W([\varepsilon])$ at constant temperature θ_o is $W([\varepsilon]) \equiv \rho_o f([\varepsilon], \theta_o) = (\frac{1}{2})\{\varepsilon\}^T[c]\{\varepsilon\}$.

The elastic moduli for adiabatic response are slightly different from those for isothermal response. In the case of the isotropic material, it is convenient to give results in terms of G and K, the isothermal shear and bulk moduli. The adiabatic moduli G and K^- are then $G = G$ and $K^- = K(1 + 9\theta_o Ka^2/\rho_o c_\varepsilon)$, where $c_\varepsilon = \theta_o \partial s([\varepsilon],\theta)/\partial\theta$, evaluated at $\theta = \theta_o$ and $[\varepsilon] = [o]$, is the specific heat at constant strain. The fractional change in the bulk modulus, given by the second term in the parentheses, is very small, typically on the order of 1 percent or less, even for metals and ceramics of relatively high a, on the order of 10^{-5}/kelvin.

The fractional change in absolute temperature during an adiabatic deformation is found to involve the same small parameter: $[(\theta - \theta_o)/\theta_o]s_{= const} = -(9\theta_o Ka^2/\rho_o c_\varepsilon) [(\varepsilon_{11} + \varepsilon_{22} + \varepsilon_{33})/3a\theta_o]$. Values of a for most solid elements and inorganic compounds are in the range of 10^{-6} to 4×10^{-5}/kelvin; room temperature is about 300 kelvins, so $3a\theta_o$ is typically in the range 10^{-3} to 4×10^{-2}. Thus, if the fractional change in volume is on the order of 1 percent, which is quite large for a metal or ceramic deforming in its elastic range, the fractional change in absolute temperature is also on the order of 1 percent. For those reasons, it is usually appropriate to neglect the alteration of the temperature field due to elastic deformation and hence to use purely mechanical formulations of elasticity in which distinctions between adiabatic and isothermal response are neglected.

FINITE ELASTIC DEFORMATIONS

When elastic response under arbitrary deformation gradients is considered—because rotations, if not strains, are large or, in a material such as rubber, because the strains are large too—it is necessary to dispense with the infinitesimal strain theory. In such cases, the combined first and second laws of thermodynamics have the form $\rho_o \theta ds + \det[F] \text{tr}([F]^{-1}[\sigma][dF]) = \rho_o de$, where $[F]^{-1}$ is the matrix inverse of the deformation gradient $[F]$. If a parcel of material is deformed by $[F]$ and then given some additional rigid rotation, the free energy f must be unchanged in that rotation. In terms of the polar decomposition $[F] = [R][U]$, this is equivalent to saying that f is independent of the rotation part $[R]$ of $[F]$, which is then equivalent to saying that f is a function of the finite strain measure $[E^M] = (\frac{1}{2})([F]^T[F] - [I])$ based on change of metric or, for that matter, on any member of the family of material strain tensors. Thus,

$$\sigma_{ij} = (1/\det[F]) \sum_{k=1}^{3} \sum_{l=1}^{3} F_{ik} F_{jl} S_{kl}([E^M], \theta), \text{ where } S_{kl}(=S_{lk})$$

is sometimes called the second Piola-Kirchhoff stress and is given by $S_{kl} = \rho_o \partial f([E^M], \theta)/\partial E^M_{kl}$, it being assumed that f has been written so as to have identical dependence on E^M_{kl} and E^M_{lk}.

INELASTIC RESPONSE

The above mode of expressing $[\sigma]$ in terms of $[S]$ is valid for solids showing viscoelastic or plastic response as well, except that $[S]$ is then to be regarded not only as a function of the present $[E^M]$ and θ but also as dependent on the prior history of both. Assuming that such materials show elastic response to sudden stress changes or to small unloading from a plastically deforming state, $[S]$ may still be expressed as a derivative of f, as above, but the derivative is understood as being taken with respect to an elastic variation of strain and is to be taken at fixed θ and with fixed prior inelastic deformation and temperature history.

Such dependence on history is sometimes represented as a dependence of f on internal state variables whose laws of evolution are part of the inelastic constitutive description. There are also simpler models of inelastic response, and the most commonly employed forms for plasticity and creep in isotropic solids are presented next.

To a good approximation, plastic deformation of crystalline solids causes no change in volume; and hydrostatic changes in stress, amounting to equal change of all normal stresses, have no effect on plastic flow, at least for changes that are of the same order or magnitude as the strength of the solid in shear. Thus, plastic response is usually formulated in terms of deviatoric stress, which is defined by $\tau_{ij} = \sigma_{ij} - \delta_{ij}(\sigma_{11} + \sigma_{22} + \sigma_{33})/3$. Following Richard von Mises, in a procedure that is found to agree moderately well with experiment, the plastic flow relation is formulated in terms of the second invariant of deviatoric stress, commonly rewritten as

$$\bar{\sigma} = \sqrt{(^3\!/_2)\mathrm{tr}([\tau][\tau])}$$

and called the equivalent tensile stress. The definition is made so that, for a state of uniaxial tension, σ equals the tensile stress, and the stress-strain relation for general stress states is formulated in terms of data from the tensile test. In particular, a plastic strain ε^p in a uniaxial tension test is defined from $\varepsilon^p = \varepsilon - \sigma/E$, where ε is interpreted as the strain in the tensile test according to the logarithmic definition $\varepsilon = \ln\lambda$, the elastic modulus E is assumed to remain unchanged with deformation, and $\sigma/E \ll 1$.

Thus, in the rate-independent plasticity version of the theory, tensile data (or compressive, with appropriate sign reversals) from a monotonic load test is assumed to define a function ε^p (σ). In the viscoplastic or high-temperature creep versions of the theory, tensile data is interpreted to define $d\varepsilon^p/dt$ as a function of σ in the simplest case, representing, for example, secondary creep, and as a function of σ and ε^p in theories intended to represent transient creep effects or rate-sensitive response at lower temperatures. Consider first the rigid-plastic material model in which elastic deformability is ignored altogether, as is sometimes appropriate for problems of large plastic flow, as in metal forming or long-term creep in Earth's mantle or for analysis of plastic collapse loads on structures. The rate of deformation tensor D_{ij} is defined by $2D_{ij} = \partial v_i/\partial x_j + \partial v_j/\partial x_i$, and in the rigid-plastic case $[D]$ can be equated to what may be considered its plastic part $[D^p]$, given as $D^p_{ij} = 3(d\varepsilon^p/dt)\tau_{ij}/2\sigma$. The numerical factors secure agreement between D^p_{11} and $d\varepsilon^p/dt$ for uniaxial tension in the 1-direction. Also, the equation implies that

$$D^p_{11} + D^p_{22} + D^p_{33} = 0 \text{ and that } d\bar{\varepsilon}^p/dt = \sqrt{(2/3)\mathrm{tr}([D^p][D^p])},$$

which must be integrated over previous history to get ε^p as required for viscoplastic models in which $d\varepsilon^p/dt$ is a function of σ and ε^p. In the rate-independent version, $[D^p]$ is defined as zero whenever σ is less than the highest value that it has attained in the previous history or when the current value of σ is the highest value but $d\sigma/dt < 0$. (In the elastic-plastic context, this means that "unloading" involves only elastic response.) For the ideally plastic solid, which is idealized to be able to flow without increase of stress when σ equals the yield strength level, $d\varepsilon^p/dt$ is regarded as an undetermined but necessarily nonnegative parameter, which can be determined (sometimes not uniquely) only through the complete solution of a solid mechanics boundary-value problem.

The elastic-plastic material model is then formulated by writing $D_{ij} = D^e_{ij} + D^p_{ij}$, where D^p_{ij} is given in terms of stress and possibly stress rate as above and where the elastic deformation rates $[D^e]$ are related to stresses by the usual linear elastic expression $D^e_{ij} = (1 + v)\sigma^*_{ij}/E - v\delta_{ij}(\sigma^*_{11} + \sigma^*_{22} + \sigma^*_{33})/E$. Here the stress rates are expressed as the Jaumann co-rotational rates

$$\dot{\sigma}^*_{ij} = \dot{\sigma}_{ij} + \sum_{k=1}^{3} (\sigma_{ik}\Omega_{kj} - \Omega_{ik}\sigma_{kj}), \text{ where } \dot{\sigma}_{ij} = d\sigma_{ij}/dt$$

is a derivative following the motion of a material point and where the spin Ω_{ij} is defined by $2\Omega_{ij} = \partial v_i/\partial x_j - \partial v_j/\partial x_i$. The co-rotational stress rates are those calculated by an observer who spins with the average angular velocity of a material element. The elastic part of the stress-strain relation should be consistent with the existence of a free energy f, as discussed above. This is not strictly satisfied by the form just given, but the differences between it and one which is consistent in that way involves additional terms that are on the order of σ/E^2 times the σ^*_{kl} and are negligible in typical cases in which the theory is used, since σ/E is usually an extremely small fraction of unity, say, 10^{-4} to 10^{-2}. A small-strain version of the theory is in common use for purposes of elastic-plastic stress analysis. In these cases, $[D]$ is replaced with $\partial[\varepsilon(X, t)]/\partial t$, where $[\varepsilon]$ is the small-strain tensor, $\partial/\partial x$ with $\partial/\partial X$ in all equations, and $[\sigma^*]$ with $\partial[\sigma(X, t)]/\partial t$. The last two steps cannot always be justified, even in cases of very small strain when, for example, in a rate-independent material, $d\sigma/d\varepsilon^p$ is not large compared to σ or when rates of rotation of material fibres can become much larger than rates of stretching, which is a concern for buckling problems even in purely elastic solids.

PROBLEMS INVOLVING ELASTIC RESPONSE

There are cases in which a deformed material body returns to its original shape and size when the forces causing the deformation are removed. A body with this ability is said to behave (or respond) elastically.

EQUATIONS OF MOTION OF LINEAR ELASTIC BODIES

The final equations of the purely mechanical theory of linear elasticity (i.e., when coupling with the temperature field is neglected, or when either isothermal or isentropic response is assumed) are obtained as follows. The stress-strain relations are used, and the strains are written in terms of displacement gradients. The final expressions for stress are inserted into the equations of motion, replacing $\partial/\partial x$ with $\partial/\partial X$ in those equations. In the case of an isotropic and homogenous solid, these reduce to

$$(\lambda + \mu)\nabla(\nabla \cdot \boldsymbol{u}) + \mu\nabla^2\boldsymbol{u} + \boldsymbol{f} = \frac{\rho\partial^2\boldsymbol{u}}{\partial t^2}, \tag{116}$$

known as the Navier equations (here, $\nabla = \boldsymbol{e}_1\partial/\partial X_1 + \boldsymbol{e}_2\partial/\partial X_2 + \boldsymbol{e}_3\partial/\partial X_3$, and ∇^2 is the Laplacian operator defined by $\nabla\cdot\nabla$, or $\partial^2/\partial x_1^2 + \partial^2/\partial x_2^2 + \partial^2/\partial x_3^2$, and, as described earlier, λ and μ are the Lamé constants, $\boldsymbol{u}$ the displacement, f the body force, and ρ the density of the material). Such equations hold in the region V occupied by the solid; on the surface S one prescribes each component of $\boldsymbol{u}$, or each component of the stress vector T (expressed in terms of $[\partial u/\partial X]$), or sometimes mixtures of components or relations between them. For example, along a freely slipping planar interface with a rigid solid, the normal component of $\boldsymbol{u}$ and the two tangential components of T would be prescribed, all as zero.

BODY WAVE SOLUTIONS

By looking for body wave solutions in the form $u(X, t) = pf$ $(n \cdot X - ct)$, where unit vector n is the propagation direction, p is the polarization, or direction of particle motion, and c is the wave speed, one may show for the isotropic material that solutions exist for arbitrary functions f if either

$$c = c_d \equiv \sqrt{(\lambda + 2\mu)/\rho} \text{ and } p = n, \text{ or } c = c_s \equiv \sqrt{\mu/\rho} \text{ and } p \cdot n = 0.$$

The first case, with particle displacements in the propagation direction, describes longitudinal, or dilatational, waves; and the latter case, which corresponds to two linearly independent displacement directions, both transverse to the propagation direction, describes transverse, or shear, waves.

LINEAR ELASTIC BEAM

The case of a beam treated as a linear elastic line may also be considered. Let the line along the 1-axis, have properties that are uniform along its length and have sufficient symmetry that bending it by applying a torque about the 3-direction causes the line to deform into an arc lying in the 1,2-plane. Make an imaginary cut through the line, and let the forces and torque acting at that section on the part lying in the direction of decreasing X_1 be denoted as a shear force V in the positive 2-direction, an axial force P in the positive 1-direction, and torque M, commonly called a bending moment, about the positive 3-direction. The linear and angular momentum principles then require

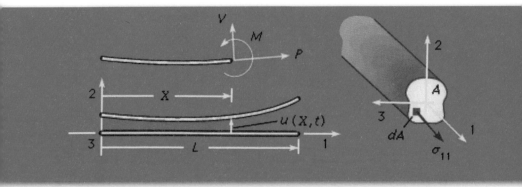

Transverse motion of an initially straight beam, shown at left as an elastic line and at right as a solid of finite section. Copyright Encyclopædia Britannica; rendering for this edition by Rosen Educational Services

that the actions at that section on the part of the line lying along the direction of increasing X_1 be of equal magnitude but opposite sign.

Now let the line be loaded by transverse force F per unit length, directed in the 2-direction, and make assumptions on the smallness of deformation consistent with those of linear elasticity. Let ρA be the mass per unit length (so that A can be interpreted as the cross-sectional area of a homogeneous beam of density ρ) and let u be the transverse displacement in the 2-direction. Then, writing X for X_1, the linear and angular momentum principles require that $\partial V/\partial X + F = \rho A\, \partial^2 u/\partial t^2$ and $\partial M/\partial X + V = 0$, where rotary inertia has been neglected in the second equation, as is appropriate for disturbances which are of a wavelength that is long compared to cross-sectional dimensions. The curvature κ of the elastic line can be approximated by $\kappa = \partial^2 u/\partial X^2$ for the small deformation situation considered, and the equivalent of the stress-strain relation is to assume that κ is a function of M at each point along the line. The function can be derived by the analysis of stress and strain in pure bending and is $M = EI\kappa$, with the moment of inertia $I = \int_A (X_2)^2 dA$ for uniform elastic properties over all the cross section and with the 1-axis passing through the section centroid. Hence, the equation relating transverse load and displacement of a linear elastic beam is $-\partial^2(EI\partial^2u/\partial X^2)/\partial X^2 + F = \rho A\partial^2u/\partial t^2$, and this is to be solved subject to two boundary conditions at each end of the elastic line. Examples are $u = \partial u/\partial X = 0$ at a completely restrained ("built in") end, $u = M = 0$ at an end that is restrained against displacement but not rotation, and $V = M = 0$ at a completely unrestrained (free) end. The beam will be reconsidered later in an analysis of response with initial stress present.

The preceding derivation was presented in the spirit of the model of a beam as the elastic line of Euler. The same equations of motion may be obtained by the following five steps: (1) integrate the three-dimensional equations of motion over a section, writing $V = \int_A \sigma_{12}dA$; (2) integrate the product of X_2 and those equations over a section, writing $M = -\int AX_2\sigma_{11}dA$; (3) assume that planes initially perpendicular to fibres lying along the 1-axis remain perpendicular during deformation, so that $\varepsilon_{11} = \varepsilon_0(X, t) - X_2\kappa(X, t)$, where $X \equiv X_1$, $\varepsilon_0(X, t)$ is the strain of the fibre along the 1-axis, and $\kappa(X, t) = \partial^2u/\partial X^2$, where $u(X, t)$ is u_2 for the fibre initially along the 1-axis; (4) assume that the stress σ_{11} relates to strain as if each point were under uniaxial tension, so that $\sigma_{11} = E\varepsilon_{11}$; and (5) neglect terms of order h^2/L^2 compared to unity, where h is a typical cross-section dimension and L is a scale length for variations along the direction of the 1-axis. In step (1) the average of u_2 over area A enters but may be interpreted as the displacement u of step (3) to the order retained in (5). The kinematic assumption (3) together with (5), if implemented under conditions such that there are no loadings to generate a net axial force P, requires that $\varepsilon_0(X, t) = 0$ and that $\kappa(X, t) = M(X, t)/EI$ when the 1-axis has been chosen to pass through the centroid of the cross section. Hence, according to these approximations, $\sigma_{11} = -X_2 M(X, t)/I = -X_2 E \partial^2 u(X, t)/\partial X^2$. The expression for σ_{11} is exact for static equilibrium under pure bending, since assumptions (3) and (4) are exact and (5) is then irrelevant. This motivates the use of assumptions (3) and (4) in a situation that does not correspond to pure bending.

Sometimes it is necessary to deal with solids that are already under stress in the reference configuration that is chosen for measuring strain. As a simple example, suppose that the beam just discussed is under an initial uniform tensile stress $\sigma_{11} = \sigma^\circ$ — that is, the axial force $P = \sigma^\circ A$. If σ° is negative and of significant magnitude, one generally refers to the beam as a column; if it is large and positive, the beam might respond more like a taut string. The initial stress σ° contributes a term to the equations of small transverse motion, which now becomes $-\partial^2(EI \partial^2 u/\partial X^2)/\partial X^2 + \sigma^\circ A \partial^2 u/\partial X^2 + F = \rho A \partial^2 u/\partial t^2$.

Free Vibrations

Suppose that the beam is of length L, is of uniform properties, and is hinge-supported at its ends at $X = 0$ and $X = L$ so that $u = M = 0$ there. Then free transverse motions of the beam, solving the above equation with $F = 0$, are described by any linear combination of the real part of solutions that have the form $u = C_n \exp(i\omega_n t)\sin(n\pi X/L)$, where n is any positive integer, C_n is an arbitrary complex constant, and where

$$\rho A \omega_n^2 = \left(\frac{n\pi}{L}\right)^4 EI\left[1 + \left(\frac{\sigma^0}{E}\right)\left(\frac{AL^2}{n^2\pi^2 I}\right)\right] \qquad (117)$$

defines the angular vibration frequency ω_n associated with the nth mode, in units of radians per unit time. The number of vibration cycles per unit time is $\omega_n/2\pi$. Equation (117) is arranged so that the term in the brackets shows the correction, from unity, of what would be the expression giving the frequencies of free vibration for a beam when there is no σ^o. The correction from unity can be quite significant, even though σ^o/E is always much smaller than unity (for interesting cases, 10^{-6} to, say, 10^{-3} would be a representative range; few materials in bulk form would remain elastic or resist fracture at higher σ^o/E, although good piano wire could reach about 10^{-2}). The correction term's significance results because σ^o/E is multiplied by a term that can become enormous for a beam that is long compared to its thickness; for a square section of side length h, that term (at its largest, when $n = 1$) is $AL^2/\pi^2 I \approx 1.2L^2/h^2$, which can combine with a small σ^o/E to produce a correction term within the brackets that is quite non-negligible compared to unity. When $\sigma^o > 0$ and L is large enough to make the bracketed expression much larger than unity, the EI term cancels out and the beam simply responds like a stretched string (here, string denotes an object that is unable to support a bending moment). When the vibration mode number n is large enough, however, the stringlike effects become negligible and beamlike response takes over; at sufficiently high n that L/n is reduced to the same order as h, the simple beam theory becomes inaccurate and should be replaced by three-dimensional elasticity or, at least, an improved beam theory that takes into account rotary inertia and shear deformability. (While the option of using three-dimensional elasticity for such a problem posed an insurmountable obstacle over most of the history of the subject, by 1990 the availability of computing power and easily used software reduced it to a routine problem that could be studied by an undergraduate engineer or physicist using the finite-element method or some other computational mechanics technique.)

BUCKLING

An important case of compressive loading is that in which $\sigma^\circ < 0$, which can lead to buckling. Indeed, if $\sigma^\circ A < -\pi^2 EI/L^2$, then the ω^2_n is negative, at least for $n = 1$, which means that the corresponding ω_n is of the form $\pm ib$, where b is a positive real number, so that the $\exp(i\omega_n t)$ term has a time dependence of a type that no longer involves oscillation but, rather, exponential growth, $\exp(bt)$. The critical compressive force, $\pi^2 EI/L^2$, that causes this type of behaviour is called the Euler buckling load; different numerical factors are obtained for different end conditions. The acceleration associated with the $n = 1$ mode becomes small in the vicinity of the critical load and vanishes at that load. Thus solutions are possible, at the buckling load, for which the column takes a deformed shape without acceleration; for that reason, an approach to buckling problems that is equivalent for what, in dynamic terminology, are called conservative systems is to seek the first load at which an alternate equilibrium solution $u = u(X)$, other than $u = 0$, may exist.

Instability by divergence—that is, with growth of displacement in the form $\exp(bt)$—is representative of conservative systems. Columns under nonconservative loadings by, for example, a follower force, which has the property that its line of action rotates so as to be always tangent to the beam centreline at its place of application, can exhibit a flutter instability in which the dynamic response is proportional to the real or imaginary part of a term such as $\exp(iat)\exp(bt)$—i.e., an oscillation with exponentially growing amplitude. Such instabilities also arise in the coupling between fluid flow and elastic structural response, as in the subfield called aeroelasticity. The prototype is the flutter of an airplane wing—that is, a torsional oscillation of the wing, of growing amplitude, which is driven by the coupling between rotation of the wing and the development of aerodynamic forces related to the angle of attack; the coupling feeds more energy into the structure with each cycle.

Of course, instability models that are based on linearized theories and predicting exponential growth in time actually reveal no more than that the system is deforming out of the range for which the mathematical model applies. Proper nonlinear theories that take account of the finiteness of rotation, and sometimes the large and possibly nonelastic strain of material fibres, are necessary to really understand the phenomena. An important subclass of such nonlinear analyses for conservative systems involves the static post-buckling response of a perfect structure, such as a perfectly straight column or perfectly spherical shell. That post-buckling analysis allows one to determine if increasing force is required for very large displacement to develop during the buckle or whether the buckling is of a more highly unstable type for which the load must diminish with buckling amplitude in order to still satisfy the equilibrium equations. The latter type of behaviour describes a structure whose maximum load (that is, the largest load it can support without collapsing) shows strong sensitivity to very small imperfections of material or geometry, as is the case with many shell structures.

CHAPTER 8
LIQUIDS AT REST

Fluid mechanics is the science concerned with the response of fluids to forces exerted upon them. It is a branch of classical physics with applications of great importance in hydraulic and aeronautical engineering, chemical engineering, meteorology, and zoology.

The most familiar fluid is of course water, and an encyclopaedia of the 19th century probably would have dealt with the subject under the separate headings of hydrostatics, the science of water at rest, and hydrodynamics, the science of water in motion. Archimedes founded hydrostatics in about 250 BCE when, according to legend, he leapt out of his bath and ran naked through the streets of Syracuse crying "Eureka!"; it has undergone rather little development since. The foundations of hydrodynamics, on the other hand, were not laid until the 18th century when mathematicians such as Leonhard Euler and Daniel Bernoulli began to explore the consequences, for a virtually continuous medium such as water, of the dynamic principles that Newton had enunciated for systems composed of discrete particles. Their work was continued in the 19th century by several mathematicians and physicists of the first rank, notably G.G. Stokes and William Thomson. By the end of the century explanations had been found for a host of intriguing phenomena having to do with the flow of water through tubes and orifices, the waves that ships moving through water leave behind them, raindrops on windowpanes, and the like. There was still no proper understanding, however, of problems as fundamental as that of water flowing past a fixed obstacle and exerting a drag force upon it; the theory of potential flow, which worked so well in other contexts, yielded results that at relatively high flow rates were grossly at variance with experiment. This problem was not properly understood until 1904, when the German physicist Ludwig Prandtl introduced the concept of the boundary layer. Prandtl's career continued into the period in which the first manned aircraft were developed. Since that time, the flow of air has been of as much interest to physicists and engineers as the flow of water, and hydrodynamics has, as a consequence, become fluid dynamics. The term fluid mechanics, as used here, embraces both fluid dynamics and the subject still generally referred to as hydrostatics.

One other representative of the 20th century who deserves mention here besides Prandtl is Geoffrey Taylor of England. Taylor remained a classical physicist while most of his contemporaries were turning their attention to the problems of atomic structure and quantum mechanics, and he made several unexpected and important discoveries in the field of fluid mechanics. The richness of fluid mechanics is due in large part to a term in the basic equation of the motion of fluids which is nonlinear—i.e., one that involves the fluid velocity twice over. It is characteristic of systems described by nonlinear equations that under certain conditions they become unstable and begin behaving in ways that seem at first sight to be totally chaotic. In the case of fluids, chaotic behaviour is very common and is called turbulence. Mathematicians have now begun to recognize patterns in chaos that can be analyzed fruitfully, and this development suggests that fluid mechanics will remain a field of active research well into the 21st century.

BASIC PROPERTIES OF FLUIDS

Fluids are not strictly continuous media in the way that all the successors of Euler and Bernoulli have assumed, for they are composed of discrete molecules. The molecules, however, are so small and, except in gases at very low pressures, the number of molecules per millilitre is so enormous that they need not be viewed as individual entities. There are a few liquids, known as liquid crystals, in which the molecules are packed together in such a way as to make the properties of the medium locally anisotropic, but the vast majority of fluids (including air and water) are isotropic. In fluid mechanics, the state of an isotropic fluid may be completely described by defining its mean mass per unit volume, or density (ρ), its temperature (T), and its velocity (v) at every point in space, and just what the connection is between these macroscopic properties and the positions and velocities of individual molecules is of no direct relevance.

A word perhaps is needed about the difference between gases and liquids, though the difference is easier to perceive than to describe. In gases the molecules are sufficiently far apart to move almost independently of one another, and gases tend to expand to fill any volume available to them. In liquids the molecules are more or less in contact, and the short-range attractive forces between them make them cohere; the molecules are moving too fast to settle down into the ordered arrays that are characteristic of solids, but not so fast that they can fly apart. Thus, samples of liquid can exist as drops or as jets with free surfaces, or they can sit in beakers constrained only by gravity, in a way that samples of gas cannot. Such samples may evaporate in time, as molecules one by one pick up enough speed to escape across the free surface and are not replaced. The lifetime of liquid drops and jets, however, is normally long enough for evaporation to be ignored.

There are two sorts of stress that may exist in any solid or fluid medium, and the difference between them may be illustrated by reference to a brick held between two hands.

If the holder moves his hands toward each other, he exerts pressure on the brick; if he moves one hand toward his body and the other away from it, then he exerts what is called a shear stress. A solid substance such as a brick can withstand stresses of both types, but fluids, by definition, yield to shear stresses no matter how small these stresses may be. They do so at a rate determined by the fluid's viscosity. This property, about which more will be said later, is a measure of the friction that arises when adjacent layers of fluid slip over one another. It follows that the shear stresses are everywhere zero in a fluid at rest and in equilibrium, and from this it follows that the pressure (that is, force per unit area) acting perpendicular to all planes in the fluid is the same irrespective of their orientation (Pascal's law). For an isotropic fluid in equilibrium there is only one value of the local pressure (p) consistent with the stated values for ρ and T. These three quantities are linked together by what is called the equation of state for the fluid.

For gases at low pressures the equation of state is simple and well known. It is

$$p = \left(\frac{RT}{M}\right)\rho, \tag{118}$$

where R is the universal gas constant (8.3 joules per degree Celsius per mole) and M is the molar mass, or an average molar mass if the gas is a mixture; for air, the appropriate average is about 29×10^{-3} kilogram per mole. For other fluids knowledge of the equation of state is often incomplete. Except under very extreme conditions, however, all one needs to know is how the density changes when the pressure is changed by a small amount, and this is described by the compressibility of the fluid—either the isothermal compressibility, β_T, or the adiabatic compressibility, β_S, according to circumstance. When an element of fluid is compressed, the work done on it tends to heat it up. If the heat has time to drain away to the surroundings and the temperature of the fluid remains essentially unchanged throughout, then β_T is the relevant quantity. If virtually none of the heat escapes, as is more commonly the case in flow problems because the thermal conductivity of most fluids is poor, then the flow is said to be adiabatic, and β_S is needed instead. (The S refers to entropy, which remains constant in an adiabatic process provided that it takes place slowly enough to be treated as "reversible" in the thermodynamic sense.) For gases that obey equation (118), it is evident that p and ρ are proportional to one another in an isothermal process, and

$$\beta_T = \rho^{-1}\left(\frac{\partial \rho}{\partial p}\right)_T = p^{-1}. \tag{119}$$

In reversible adiabatic processes for such gases, however, the temperature rises on compression at a rate such that

$$T \propto \rho^{(\gamma-1)}, \quad p \propto \rho^{\gamma}, \tag{120}$$

and

$$\beta_S = \rho^{-1}\left(\frac{\partial \rho}{\partial p}\right)_S = (\gamma p)^{-1} = \frac{\beta_T}{\gamma}, \tag{121}$$

where γ is about 1.4 for air and takes similar values for other common gases. For liquids the ratio between the isothermal and adiabatic compressibilities is much closer to unity. For liquids, however, both compressibilities are normally much less than p^{-1}, and the simplifying assumption that they are zero is often justified.

The factor γ is not only the ratio between two compressibilities; it is also the ratio between two principal specific heats. The molar specific heat is the amount of heat required to raise the temperature of one mole through one degree. This is greater if the substance is allowed to expand as it is heated, and therefore to do work, than if its volume is fixed. The principal molar specific heats, C_P and C_V, refer to heating at constant pressure and constant volume, respectively, and

$$\gamma = \frac{C_P}{C_V}.\tag{122}$$

For air, C_P is about 3.5 R.

Solids can be stretched without breaking, and liquids, though not gases, can withstand stretching, too. Thus, if the pressure is steadily reduced in a specimen of very pure water, bubbles will ultimately appear, but they may not do so until the pressure is negative and well below -10^7 newton per square metre; this is 100 times greater in magnitude than the (positive) pressure exerted by Earth's atmosphere. Water owes its high ideal strength to the fact that rupture involves breaking links of attraction between molecules on either side of the plane on which rupture occurs; work must be done to break these links. However, its strength is drastically reduced by anything that provides a nucleus at which the process known as cavitation (formation of vapour- or gas-filled cavities) can begin, and a liquid containing suspended dust particles or dissolved gases is liable to cavitate quite easily.

Work also must be done if a free liquid drop of spherical shape is to be drawn out into a long thin cylinder or deformed in any other way that increases its surface area. Here again work is needed to break intermolecular links. The surface of a liquid behaves, in fact, as if it were an elastic membrane under tension, except that the tension exerted by an elastic membrane increases when the membrane is stretched in a way that the tension exerted by a liquid surface does not. Surface tension is what causes liquids to rise up capillary tubes, what supports hanging liquid drops, what limits the formation of ripples on the surface of liquids, and so on.

HYDROSTATICS

It is common knowledge that the pressure of the atmosphere (about 10^5 newtons per square metre) is due to the weight of air above Earth's surface, that this pressure falls as one climbs upward, and, correspondingly, that pressure increases as one dives deeper into a lake (or comparable body of water). Mathematically, the rate at which the pressure in a stationary fluid varies with height z in a vertical gravitational field of strength g is given by

$$\frac{dp}{dz} = -\rho g. \tag{123}$$

If ρ and g are both independent of z, as is more or less the case in lakes, then

$$p(z) = p(0) - \rho g z. \tag{124}$$

This means that, since ρ is about 10^3 kilograms per cubic metre for water and g is about 10 metres per second squared, the pressure is already twice the atmospheric value at a depth of 10 metres. Applied to the atmosphere, equation (124) would imply that the pressure falls to zero at a height of about 10 kilometres. In the atmosphere, however, the variation of ρ with z is far from negligible and equation (124) is unreliable as a consequence.

DIFFERENTIAL MANOMETERS

Instruments for comparing pressures are called differential manometers, and the simplest such instrument is a U-tube containing liquid. The two pressures of interest, p_1 and p_2, are transmitted to the two ends of the liquid column through an inert gas — the density of which is negligible by comparison with the liquid density, ρ — and the difference of height, h, of the two menisci is measured. It is a consequence of equation (124) that

$$p_1 - p_2 = \rho g h. \tag{125}$$

A barometer for measuring the pressure of the atmosphere in absolute terms is simply a manometer in which p_2 is made zero, or as close to zero as is feasible. The barometer invented in the 17th century by the Italian physicist and mathematician Evangelista Torricelli, and still in use today, is a U-tube that is sealed at one end. It may be filled with liquid, with the sealed end downward, and then inverted. On inversion, a negative pressure may momentarily develop at the top of the liquid column if the column is long enough; however, cavitation normally occurs there and the column falls away from the sealed end of the tube, as shown in the figure. Between the two exists what Torricelli thought of as a vacuum, though it may be very far from that condition if the barometer has been filled without scrupulous precautions to ensure that all dissolved or adsorbed gases, which would otherwise collect in this space, have first been removed. Even if no contaminating gas is present, the Torricellian vacuum always contains the vapour of the liquid, and this exerts a pressure which may be small but is never quite zero. The liquid conventionally used in a Torricelli barometer is of course mercury, which has a low vapour pressure and a

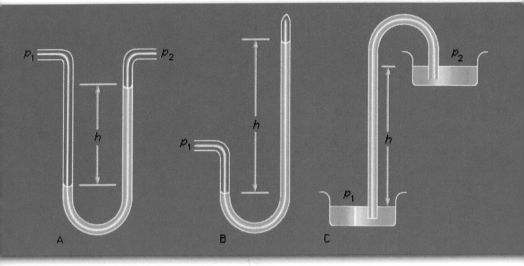

Schematic representations of (A) a differential manometer, (B) a Torricellian barometer, and (C) a siphon. Copyright Encyclopædia Britannica; rendering for this edition by Rosen Educational Services

high density. The high density means that h is only about 760 millimetres; if water were used, it would have to be about 10 metres instead.

Consider the principle of the siphon, two containers of differing heights connected by a tube. The top container is open to the atmosphere, and the pressure in it, p_2, is therefore atmospheric. To balance this and the weight of the liquid column in between, the pressure p_1 in the bottom container ought to be greater by $\rho g h$. If the bottom container is also open to the atmosphere, then equilibrium is clearly impossible; the weight of the liquid column prevails and causes the liquid to flow downward. The siphon operates only as long as the column is continuous; it fails if a bubble of gas collects in the tube or if cavitation occurs. Cavitation therefore limits the level differences over which siphons can be used, and it also limits (to about 10 metres) the depth of wells from which water can be pumped using suction alone.

ARCHIMEDES' PRINCIPLE

Consider now a cube of side d totally immersed in liquid with its top and bottom faces horizontal. The pressure on the bottom face will be higher than on the top by $\rho g d$, and, since pressure is force per unit area and the area of a cube face is d^2, the resultant upthrust on the cube is $\rho g d^3$. This is a simple example of the so-called Archimedes' principle, which states that the upthrust experienced by a submerged or floating body is always equal to the weight of the liquid that the body displaces. As Archimedes must have realized, there is no need to prove this by detailed examination of the pressure difference between top and bottom. It is obviously true, whatever the body's shape. It is obvious because, if the solid body could somehow be removed and if the cavity thereby created could somehow be filled with more fluid instead, the whole system would still be in equilibrium. The extra fluid would, however, then be experiencing the upthrust previously experienced by the solid body, and it would not be in equilibrium unless this were just sufficient to balance its weight.

Archimedes' problem was to discover, by what would nowadays be called a nondestructive test, whether the crown of King Hieron II was made of pure gold or of gold diluted with silver. He understood that the pure metal and the alloy would differ in density and that he could determine the density of the crown by weighing it to find its mass and making a separate measurement of its volume. Perhaps the inspiration that struck him (in his bath) was that one can find the volume of any object by submerging it in liquid in something like a measuring cylinder (i.e., in a container with vertical sides that have been suitably graduated) and measuring the displacement of the liquid surface. If so, he no doubt realized soon afterward that a more elegant and more accurate method for determining density can be based on the principle that bears his name. This method involves weighing the object twice, first, when it is suspended in a vacuum (suspension in air will normally suffice) and, second, when it is totally submerged in a liquid of density ρ. If the density of the object is ρ', the ratio between the two weights must be

$$\frac{W_2}{W_1} = \frac{(\rho' - \rho)}{\rho'}. \qquad (126)$$

If ρ' is less than ρ, then W_2, according to equation (126), is negative. What that means is that the object does not submerge of its own accord; it has to be pushed downward to make it do so. If an object with a mean density less than that of water is placed in a lake and not subjected to any downward force other than its own weight, it naturally floats on the surface, and Archimedes' principle shows that in equilibrium the volume of water which it displaces is a fraction ρ'/ρ of its own volume. A hydrometer is an object graduated in such a way that this fraction may be measured. By floating a hydrometer first in water of density ρ_0 and then in some other liquid of density ρ_1 and comparing the readings, one may determine the ratio ρ_1/ρ_0—i.e., the specific gravity of the other liquid.

SURFACE TENSION OF LIQUIDS

Of the many hydrostatic phenomena in which the surface tension of liquids plays a role, the most significant is probably capillarity. Consider what happens when a tube of narrow bore, often called a capillary tube, is dipped into a liquid. If the liquid "wets" the tube (with zero contact angle), the liquid surface inside the tube forms a concave meniscus, which is a virtually spherical surface having the same radius, r, as the inside of the tube. The tube experiences a downward force of magnitude $2\pi r d\sigma$, where σ is the surface tension of the liquid, and the liquid experiences a reaction of equal magnitude that lifts the meniscus through a height h such that

$$2\pi r\sigma = \pi r^2 h\rho g \qquad (127)$$

—i.e., until the upward force for which surface tension is responsible is balanced by the weight of the column of liquid that has been lifted. If the liquid does not wet the tube, the meniscus is convex and depressed through the same distance h. A simple method for determining surface tension involves the measurement of h in one or the other of these situations and the use of equation (127) thereafter.

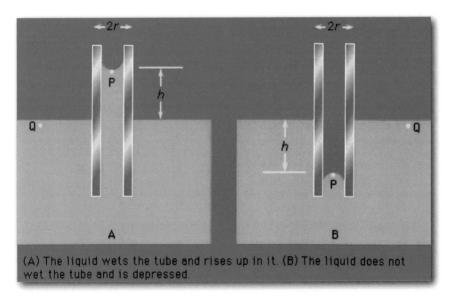

(A) The liquid wets the tube and rises up in it. (B) The liquid does not wet the tube and is depressed.

Capillarity. Copyright Encyclopædia Britannica; rendering for this edition by Rosen Educational Services

It follows from equations (124) and (127) that the pressure at a point P in the tube just below the meniscus differs from the pressure at Q outside of the tube by an amount

$$\rho g h = \frac{2\sigma}{r}; \qquad (128)$$

it is less than the pressure at Q in the case in which the liquid wets the tube and rises up in it and greater than the pressure at Q in the other case in which the liquid does not wet the tube and is depressed. Since the pressure at Q is just the atmospheric pressure, it is equal to the pressure at a point immediately above the meniscus. Hence, in both instances there is a pressure difference of $2\sigma/r$ between the two sides of the curved meniscus, and in both the higher pressure is on the inner side of the curve. Such a pressure difference is a requirement of equilibrium wherever a liquid surface is curved. If the surface is curved but not spherical, the pressure difference is

$$\sigma(r_1^{-1} + r_2^{-1}), \qquad (129)$$

where r_1 and r_2 are the two principal radii of curvature. If it is cylindrical, one of these radii is infinite, and, if it is curved in opposite directions, then for the purposes of (129) they should be treated as being of opposite sign.

The preceding analysis applies equally well to two vertical parallel plates that are partly submerged in the liquid a small distance apart. Consideration of how the pressure varies with height shows that over the range of height h the plates experience a greater pressure on their outer surfaces than on their inner surfaces; this is true whether the liquid wets both plates or not. It is a matter of observation that small objects floating near one another on the surface of a liquid tend to move toward one another, and it

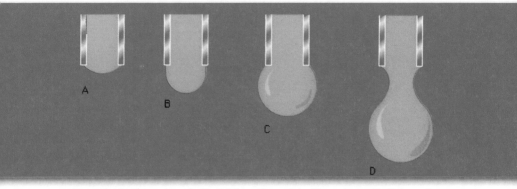

Stages in the formation of a liquid drop. Copyright Encyclopædia Britannica; rendering for this edition by Rosen Educational Services

is the pressure difference just referred to that makes them behave in this way.

One other problem having to do with surface tension will be examined here. Consider the stages in the growth of a liquid drop on the end of a tube which the liquid is supposed to wet. In the beginning, by which time the drop is roughly hemispheric in shape, the radius of curvature of the drop diminishes; and it follows from equation (128) that, to bring about this growth, one must slowly increase the pressure of the liquid inside the tube. If the pressure could be held steady, the drop would then become unstable, because any further growth (e.g., to a more or less spherical shape) would involve an increase in radius of curvature. The applied pressure would then exceed that required to hold the drop in equilibrium, and the drop would necessarily grow bigger still. In practice, however, it is easier to control the rate of flow of water through the tube, and hence the rate of growth of the drop, than it is to control the pressure. If the rate of flow is very small, drops will form nonspherical shapes before they detach themselves and fall. It is not an easy matter to analyze the shape of a drop on the point of detachment, and there is no simple formula for the volume of the drop after it is detached.

CHAPTER 9
LIQUIDS IN MOTION

This chapter deals with fluids that are in motion in a steady fashion such that the fluid velocity at each given point in space is not changing with time. Any flow pattern that is steady in this sense may be seen in terms of a set of streamlines, the trajectories of imaginary particles suspended in the fluid and carried along with it. In steady flow, the fluid is in motion but the streamlines are fixed. Where the streamlines crowd together, the fluid velocity is relatively high; where they open out, the fluid becomes relatively stagnant.

BERNOULLI'S LAW

When Euler and Bernoulli were laying the foundations of hydrodynamics, they treated the fluid as an idealized inviscid substance in which, as in a fluid at rest in equilibrium, the shear stresses associated with viscosity are zero and the pressure p is isotropic. They arrived at a simple law relating the variation of p along a streamline to the variation of v (the principle is credited to Bernoulli, but Euler seems to have arrived at it first), which serves to explain many of the phenomena that real fluids in steady motion display. To the inevitable question of when and why it is justifiable to neglect viscosity, there is no single answer.

Consider a small element of fluid of mass m, which—apart from the force on it due to gravity—is acted on only by a pressure p. The latter is isotropic and does not vary with time but may vary from point to point in space. It is a well-known consequence of Newton's laws of motion that, when a particle of mass m moves under the influence of its weight mg and an additional force F from a point P where its speed is v_P and its height is z_P to a point Q where its speed is v_Q and its height is z_Q, the work done by the additional force is equal to the increase in kinetic and potential energy of the particle—i.e., that

$$\int_P^Q \boldsymbol{F} \cdot d\boldsymbol{s} = \left(\frac{1}{2}\right) m(v_Q^2 - v_P^2) + mg(z_Q - z_P). \tag{130}$$

In the case of the fluid element under consideration, F may be related in a simple fashion to the gradient of the pressure, and one finds

$$\int_P^Q \boldsymbol{F} \cdot d\boldsymbol{s} = -m \int_P^Q \rho^{-1} dp. \tag{131}$$

If the variations of fluid density along the streamline from P to Q are negligibly small, the factor ρ^{-1} may be taken outside the integral on the right-hand side of equation (131), which thereupon reduces to $\rho^{-1}(p_Q - p_P)$. Then equations (130) and (131) can be combined to obtain

$$\frac{p_P}{\rho} + \frac{v_P^2}{2} + gz_P = \frac{p_Q}{\rho} + \frac{v_Q^2}{2} + gz_Q. \tag{132}$$

Since this applies for any two points that can be visited by a single element of fluid, one can immediately deduce Bernoulli's (or Euler's) important result that along each streamline in the steady flow of an inviscid fluid the quantity

$$\left(\frac{p}{\rho} + \frac{v^2}{2} + gz \right) \tag{133}$$

is constant.

Under what circumstances are variations in the density negligibly small? When they are very small compared with the density itself—i.e., when

$$\left(\frac{\Delta \rho}{\rho}\right) = \beta_S \Delta p = (\beta_S \rho) \Delta \left(\frac{v^2}{2} + gz\right) = \frac{\Delta\left(\frac{v^2}{2} + gz\right)}{V_S^2} \ll 1, \quad (134)$$

where the symbol Δ is used to represent the extent of the change along a streamline of the quantity that follows it, and where V_s is the speed of sound. If the fluid is air, it is adequately satisfied provided that the largest excursion in z is on the order of metres rather than kilometres and provided that the fluid velocity is everywhere less than about 100 metres per second.

Bernoulli's law indicates that, if an inviscid fluid is flowing along a pipe of varying cross section, then the pressure is relatively low at constrictions where the velocity is high and relatively high where the pipe opens out and the fluid stagnates. Many people find this situation paradoxical when they first encounter it. Surely, they say, a constriction should increase the local pressure rather than diminish it? The paradox evaporates as one learns to think of the pressure changes along the pipe as cause and the velocity changes as effect, instead of the other way around; it is only because the pressure falls at a constriction that the pressure gradient upstream of the constriction has the right sign to make the fluid accelerate.

Paradoxical or not, predictions based on Bernoulli's law are well-verified by experiment. Try holding two sheets of paper so that they hang vertically two centimetres or so apart and blow downward so that there is a current of air between them. The sheets will be drawn together by the reduction in pressure associated with this current. Ships are drawn together for much the same reason if they are moving through the water in the same direction at the same speed with a small distance between them. In this case, the current results from the displacement of water by each ship's bow, which has to flow backward to fill the space created as the stern moves forward, and the current between the ships, to which they both contribute, is stronger than the current moving past their outer sides. As another simple experiment, listen to the hissing sound made by a tap that is almost, but not quite, turned off. What happens in this case is that the flow is so constricted and the velocity within the constriction so high that the pressure in the constriction is actually negative. Assisted by the dissolved gases that are normally present, the water cavitates as it passes through, and the noise that is heard is the sound of tiny bubbles collapsing as the water slows down and the pressure rises again on the other side.

Two practical devices that are used by hydraulic engineers to monitor the flow of liquids though pipes are based on Bernoulli's law. One is the venturi tube, a short length with a constriction in it of standard shape, which may be inserted into the pipe proper. If the velocity at a point P before the constriction, where the tube has a cross-sectional area A_P, is v_P and the velocity in the constriction, where the area is A_Q, is v_Q, the continuity condition—the condition that the mass flowing through the pipe per unit time has to be the same at all points along its length—suggests that $\rho_P A_P v_P = \rho_Q A_Q v_Q$, or that $A_P v_P = A_Q v_Q$ if the difference between ρ_P and ρ_Q is negligible. Then Bernoulli's law indicates

$$\rho g h = (p_P - p_Q) = \left(\frac{1}{2}\right)\rho v_P^2 \left[\left(\frac{A_P}{A_Q}\right)^2 - 1\right]. \qquad (135)$$

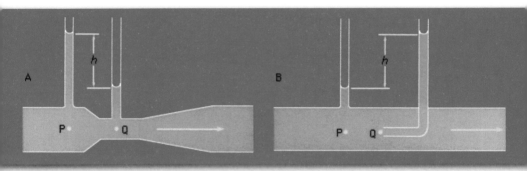

Schematic representation of (A) a venturi tube and of (B) a pitot tube. Copyright Encyclopædia Britannica; rendering for this edition by Rosen Educational Services

Thus one should be able to find v_P, and hence the quantity $Q(=A_P v_P)$ that engineers refer to as the rate of discharge, by measuring the difference of level h of the fluid in the two side tubes shown in the diagram. At low velocities the pressure difference $(p_P - p_Q)$ is greatly affected by viscosity, and equation (135) is unreliable in consequence. The venturi tube is normally used, however, when the velocity is large enough for the flow to be turbulent. In such a circumstance, equation (135) predicts values for Q that agree with values measured by more direct means to within a few parts percent, even though the flow pattern is not really steady at all.

The other device is the pitot tube. It consists of a tube with a short, right-angled bend, which is placed vertically in a moving fluid with the mouth of the bent part directed upstream. The fluid streamlines divide as they approach the blunt end of this tube, and at the point Q, just before the end of the tube, there is complete stagnation, since the fluid at this point is moving neither up nor down nor to the right. It follows immediately from Bernoulli's law that

$$\rho g h = (p_Q - p_P) = \left(\frac{1}{2}\right)\rho v_P^2. \qquad (136)$$

As with the venturi tube, one should therefore be able to find v_p from the level difference h. One other simple result deserves mention here. It concerns a jet of fluid emerging through a hole in the wall of a vessel filled with liquid under pressure. Observation of jets shows that after emerging they narrow slightly before settling down to a more or less uniform cross section known as the vena contracta. They do so because the streamlines are converging on the hole inside the vessel and are obliged to continue converging for a short while outside. It was Torricelli who first suggested that, if the pressure excess inside the vessel is generated by a head of liquid h, then the velocity v at the vena contracta is the velocity that a free particle would reach on falling through a height h—i.e., that

$$v = \sqrt{(2gh)} . \tag{137}$$

This result is an immediate consequence, for an inviscid fluid, of the principle of energy conservation that Bernoulli's law enshrines.

In the following section, Bernoulli's law is used in an indirect way to establish a formula for the speed at which disturbances travel over the surface of shallow water. The explanation of several interesting phenomena having to do with water waves is buried in this formula. Analogous phenomena dealing with sound waves in gases are discussed later in the section on compressible flow in gases, where an alternative form of Bernoulli's law is introduced. This form of the law is restricted to gases in steady flow but is not restricted to flow velocities that are much less than the speed of sound. The complication that viscosity represents is again ignored throughout these two sections.

WAVES ON SHALLOW WATER

Imagine a layer of water with a flat base that has a small step on its surface, dividing a region in which the depth of the water is uniformly equal to D from a region in which it is uniformly equal to $D(1 + \varepsilon)$, with $\varepsilon \ll 1$. Let the water in the shallower region flow toward the step with some uniform speed V, and let this speed be just sufficient to hold the step in the same position so that the flow pattern is a steady one. The continuity condition (i.e., the condition that as much water flows out to the left per unit time as flows in from the right) indicates that in the deeper region the speed of the water is $V(1 + \varepsilon)^{-1}$. Hence by applying Bernoulli's law to points P and Q, which lie on the same streamline and at both of which the pressure is atmospheric but with P at a height εD lower than Q, one may deduce that

$$g \varepsilon D = \left(\frac{1}{2}\right) V^2 [1 - (1 + \varepsilon)^{-2}] \approx \varepsilon V^2$$

—i.e., that

(138)

$$V = \sqrt{(gD)} .$$

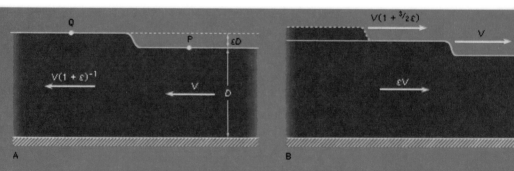

In (A) the water is moving and the step is stationary. In (B) the water is stationary in front of the first step and the step is therefore moving; the second step (dotted line) is catching up to the first.

Steps on the surface of shallow water. Copyright Encyclopædia Britannica; rendering for this edition by Rosen Educational Services

This result shows that, if the water in the shallower region is in fact stationary, the step advances over it with the speed V that equation (138) describes, and it reveals incidentally that behind the step the deeper water follows up with speed $V[1 - (1 + \varepsilon)^{-1}] \approx \varepsilon V$. The argument may readily be extended to disturbances of the surface that are undulatory rather than steplike. Provided that the distance between successive crests—a distance known as the wavelength and denoted by λ—is much greater than the depth of the water, D, and provided that its amplitude is very much less than D, a wave travels over stationary water at a speed given by equation (138). Because their speed does not depend on wavelength, the waves are said to be nondispersive.

Evidently waves that are approaching a shelving beach should slow down as D diminishes. If they are approaching it at an angle, the slowing-down effect bends, or refracts, the wave crests so that they are nearly parallel to the shore by the time they ultimately break.

Suppose now that a small step of height εD ($\varepsilon \ll 1$) is traveling over stationary water of uniform depth D and that behind it is a second step of much the same height traveling in the same direction. Because the second step is traveling on a base that is moving at $\varepsilon\sqrt{(gD)}$ and because the thickness of that base is $(1 + \varepsilon)D$ rather than D, the speed of the second step is approximately $(1 + 3\varepsilon/2)\sqrt{(gD)}$. Since this is greater than $\sqrt{(gD)}$, the second step is bound to catch up with the first. Hence, if there are a succession of infinitesimal steps that raise the depth continuously from D to some value D', which differs significantly from D, then the ramp on the surface is bound to become steeper as it advances. It may be shown that if D' exceeds about $1.3D$, the ramp ultimately becomes a vertical step of finite height and that the step then "breaks." A finite step that has broken dissipates energy as heat in the resultant foaming motion, and Bernoulli's equation is no longer applicable to it. A simple argument based on conservation of momentum rather than energy, however, suffices to show that its velocity of propagation is

$$\sqrt{\left(\frac{gD'(D'+D)}{2D}\right)}. \tag{139}$$

Tidal bores, which may be observed on some estuaries, are examples on the large scale of the sort of phenomena to which equation (139) applies. Examples on a smaller scale include the hydraulic jumps that are commonly seen below weirs and sluice gates where a smooth stream of water suddenly rises at a foaming front. In this case, equation (139) describes the speed of the water, since the front itself is more or less stationary.

When water is shallow but not extremely shallow, so that correction terms of the order of $(D/\lambda)^2$ are significant, waves of small amplitude become slightly dispersive. In this case, a localized disturbance on the surface of a river or canal, which is guided by the banks in such a way that it can propagate in one direction only, is liable to spread as it propagates. If its amplitude is not small, however, the tendency to spread due to dispersion may in special circumstances be subtly balanced by the factors that cause waves of relatively large amplitude to form bores, and the result is a localized hump in the surface, of symmetrical shape, which does not spread at all. The phenomenon was first observed on a canal near Edinburgh in 1834 by a Scottish engineer named Scott Russell; he later wrote a graphic account of following on horseback, for well over a kilometre, a "large solitary elevation . . . which continued its course along the channel apparently without change of form." What Scott Russell saw is now called a soliton. Solitons on canals can have various widths, but the smaller the width the larger the height must be and the faster the soliton travels. Thus,

Interaction of two solitons. Copyright Encyclopædia Britannica; rendering for this edition by Rosen Educational Services

if a high, narrow soliton is formed behind a low, broad one, it will catch up with the low one. It turns out that, when the high soliton does so, it passes through the low one and emerges with its shape unchanged.

It is now recognized that many of the nonlinear differential equations that appear in diverse branches of physics have solutions of large amplitude corresponding to solitons and that the remarkable capacity of solitons for surviving encounters with other solitons is universal. This discovery has stimulated much interest among mathematicians and physicists, and understanding of solitons is expanding rapidly.

COMPRESSIBLE FLOW IN GASES

Compressible flow refers to flow at velocities that are comparable to, or exceed, the speed of sound. The compressibility is relevant because at such velocities the variations in density that occur as the fluid moves from place to place cannot be ignored.

Suppose that the fluid is a gas at a low enough pressure for the ideal equation of state, equation (118), to apply and that its thermal conductivity is so poor that the compressions and rarefactions undergone by each element of the gas may be treated as adiabatic. In this case, it follows from equation (120) that the change of density accompanying any small change in pressure, dp, is such that

$$\rho^{-1} dp = \left(\frac{\gamma}{\gamma-1}\right) d\left(\frac{p}{\rho}\right). \tag{140}$$

This makes it possible to integrate the right-hand side of equation (131), and one thereby arrives at a version of Bernoulli's law for a steady compressible flow of gases which states that

$$\left(\frac{\gamma p}{(\gamma-1)\rho}\right) + \frac{v^2}{2} + gz \tag{141}$$

is constant along a streamline. An equivalent statement is that

$$\frac{C_p T}{M} + \frac{v^2}{2} + gz \tag{142}$$

is constant along a streamline. It is worth noting that, when a gas flows through a nozzle or through a shock front, the flow, though adiabatic, may not be reversible in the thermodynamic sense. Thus the entropy of the gas is not necessarily constant in such flow, and as a consequence the application of equation (120) is open to question. Fortunately, the result expressed by equation (141) or (142) can be established by arguments that do not involve integration of equation (131). It is valid for steady adiabatic flow whether this is reversible or not.

Bernoulli's law in the form of equation (142) may be used to estimate the variation of temperature with height in Earth's atmosphere. Even on the calmest day the atmosphere is normally in motion because convection currents are set up by heat derived from sunlight that is released at Earth's surface. The currents are indeed adiabatic to a good approximation, and their velocity is generally small enough for the term v^2 in equation (142) to be negligible. One can therefore deduce without more ado that the temperature of the atmosphere should fall off in a linear fashion—i.e., that

$$T(z) = T(0) - \beta z = T(0) - \left(\frac{Mg}{C_p}\right)z. \tag{143}$$

Here β is used to represent the temperature lapse rate, and the value suggested for this quantity, (Mg/C_p), is close to $10°$ C per kilometre for dry air.

This prediction is not exactly fulfilled in practice. Within the troposphere (i.e., to the heights of about 10 kilometres to which convection currents extend), the mean temperature does decrease with height in a linear fashion, but β is only about $6.5°$ C per kilometre. It is the water vapour in the atmosphere, which condenses as the air rises and cools, that lowers the lapse rate to this value by increasing the effective value of C_p. The fact that the lapse rate is smaller for moist air than for dry air means that a stream of moist air which passes over a mountain range and which deposits its moisture as rain or snow at the summit is warmer when it descends to sea level on the other side of the range than it was when it started. The foehn wind of the Alps owes its warmth to this effect.

The variation of the pressure of the atmosphere with height may be estimated in terms of β, using the equation

$$p(z) = p(0)\left[1 - \frac{\beta z}{T(0)}\right]^{Mg/R\beta}. \tag{144}$$

This is obtained by integration of equation (123), using equations (118) and (143).

In the form of equation (141), Bernoulli's law may be used to calculate the speed of sound in gases. The argument is directly analogous to that for waves on shallow water. The results of the argument will be stated without proof. If there exists an infinitesimal step in the density of the gas, it will remain stationary provided that the gas flows uniformly through it toward the region of higher density, with a velocity

$$V_s = \sqrt{\left|\frac{\gamma p}{\rho}\right|}. \tag{145}$$

If the gas is stationary, then equation (145) describes the velocity with which the step moves. It also describes the speed of propagation of the sort of undulatory variation of density that constitutes a sound wave of fixed frequency or pitch. Because the speed of sound is independent of pitch, sound waves, like waves on shallow water, are nondispersive. This is just as well. It is only because there is no dispersion that one can understand the words of a distant speaker or listen to a symphony orchestra with pleasure from the back of an auditorium as well as from the front.

It should be noted that the formula for the speed of sound in gases may be proved in other ways, and Newton came close to it a century before Bernoulli's time. However, because Newton failed to appreciate the distinction between adiabatic and isothermal flow, his answer lacked the factor γ occurring in equation (145). The first person to correct this error was Pierre-Simon Laplace.

The above statements apply to density steps or undulations, the amplitude of which is infinitesimal, and they need some modification if the amplitude is large. In the first place it is found, as for waves on shallow water and for very much the same reasons, that, where two small density steps are moving parallel to one another, the second is bound to catch up with the first. It follows that, if there exists a propagating region in which the density rises in a continuous fashion from ρ to ρ', where ($\rho' - \rho$) is not necessarily small, then the width of this region is bound to diminish as time passes. Ultimately a shock front develops over which the density—and hence the pressure and temperature—rises almost discontinuously. There are processes within the shock front, vaguely analogous on the molecular scale to the foaming of a breaking water wave, by which energy is dissipated as heat. The speed of propagation, V_{sh}, of a shock front in a gas that is stationary in front of it may be expressed in terms of V_s and V_s', the velocities of small-amplitude sound waves in front of the shock and behind it, respectively, by the equation

$$2V_{sh}^2 = \left[\frac{(\gamma + 1)\rho'}{\gamma\rho} \right] V_s'^2 + V_s^2. \tag{146}$$

Thus, if the shock is a strong one ($\rho' \gg \rho$), V_{sh} may be significantly greater than both V_s and V_s'.

Even the gentlest sound wave, in which density and pressure initially oscillate in a smooth and sinusoidal fashion, develops into a succession of weak shock fronts in time. More noticeable shock fronts are a feature of the flow of gases at supersonic speeds through the nozzles of jet engines and accompany projectiles that are moving through stationary air at supersonic speeds. In certain circumstances when a supersonic aircraft is following a curved path, the accompanying shock wave may accidentally reinforce itself in places and thereby become offensively noticeable as a "sonic boom," which may break windowpanes and cause other damage. Strong shock fronts also occur immediately after explosions, of course, and when windowpanes are broken by an explosion, the broken glass tends to fall outward rather than inward. Such is the case because the glass is sucked out by the relatively low density and pressure that succeed the shock itself.

Viscosity

A number of phenomena of considerable physical interest can be discussed using little more than the law of conservation of energy, as expressed by Bernoulli's law. However, the argument has so far been restricted to cases of steady flow. To discuss cases in which the flow is not steady, an equation of motion for fluids is needed, and one cannot write down a realistic equation of motion without facing up to the problems presented by viscosity, which have so far been deliberately set aside.

Stresses in Laminar Motion

The concept of viscosity was first formalized by Newton, who considered the shear stresses likely to arise when a fluid undergoes what is called laminar motion; the laminae here are planes normal to the x_2-axis, and they are moving in the direction of the x_1-axis with a velocity v_1, which increases in a linear fashion with x_2. Newton suggested that, as each lamina slips over the one below, it exerts a sort of frictional force upon the latter in the forward direction, in which case the upper lamina is bound to

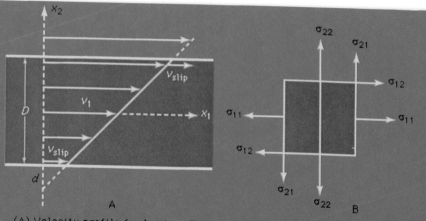

(A) Velocity profile for laminar flow between two plates, driven by motion of the upper plate, (B) an enlarged view of a cubic element of the fluid between the plates, showing the stresses that act upon it.

Laminar motion and associated stresses. Copyright Encyclopædia Britannica; rendering for this edition by Rosen Educational Services

experience an equal reaction in the backward direction. The strength of these forces per unit area constitutes the component of shear stress normally written as σ_{12} (not to be confused with surface tension, for which the symbol σ has been used above). Consider an infinitesimal element of the fluid of cubic shape and the directions of the forces experienced by this cube associated with σ_{12}. The directions of the forces associated with the so-called normal stresses σ_{11} and σ_{22} in the absence of motion of the fluid would both be equal, by Pascal's law, to $-p$. Now σ_{12} is clearly zero when the rate of variation of velocity, $\partial v_1/\partial x_2$, is zero, for then there is no slip, and presumably it increases monotonically as $\partial v_1/\partial x_2$ increases. Newton made the plausible assumption that the two are linearly related—i.e., that

$$\sigma_{12} = \eta\left(\frac{\partial v_1}{\partial x_2}\right).$$

(147)

The full name for the coefficient η is shear viscosity to distinguish it from the bulk viscosity, b. The word "shear," however, is frequently omitted in this context.

Now if the only shear stress acting on the cubic element of fluid were σ_{12}, the cube would experience a torque tending to make it twist in a clockwise sense. Since the magnitude of the torque would vary like the third power of the linear dimensions of the cube, whereas the moment of inertia of the element would vary like the fifth power, the resultant angular acceleration for an infinitesimal cube would be infinite. One may infer that any tendency to twist in a clockwise sense gives rise instantaneously to an additional shear stress σ_{21}, the direction of which is indicated in the diagram, and that σ_{12} and σ_{21} are equal at all times. It follows that equation (147) cannot be a complete expression for these shear stresses, for it does not include the possibility that the fluid is moving in the x_2 direction, with a velocity v_2 that varies with x_1. The complete expression for what is called a Newtonian fluid is

$$\sigma_{12} = \sigma_{21} = \eta\left[\left(\frac{\partial v_1}{\partial x_2}\right) + \left(\frac{\partial v_2}{\partial x_1}\right)\right]. \tag{148}$$

Similar expressions may be written down for σ_{23} $(= \sigma_{32})$ and σ_{31} $(= \sigma_{13})$. Since Newton's day these hypothetical expressions have been fully substantiated for gases and simple liquids, not only by experiment but also by analysis of the molecular motions and molecular interactions in such fluids undergoing shear, and for such fluids one can even predict the magnitude of η with reasonable success. There do exist, however, more complicated fluids for which the Newtonian description of shear stress is inadequate, and some of these are very familiar in the home. In the whites of eggs, for example, and in most shampoos, there are long-chain molecules that become entangled with one another, and entanglement may hinder their efforts to respond to changes of environment associated with flow. As a result, the stresses acting in such fluids may reflect the deformations experienced by the fluid in the recent past as much as the instantaneous rate of deformation. Moreover, the relation between stress and rate of deformation may be far from linear. Non-Newtonian effects, interesting though they are, lie outside the scope of the present discussion, however.

The sort of velocity profile may be established by containing the fluid between two parallel flat plates and moving one plate relative to the other. The possibility exists that in this situation the layers of fluid immediately in contact with each plate will slip over them with some finite velocity (indicated in the diagram by an arrow labeled v_{slip}). If so, the frictional stresses associated with this slip must be such as to balance the shear stress $\eta(\partial v_1/\partial x_2)$ exerted on each of these layers by the rest of the fluid. Little is known about fluid-solid frictional stresses, but intelligent guesswork suggests that they are proportional in magnitude to v_{slip} and that, in the circumstances of laminar motion, the distance d below the surface of the stationary bottom plate at which the variation of v_1 with x_2 extrapolates to zero should be of the same order of magnitude as the diameter of a molecule if the fluid is a liquid or as the molecular "mean free path" if it is a gas. These distances are normally very small compared with the separation of the plates, D. Accordingly, fluid flow patterns may normally be treated as subject to the boundary condition that at a fluid-solid interface the relative velocity of the fluid is zero. No reliable evidence for failure of predictions based on this no-slip boundary condition has yet been found, except in the case of what is called Knudsen flow of gases (i.e., flow at such low pressures that the mean free path is comparable in length with the dimensions of the apparatus).

If a fluid is flowing steadily between two parallel plates that are both stationary and if its velocity must be zero in contact with both of them, the velocity profile must necessarily have the form in which the velocity is a maximum midway between the two plates. A force in the forward direction due to the shear stress $\eta(\partial v_1/\partial x_2)$ is transmitted to the plates, and an equal force in the backward direction acts on the fluid. The motion therefore cannot be maintained unless the pressure acting on the fluid is greater on the left of the diagram than it is on the right. A full analysis shows the velocity profile to be parabolic, and it indicates that the rate of discharge is related to the pressure gradient by the equation

$$Q = -\left(\frac{WD^3}{12\eta}\right)\left(\frac{dp}{dx_1}\right), \qquad (149)$$

where $W (>> D)$ is the width of the plates. A similar analysis of the problem of steady flow through a (horizontal)

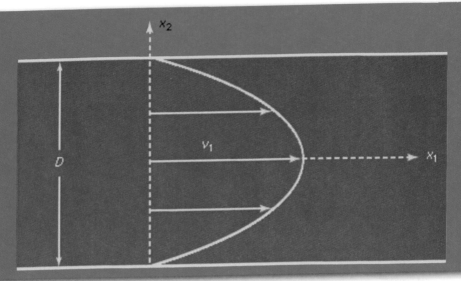

Velocity profile for laminar flow between two plates (or inside a cylindrical tube), driven by a pressure gradient. Copyright Encyclopædia Britannica; rendering for this edition by Rosen Educational Services

cylindrical pipe of uniform diameter D shows the rate of discharge in this case to be given by

$$Q = -\left(\frac{\pi D^4}{128\eta}\right)\left(\frac{dp}{dx_1}\right); \tag{150}$$

this famous result is known as Poiseuille's equation, and the type of flow to which it refers is called Poiseuille flow.

BULK VISCOSITY

Viscosity may affect the normal stress components, σ_{11}, σ_{22}, and σ_{33}, as well as the shear stress components. To see why this is so, one needs to examine the way in which stress components transform when one's reference axes are rotated. Here, the result will be stated without proof that the general expression for σ_{11} consistent with equation (148) is

$$\sigma_{11} = -p + \left(b + \frac{4\eta}{3}\right)\left(\frac{\partial v_1}{\partial x_1}\right) + \left(b - \frac{2\eta}{3}\right)\left(\frac{\partial v_2}{\partial x_2}\right)$$
$$+ \left(b - \frac{2\eta}{3}\right)\left(\frac{\partial v_3}{\partial x_3}\right). \tag{151}$$

On the right-hand side of this equation, p represents the equilibrium pressure defined in terms of local density and temperature by the equation of state, and b is another viscosity coefficient known as the bulk viscosity.

The bulk viscosity is relevant only where the density is changing. Thus it plays a role in attenuating sound waves in fluids and may be estimated from the magnitude of the attenuation. If the fluid is effectively incompressible, however, so that changes of density may be ignored, the flow is everywhere subject to the continuity condition that

$$\left(\frac{\partial v_1}{\partial x_1}\right) + \left(\frac{\partial v_2}{\partial x_2}\right) + \left(\frac{\partial v_3}{\partial x_3}\right) [\equiv \nabla \cdot \boldsymbol{v} \text{ or div } \boldsymbol{v}] = 0. \quad (152)$$

The terms in equation (151) that involve b then cancel, and the expression simplifies to

$$\sigma_{11} = -p + 2\eta \left(\frac{\partial v_1}{\partial x_1}\right). \quad (153)$$

Similar equations may be written down for σ_{22} and σ_{33}. These simpler expressions provide the basis for the argument that follows, and the bulk viscosity can be left on one side.

MEASUREMENT OF SHEAR VISCOSITY

A variety of methods are available for the measurement of shear viscosity. One standard method involves measurement of the pressure gradient along a pipe for various rates of flow and application of Poiseuille's equation. Other methods involve measurement either of the damping of the torsional oscillations of a solid disk supported between two parallel plates when fluid is admitted to the space between the plates, or of the effect of the fluid on the frequency of the oscillations.

The Couette viscometer deserves a fuller explanation. In this device, the fluid occupies the space between two coaxial cylinders of radii a and b ($> a$); the outer cylinder is rotated with uniform angular velocity ω_o, and the resultant torque transmitted to the inner stationary cylinder is measured. If both the terms on the right-hand side of equation (148) are taken into account, the shear stress in the circulating fluid is found to be proportional to $r(d\omega/dr)$ rather than to (dv/dr)—not an unexpected result, since it is only if ω, the angular velocity of the fluid, varies with radius r

that there is any slip between one cylindrical lamina of fluid and the next. The torque transmitted through the fluid is therefore proportional to $r^3(d\omega/dr)$. In the steady state, the opposing torques acting on the inner and outer surfaces of each cylindrical lamina of fluid must be of equal magnitude—otherwise the laminae accelerate—and this means that $r^3(d\omega/dr)$ must be independent of r. There are two basic modes of motion for a circulating fluid that satisfy this condition: in one, the liquid rotates as a solid body would, with an angular velocity that does not vary with r, and the torque is everywhere zero; in the other, ω varies like r^{-2}. The angular velocity of the fluid in a Couette viscometer can be viewed as a mixture of these two modes in proportions that satisfy the boundary conditions at $r = a$ and $r = b$. The torque transmitted per unit length of the cylinders turns out to be given by

$$4\pi\eta\omega_0 \left[\frac{b^2 a^2}{(b^2 - a^2)} \right]. \tag{154}$$

It may be added that if the inner cylinder is absent, the steady flow pattern consists only of the first mode—i.e., the fluid rotates like a solid body with uniform angular velocity ω_0. If the outer cylinder is absent, however, and the inner one rotates, it then consists only of the second mode. The angular velocity falls off like r^{-2}, and the velocity v falls off like r^{-1}.

In the equation of motion given in the following section, the shear viscosity occurs only in the combination (η/ρ). This combination occurs so frequently in arguments of fluid dynamics that it has been given a special name—kinetic viscosity. The kinetic viscosity at normal temperatures and pressures is about 10^{-6} square metre per second for water and about 1.5×10^{-5} square metre per second for air.

NAVIER-STOKES EQUATION

One may have a situation where σ_{11} increases with x_1. The force that this component of stress exerts on the right-hand side of the cubic element of fluid will then be greater than the force in the opposite direction that it exerts on the left-hand side, and the difference between the two will cause the fluid to accelerate along x_1. Accelerations along x_1 will also result if σ_{12} and σ_{13} increase with x_2 and x_3, respectively. These accelerations, and corresponding accelerations in the other two directions, are described by the equation of motion of the fluid. For a fluid moving so slowly compared with the speed of sound that it may be treated as incompressible and in which the variations of temperature from place to place are insufficient to cause significant variations in the shear viscosity η, this equation takes the form

$$-\nabla\left(\frac{p}{\rho}+gz\right)-\left(\frac{\eta}{\rho}\right)[\nabla\times(\nabla\times\boldsymbol{v})]=\frac{D\boldsymbol{v}}{Dt}$$

$$(155)$$

$$=\frac{\partial\boldsymbol{v}}{\partial t}+(\boldsymbol{v}\cdot\nabla)\boldsymbol{v}.$$

Euler derived all the terms in this equation except the one on the left-hand side proportional to (η/ρ), and without that term the equation is known as the Euler equation. The whole is called the Navier-Stokes equation.

The equation is written in a compact vector notation which many readers will find totally impenetrable, but a few words of explanation may help some others. The symbol ∇ represents the gradient operator, which, when preceding a scalar quantity X, generates a vector with components $(\partial X/\partial x_1, \partial X/\partial x_2, \partial X/\partial x_3)$. The vector product of this operator and the fluid velocity $\boldsymbol{v}$—i.e., $(\nabla\times\boldsymbol{v})$—is sometimes designated as **curl** $\boldsymbol{v}$ [and $\nabla\times(\nabla\times\boldsymbol{v})$ is also *curl curl v*]. Another name for $(\nabla \times v)$, which expresses particularly vividly the characteristics of the local flow pattern that it represents, is vorticity. In a sample of fluid that is rotating like a solid body with uniform angular velocity ω_o, the vorticity lies in the same direction as the axis of rotation, and its magnitude is equal to $2\omega_o$. In other circumstances the vorticity is related in a similar fashion to the local angular velocity and may vary from place to place. As for the right-hand side of equation (155), Dv/Dt represents the rate of change of velocity that one would see if the motion of a single element of the fluid could be followed—that is, it represents the acceleration of the element—while $\partial v/\partial t$ represents the rate of change at a fixed point in space. If the flow is steady, then $\partial v/\partial t$ is everywhere zero, but the fluid may be accelerating all the same, as individual fluid elements move from regions where the streamlines are widely spaced to regions where they are close together. It is the difference between Dv/Dt and $\partial v/\partial t$—i.e., the final $(v \cdot \nabla)v$ term in equation (155)— that introduces into fluid dynamics the nonlinearity that makes the subject so rife with surprises.

POTENTIAL FLOW

This section is concerned with an important class of flow problems in which the vorticity is everywhere zero, and for such problems the Navier-Stokes equation may be greatly simplified. For one thing, the viscosity term drops out of it. For another, the nonlinear term, $(v \cdot \nabla)v$, may be transformed into $\nabla(v^2/2)$. Finally, it may be shown that, when $(\nabla \times v)$ is zero, one may describe the velocity by means of a scalar potential ϕ, using the equation

$$v = \nabla\varphi \,[\equiv \text{grad } \varphi]. \tag{156}$$

Thus equation (155) becomes

$$-\nabla\left(\frac{p}{\rho} + gz + \frac{v^2}{2} + \frac{\partial\varphi}{\partial t}\right) = 0,$$

which may at once be integrated to show that

$$\left(\frac{p}{\rho} + gz + \frac{v^2}{2} + \frac{\partial\varphi}{\partial t}\right) = \text{constant.} \tag{157}$$

This result incorporates Bernoulli's law for an effectively incompressible fluid (equation [133]), as was to be expected from the disappearance of the viscosity term. It is more powerful than equation (133), however, because it can be applied to nonsteady flow in which $\partial\phi/\partial t$ is not zero and because it shows that in cases of potential flow the left-hand side of equation (157) is constant everywhere and not just constant along each streamline.

Vorticity-free, or potential, flow would be of rather limited interest were it not for the theorem, first proved by Thomson, that, in a body of fluid which is free of vorticity initially, the vorticity remains zero as the fluid moves. This theorem seems to open the door for relatively painless solutions to a great range of problems. Consider, for example, a stream of fluid in uniform motion approaching an obstacle of some sort. Well upstream of the obstacle the fluid is certainly vorticity-free, so it should, according to Thomson's theorem, be vorticity-free around the obstacle and downstream as well. In this case a flow potential should exist; and, if the fluid is effectively incompressible, it follows from equations (152) and (156) that it satisfies Laplace's equation,

$$\left(\frac{\partial^2\varphi}{\partial x_1^2}\right) + \left(\frac{\partial^2\varphi}{\partial x_2^2}\right) + \left(\frac{\partial^2\varphi}{\partial x_3^2}\right)[\equiv \nabla^2\varphi] = 0. \tag{158}$$

This is perhaps the most frequently occurring differential equation in physics, and methods for solving it, subject to appropriate boundary conditions, are very well established. Given a solution for ϕ, the fluid velocity v follows at once, and one may then discover how the pressure varies with position and time from equation (157).

The physicists and mathematicians who developed fluid dynamics during the 19th century relied heavily on this reasoning. They based splendid achievements upon it, a notable example being the theory of waves on deep water. There was a touch of unreality, however, about some of their theorizing. If carried to extremes, the argument of the previous section implies that water initially stationary in a beaker can never be set into rotation by rotating the beaker or by stirring it with a spoon, and this is clearly nonsense. It suggests that vorticity-free water remains vorticity-free if it is squeezed into a narrow pipe, and this too is plainly nonsensical, for the well-established parabolic profile for laminar flow in a tube is not vorticity-free. What is misleading about the argument in situations like these is that it pays inadequate attention to what happens at interfaces. Following the work of Prandtl, physicists now appreciate that vorticity is liable to be fed into the fluid at interfaces, whether these are interfaces between the fluid and some solid object or the free surfaces of a liquid. Once the slightest trace of vorticity is present, it destroys the conditions on which the proof of Thomson's theorem depends. Moreover, vorticity admitted at interfaces spreads into the fluid in much the same way that a dye would spread, and whether or not the results of potential theory are useful depends on how much of the fluid is contaminated in the particular circumstances under discussion.

POTENTIAL FLOW WITH CIRCULATION: VORTEX LINES

The proof of Thomson's theorem depends on the concept of circulation, which Thomson introduced. This quantity is defined for a closed loop which is embedded in, and moves with, the fluid; denoted by K, it is the integral around the loop of $v \cdot dl$, where dl is an element of length along the loop. If the vorticity is everywhere zero, then so is the circulation around all possible loops, and vice versa. Thomson showed that K cannot change if the viscous term in equation (155) contributes nothing to the local acceleration, and it follows that both K and vorticity remain zero for all time.

Reference was made earlier to the sort of steady flow pattern that may be set up by rotating a cylindrical spindle in a fluid; the streamlines are circles around the spindle, and the velocity falls off like r^{-1}. This pattern of flow occurs naturally in whirlpools and typhoons, where the role of the spindle is played by a "core" in which the fluid rotates like a solid body; the axis around which the fluid circulates is then referred to as a vortex line. Each small element of fluid outside the core, if examined in isolation for a short interval of time, appears to be undergoing translation without rotation, and the local vorticity is zero. Were it not so, the viscous torques would not cancel and the flow pattern would not be a steady one. Nevertheless, the circulation is not zero if the loop for which it is defined is one that encloses the spindle or core. In such situations, a potential that obeys Laplace's equation outside the spindle or core can be found, but it is no longer, to use a technical term that may be familiar to some readers, single-valued.

Readers who recognize this term are likely to have encountered it in the context of electromagnetism, and it is worth remarking that all the results of potential flow theory have electromagnetic analogues, in which stream-lines become the lines of force of a magnetic field and vortex lines become lines of electric current. The analogy may be illustrated by reference to the Magnus effect.

This effect (named for the German physicist and chemist H.G. Magnus, who first investigated it experimentally) arises when fluid flows steadily past a cylindrical spindle, with a velocity that at large distances from the spindle is perpendicular to the spindle's axis and uniformly equal to, say, v_o, while the spindle itself is steadily rotated. Rotation is communicated to the fluid, and in the steady state the circulation around any loop that encloses the spindle (and encloses a layer of fluid adjacent to the spindle within which the vorticity is nonzero and potential theory is inapplicable) has some nonzero value K. The details of the

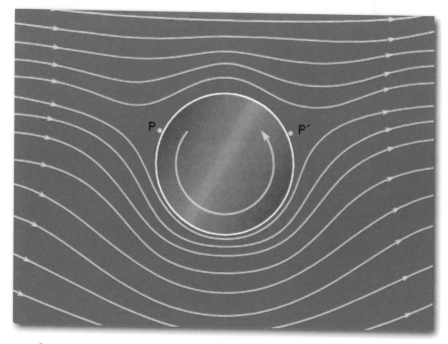

Streamlines for potential flow with circulation past a rotating cylinder. The cylinder experiences a downward Magnus force. Copyright Encyclopædia Britannica; rendering for this edition by Rosen Educational Services

streamlines that describe the steady flow pattern (outside that "boundary layer") naturally depend on the magnitude of v_0 and K. The flow pattern has two stagnation points at P and P' and, since the pressure is high at such points, the spindle may be expected to experience a downward force perpendicular both to its axis and to the direction of v_0. Detailed calculations confirm this expectation and show that the magnitude of the force, per unit length of the spindle, is

$$\rho v_0 K. \tag{159}$$

This so-called Magnus force is directly analogous to the force that a transverse magnetic field B_0 exerts upon a wire carrying an electric current I, the magnitude of which, per unit length of the wire, is $B_0 I$.

The Magnus force on rotating cylinders has been utilized to propel experimental yachts, and it is closely related to the lift force on airfoils that enables airplanes to fly. The transverse forces that cause spinning balls to swerve in flight are, however, not Magnus forces, as is sometimes asserted. They are due to the asymmetrical nature of the eddies that develop at the rear of a spinning sphere. Cricket balls, unlike the balls used for baseball, tennis, and golf, have a raised equatorial seam that plays an important part in making the eddies asymmetric. A bowler in cricket who wants to make the ball swerve imparts spin to it, but he does so chiefly to ensure that the orientation of this seam remains steady as the ball moves toward the batsman.

It may be shown, by reference to the magnetic analogue or in other ways, that straight vortex lines of equal but opposite strength, $\pm K$, which are parallel and separated by a distance d, will drift sideways together through the fluid at a speed given by $K/2\pi d$. Similarly, a vortex line that has joined up on itself to form a closed vortex ring of radius a drifts along its axis with a speed given by

$$\left(\frac{K}{4\pi a}\right)\ln\left(\frac{a}{c}\right),\qquad(160)$$

where c is the radius of the line's core, with ln standing for natural logarithm. This formula applies, for example, to smoke rings. The fact that such rings slow down as they propagate can be explained in terms of the increase of c with time, due to viscosity.

WAVES ON DEEP WATER

One particular solution of Laplace's equation that describes wave motion on the surface of a lake or of the ocean is

$$\varphi = \varphi_0 \cos\left\{2\pi\left[\left(\frac{x}{\lambda}\right) - ft\right]\right\} \sinh\left[2\pi\frac{(D+z)}{\lambda}\right].\qquad(161)$$

In this case the x-axis is the direction of propagation and the z-axis is vertical; $z = 0$ describes the free surface of the water when it is undisturbed and $z = -D$ describes the bottom surface; ϕ_0 is an arbitrary constant that determines the amplitude of the motion; and f is the frequency of the waves and λ their wavelength. If λ is more than a few centimetres, surface tension is irrelevant and the pressure in the liquid just below its free surface is atmospheric for all values of x. It can be shown that in these circumstances the wave motion described by equation (161) is consistent with equation (157) only if the frequency and wavelength are related by the equation

$$f^2 = \left(\frac{2\pi g}{\lambda}\right)\tanh\left(\frac{2\pi D}{\lambda}\right),\qquad(162)$$

and an expression for the speed of the waves may be deduced from this, since $V = f\lambda$. For shallow water ($D \ll \lambda$) one obtains the answer already quoted as equation (138), but for deep water ($D \gg \lambda$) the answer is

$$V = \sqrt{\left(\frac{g\lambda}{2\pi}\right)}. \tag{163}$$

Waves on deep water are evidently dispersive, and surfers rely on this fact. A storm in the middle of the ocean disturbs the surface in a chaotic way that would be useless for surfing, but as the component waves travel toward the shore they separate; those with long wavelengths move ahead of those with short wavelengths because they travel faster. As a result, the waves seem nicely regular by the time that they arrive.

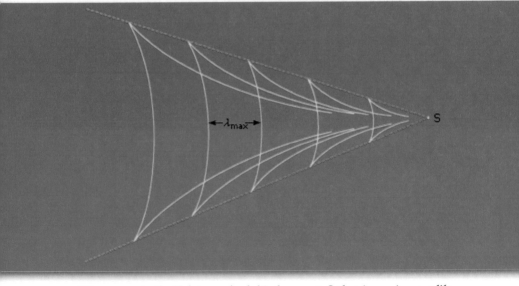

Wave crests in the Kelvin wedge behind a source S that is moving steadily from left to right. The maximum wavelength λ_{max} depends on the speed of the source, but the angle of the wedge does not. Copyright Encyclopædia Britannica; rendering for this edition by Rosen Educational Services

Anyone who has observed the waves behind a moving ship will know that they are confined to a V-shaped area of the water's surface, with the ship at its apex. The waves are particularly prominent on the arms of the V, but they can also be discerned between these arms where the wave crests curve. It seems to be widely believed that the angle of the V becomes more acute as the boat speeds up, much in the way that the conical shock wave accompanying a supersonic projectile becomes more acute. That is not the case; the dispersive character of waves on deep water is such that the V has a fixed angle of $2 \sin^{-1}(1/3) = 39°$. Thomson (Lord Kelvin) was the first to explain this, and so the V-shaped area is now known as the Kelvin wedge.

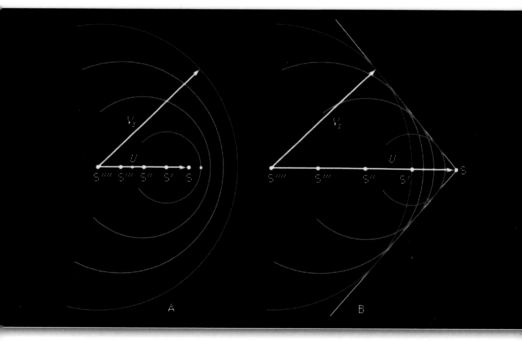

Mach's explanation of the shock front from a supersonic projectile. (A) Source speed U *less than speed of sound* V_S, *(B)* U *greater than* V_S. Copyright Encyclopædia Britannica; rendering for this edition by Rosen Educational Services

Consider a situation in which S (the "source") represents the bow of the ship which is moving from left to right with uniform speed U, and lines labeled C, C', C", etc., represent a set of parallel wave crests which are also moving from left to right. It can be shown that S will create this set of crests if, but only if, it rides continuously on the one labeled C. (It also can be shown that, though the crests in the set continue indefinitely to the left of C, there can be none to the right of this one.) The condition that S and C move together indicates that there is a relation between wavelength λ and inclination α expressed by the equation

$$\sin \alpha = \frac{V}{U} = \sqrt{\frac{g\lambda}{2\pi U^2}} \; . \qquad (164)$$

This condition can evidently be satisfied by many other sets of crests—e.g., by the set with slightly shorter wavelength λ' that is represented by broken lines. When one takes into consideration all the sets that satisfy equation (164) and have wavelengths intermediate between λ and λ', it becomes apparent that over most of the area behind

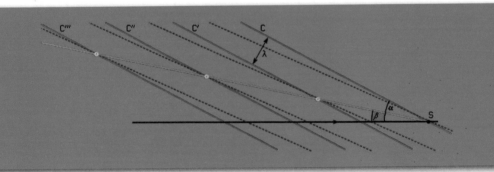

The curved wave crests in the Kelvin wedge (depicted in the first image in this section) result from the superposition of many sets of straight wave crests like the two shown here. These two sets and others that are intermediate in wavelength reinforce one another near the line of inclination β and interfere destructively elsewhere. Copyright Encyclopædia Britannica; rendering for this edition by Rosen Educational Services

the source they interfere destructively. They reinforce one another, however, near several intersections. These intersections lie on a line through S of inclination β, where

$$\tan \beta = \frac{\tan \alpha}{(2 + \tan^2 \alpha)}. \qquad (165)$$

It follows that, though the angle α can take any value between $90°$ (corresponding to $\lambda = \lambda_{max} = 2\pi U^2/g$) and zero, $\tan \beta$ can never exceed $\frac{1}{2}\sqrt{2}$, and $\sin \beta$ can never exceed $\frac{1}{3}$.

Ships lose energy to the waves in the Kelvin wedge, and they experience additional resistance on that account. The resistance is particularly high when the wave system created by the bow, where water is pushed aside, reinforces the wave system created by the "anti-source" at the stern, where the water closes in again. Such reinforcement is liable to occur when the effective length of the boat, L, is equal to $(2n + 1)\lambda_{max}/2$ (with $n = 0, 1, 2, \ldots$) and therefore when the Froude number, $U/\sqrt{(Lg)}$, takes one of the values $[\sqrt{(2n + 1)\pi}]^{-1}$. However, once a boat has been accelerated past $U = \sqrt{(Lg/\pi)}$, the bow and stern waves tend to cancel, and the resistance resulting from wave creation diminishes.

Waves on deep water whose wavelength is a few centimetres or less are generally referred to as ripples. In such waves, the pressure differences across the curved surface of the water associated with surface tension (see equation [129]) are not negligible, and the appropriate expression for their speed of propagation is

$$V = \sqrt{\left[\left(\frac{g\lambda}{2\pi}\right) + \left(\frac{2\pi\sigma}{\lambda\rho}\right)\right]}. \qquad (166)$$

The wave velocity is therefore large for very short wavelengths as well as for very long ones. For water at normal temperatures, V has a minimum value of about 0.23 metre per second where the wavelength is about 17 millimetres, and it follows (note that equation [164] has no real root for α unless U exceeds V) that an object moving through water can create no ripples at all unless its speed exceeds 0.23 metre per second. A wind moving over the surface of water likewise creates no ripples unless its speed exceeds a certain critical value, but this is a more complicated phenomenon, and the critical speed in question is distinctly higher.

BOUNDARY LAYERS AND SEPARATION

It should be reiterated that vorticity is liable to enter a fluid that is initially undergoing potential flow where it makes contact with a solid and also at its free surface. The way in which, having entered, it spreads, may be illustrated by a simple example. Consider a large body of fluid, initially stationary, being set into motion by the movement in its own plane of a large solid plate that is immersed within the fluid. The motion is communicated from solid to fluid

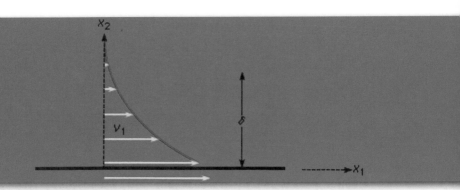

Velocity profile established by motion of a plate through stationary fluid. Copyright Encyclopædia Britannica; rendering for this edition by Rosen Educational Services

by the frictional forces that prevent slip between the two. The development of the velocity profile with time turns out to be described by the partial differential equation

$$\rho\left(\frac{\partial v_1}{\partial t}\right) = \eta\left(\frac{\partial^2 v_1}{\partial x_2^2}\right).$$

$$(167)$$

In this situation the vorticity, which may be denoted by the symbol Ω, has one nonzero component, directed along the axis perpendicular to x_1 and x_2; it is $\Omega_3 = -(\partial v_1/\partial x_2)$. Differentiation of equation (167) with respect to x_2 shows at once that

$$\rho\left(\frac{\partial \Omega_3}{\partial t}\right) = \eta\left(\frac{\partial^2 \Omega_3}{\partial x_2^2}\right).$$

$$(168)$$

This is a diffusion equation. It indicates that, if the plate oscillates to and fro with frequency f, then the so-called boundary layer within which Ω_3 is nonzero has a thickness δ given by

$$\delta \approx \sqrt{\left(\frac{\eta}{\pi \rho f}\right)},$$

$$(169)$$

and in most instances of oscillatory motion this is small enough for the boundary layer to be neglected. For example, the boundary layer on the surface of the ocean has a thickness of less than one millimetre when a wave with a frequency of about one hertz passes by; because the effects of viscosity are confined to this layer, they are too slight to affect the propagation of the wave to any significant degree. If the plate is kept moving at a uniform rate, however, the thickness of the boundary layer, as described by equation (168), will increase with the time t that has elapsed since the motion of the plate began, according to the equation

$$\delta \approx \sqrt{\left(\frac{2\eta t}{\rho}\right)}. \qquad (170)$$

Prandtl suggested that when a stream of fluid flows steadily past an obstacle of finite extent, such as a sphere, the time that matters is the time for which fluid on a streamline just outside the boundary layer remains in contact with it. This time is of order D/v_o, where D is the diameter of the sphere and v_o is the speed of the fluid well upstream. Hence, one would expect the thickness of the boundary layer at the rear of the sphere to be something like

$$\sqrt{\left(\frac{\eta D}{\rho v_0}\right)}. \qquad (171)$$

If the velocity v_o is so low that equation (170) is comparable with or greater than the diameter D, the flow pattern must be so contaminated by vorticity that the neglect of viscosity and reliance on Bernoulli's equation and on the other results of potential theory is clearly unjustified. If the velocity is high and equation (171) is much less than D, however, the boundary layer would seem to be of little importance. Surely then the results of potential theory are to be trusted?

Alas, that optimistic conclusion is not confirmed by experiment. What happens at high velocities is that the boundary layer comes unstuck from the surface of the sphere—it is said to separate. Evidently the fluid velocity is higher near the equator of the sphere, at Q, than it is at either of the two poles, P and P'. Thus according to Bernoulli's equation, which can be relied on outside the

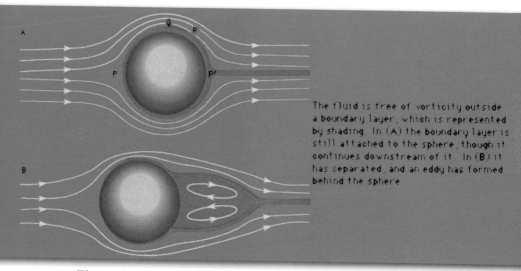

The fluid is free of vorticity outside a boundary layer, which is represented by shading. In (A) the boundary layer is still attached to the sphere, though it continues downstream of it. In (B) it has separated, and an eddy has formed behind the sphere.

Flow past a stationary solid sphere. Copyright Encyclopædia Britannica; rendering for this edition by Rosen Educational Services

boundary layer, the pressure near Q is less than it is near P and P'. The pressure gradient acts on the fluid in the boundary layer, accelerating it between P and Q but decelerating it between Q and P'. As the flow velocity increases, so does the pressure gradient, and at a certain stage the decelerating effect between Q and P' becomes so large that the direction of flow within the boundary layer reverses in sign near the point labeled R in the diagram. The backflow of fluid near R causes an accumulation of fluid that obliges the oncoming boundary layer to separate, and the fluid behind the sphere circulates slowly within the boundary layer as a ring-shaped eddy.

This analysis might well refer to a cylinder rather than a sphere. If such were the case, however, the regions of circulating flow behind the obstacle would form parts of two separate straight eddies instead of a single ring-shaped one. At high velocities the eddies behind a cylinder become so large that they are blown off by the current and disappear downstream while new eddies form in their place; they are said to have been shed. The top and bottom eddies are shed alternately, and the cylinder experiences an oscillating force as a consequence. If the cylinder is something flexible like a telephone or power cable, it will move to and fro under this force; the singing noise produced by cables in high winds is due to a resonance between their natural frequency of transverse oscillation and the frequency of eddy shedding. Similar processes are liable to occur behind obstacles of any shape, and the occurrence of eddies behind rocks or walls that interrupt the smooth flow of rivers is a familiar phenomenon.

DRAG

A fluid stream exerts a drag force F_D on any obstacle placed in its path, and the same force arises if the obstacle moves and the fluid is stationary. How large it is and how it may be reduced are questions of obvious importance to designers of moving vehicles of all sorts and equally to designers of cooling towers and other structures who want to be certain that the structures will not collapse in the face of winds.

An expression for the drag force on a sphere which is valid at such low velocities that the v^2 term in the Navier-Stokes equation is negligible, and thus at velocities such that the boundary layer thickness described by equation (171) is larger than the sphere diameter D, was first obtained by Stokes. Known as Stokes's law, it may be written as

$$F_D = 3\pi\eta D v_0. \tag{172}$$

One-third of this force is transmitted to the sphere by shear stresses near the equator, and the remaining two-thirds are due to the pressure being higher at the front of the sphere than at the rear.

As the velocity increases and the boundary layer decreases in thickness, the effect of the shear stresses (or of what is sometimes called skin friction in this context) becomes less and less important compared with the effect of the pressure difference. It is impossible to calculate that difference precisely, except in the limit to which Stokes's law applies, but there are grounds for expecting that once eddies have formed it is about $\rho v_o^2/2$. Hence at high velocities one may expect

$$F_D = \left(\frac{\rho v_0^2}{2}\right) A',$$ (173)

where A' is some effective cross-sectional area, presumably comparable to its true cross-sectional area A (which is $\pi D^2/4$ for a sphere) but not necessarily exactly equal to this. It is conventional to describe drag forces in terms of a dimensionless quantity called the drag coefficient; this is defined, irrespective of the shape of the body, as the ratio $[F_D/(\rho v_o^2/2)A]$ and is denoted by C_D. At high velocities, C_D is clearly the same thing as the ratio (A'/A) and should therefore be of order unity.

This is as far as theory can go with this problem. The principles of dimensional analysis can be invoked to show that, provided the compressibility of the fluid is irrelevant (i.e., provided the flow velocity is well below the speed of sound), the drag coefficient must be some universal function of another dimensionless quantity known as the Reynolds number and defined as

$$R = \frac{\rho v_0 D}{\eta}.$$ (174)

One must, however, resort to experiments to discover the form of this function. Fortunately, a limited number of experiments will suffice because the function is universal. They can be performed using whatever liquids and spheres are most convenient, provided that the whole range of R that is likely to be important is covered. Once the results have been plotted on a graph of C_D versus R, the graph can be used to predict the drag forces experienced by other spheres in other liquids at velocities that may be quite different from those so far employed. This point is worth emphasizing because it enshrines the principle of dynamic similarity, which is heavily relied on by engineers whenever they use results obtained with models to predict the behaviour of much larger structures.

The C_D versus R curve for spheres, plotted with logarithmic scales, is shown in Stokes's law, re-expressed in terms of C_D and R, becomes $C_D = 24/R$. This law evidently fails when R exceeds about 1. For a diagram of C_D versus R for spheres, there is a considerable range of R beginning at about 10^3 over which C_D is about 0.5, but when R reaches about 3×10^5 it falls dramatically, to about 0.1. The curve

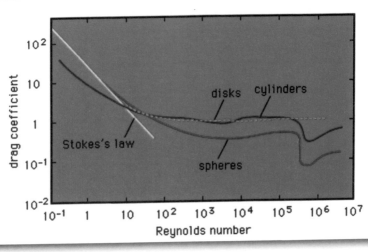

Variation of drag coefficient with Reynolds number for spheres, cylinders, and disks. Copyright Encyclopædia Britannica; rendering for this edition by Rosen Educational Services

for cylinders of diameter D whose axes are transverse to the direction of flow is similar to that for spheres (though it has no straight-line part at low Reynolds number to correspond to Stokes's law), but the curve for transverse disks of diameter D is noticeably flatter. This flatness is linked to the fact that a disk has sharp edges around which the streamlines converge and diverge rapidly. The resulting large pressure gradients near the edge favour the formation and shedding of eddies. The drag force on a transverse flat plate of any shape can normally be estimated quite accurately, provided its edges are sharp, by assuming the drag coefficient to be unity.

Since sharp edges favour the formation and shedding of eddies, and thereby increase the drag coefficient, one may hope to reduce the drag coefficient by streamlining the obstacle. It is at the rear of the obstacle that separation occurs, and it is therefore the rear that needs streamlining. By stretching the rear of the sphere out, the pressure gradient acting on the boundary layer behind the obstacle can be much reduced. There are other methods of reducing drag that have some practical applications. When the obstacle is the wing of an aircraft with a slot

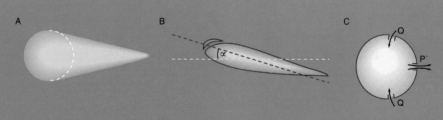

Each diagram represents a solid object that is stationary in the path of a fluid flowing from left to right, or that is moving from right to left through a fluid which is stationary: (A) a sphere that has been streamlined; (B) an aircraft wing, inclined at angle ∝, which is slotted along its leading edge; (C) a sphere equipped with an internal pump, which draws fluid in near Q and expels it at P.

Methods for reducing drag. Copyright Encyclopædia Britannica; rendering for this edition by Rosen Educational Services

through its leading edge, the current of air channeled through this slot imparts forward momentum to the fluid in the boundary layer on the upper surface of the wing to hinder this fluid from moving backward. The cowls that are often fitted to the leading edges of aircraft wings have a similar purpose. In another case, the spherical obstacle is equipped with an internal device—a pump of some sort—that prevents the accumulation of boundary-layer fluid that would otherwise lead to separation by sucking it in through small holes in the surface of the obstacle; the fluid may be ejected again through holes in the rear, where it will do no harm.

It should be stressed that the curves of C_D versus R are universal only so long as the velocity v_o is much less than the speed of sound. When v_o is comparable with the speed of sound, V_S, the compressibility of the fluid becomes relevant, which means that the drag coefficient has to be regarded as dependent on the dimensionless ratio $M = v_o/V_S$, known as the Mach number, as well as on the Reynolds number. The drag coefficient always rises as M approaches unity but may thereafter fall. To reduce drag in the supersonic region, it pays to streamline the front of obstacles or projectiles rather than the rear, as this reduces the intensity of the shock cone.

LIFT

If an aircraft wing, or airfoil, is to fulfill its function, it must experience an upward lift force, as well as a drag force, when the aircraft is in motion. The lift force arises because the speed at which the displaced air moves over the top of the airfoil (and over the top of the attached boundary layer) is greater than the speed at which it moves over the bottom and because the pressure acting on the airfoil from below is therefore greater than the pressure from above. It also can be seen, however, as an inevitable consequence of the finite circulation that exists around the airfoil. One way to establish circulation around an obstacle is to rotate it, as was seen earlier in the description of the Magnus effect. The circulation around an airfoil, however, is created by its forward motion; it arises as soon as the airfoil moves fast enough to shed its first eddy.

The lift force on an airfoil moving through stationary air at a steady speed v_o is the same as the lift force on an identical airfoil that is stationary in air moving at v_o the other way; the latter is easier to represent pictorially. The pattern of the set of streamlines representing potential flow past a stationary inclined plate before any eddy has been shed is a symmetrical one, and the pressure variations associated with it generate neither drag nor lift. At the rear of the plate, however, the streamlines diverge rapidly, so conditions exist for the formation of an eddy there, and the sense of its rotation will be counterclockwise. It grows more easily and is shed more quickly because the edges of the plate are sharp. The circulation around the closed loop that encloses both the plate and the eddy was zero before the eddy formed and, according to Thomson's

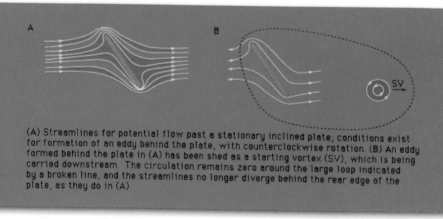

(A) Streamlines for potential flow past a stationary inclined plate; conditions exist for formation of an eddy behind the plate, with counterclockwise rotation. (B) An eddy formed behind the plate in (A) has been shed as a starting vortex (SV), which is being carried downstream. The circulation remains zero around the large loop indicated by a broken line, and the streamlines no longer diverge behind the rear edge of the plate, as they do in (A)

Generation of lift force. Copyright Encyclopædia Britannica; rendering for this edition by Rosen Educational Services

theorem, it must still be zero. Passing through this loop, there thus must be a vortex line having clockwise circulation -K to compensate for the circulation +K of the starting vortex. This other line, known as the bound vortex, is not immediately apparent in the diagram because it is attached to the plate, and it remains thus attached as the starting vortex is swept away downstream. It does show up, however, in a modification of the flow pattern immediately behind the plate, where the streamlines no longer diverge. Because the divergence here has been eliminated, no further eddies are likely to be formed.

Earlier, the formula $\rho v_o K$ was quoted for the strength of the Magnus force per unit length of a rotating cylinder, and the same formula can be applied to the inclined plate or to any airfoil that has shed a starting vortex and around which, consequently, there is circulation. The validity of the formula does not depend in any way on the precise shape of the airfoil, any more than the force exerted by a magnetic field on a wire carrying a current depends on the cross-sectional shape of the wire. The design of the airfoil, nevertheless, has a critical effect on the magnitude of the lift force because it determines the magnitude of K. The rear edge is made as sharp as possible for reasons that have already been explained, and it may take the form of hinged flaps that are lowered at takeoff. Lowering the flaps increases K and therefore also the lift, but the flaps need to be raised when the aircraft has reached its cruising altitude because they cause undesirable drag. The circulation and the lift can also be increased by increasing the angle α at which the main part of the airfoil is inclined to the direction of motion. There is a limit to the lift that can be generated in this way, however, for if the inclination is too great the boundary layer separates behind the wing's leading edge, and the bound vortex, on which the lift depends, may be shed as a result. The aircraft is then said to stall. The leading edge is made as smooth and rounded as possible to discourage stalling.

Thomson's theorem can be used to prove that if the airfoil is of finite length then the starting vortex and the bound vortex must both be parts of a single, continuous vortex ring. They are joined by two trailing vortices, which run backward from the ends of the airfoil. As time passes, these trailing vortices grow steadily longer, and more and more energy is needed to feed the swirling motion of the fluid around them. It is clear, at any rate in the case where the airfoil is moving and the air is stationary, that this energy can come only from whatever agency propels the airfoil forward, and hence that the trailing vortices are a source of additional drag. The magnitude of the additional drag is proportional to K^2 but it does not increase, as the lift force does, if the airfoil is made longer while K is kept the same. For this reason, designers who wish to maximize the ratio of lift to drag will make the wings of their aircraft as long as they can—as long, that is, as is consistent with strength and rigidity requirements.

When a yacht is sailing into the wind, its sail acts as an airfoil of which the mast is the leading edge, and the considerations that favour long wings for aircraft favour tall masts as well.

TURBULENCE

The nonlinear nature of the $(v \cdot \nabla)v$ term in the Navier-Stokes equation—equation (155)—means that solutions of this equation cannot be superposed. The fact that $v_1(R, t)$ and $v_2(R, t)$ satisfy the equation does not ensure that $(v_1 + v_2)$ does so too. The nonlinear term provides a contact, in fact, through which two different modes of motion may exchange energy, so that one grows in amplitude at the expense of the other. A great deal of experimental and theoretical work has shown, in particular, that if a fluid is undergoing regular laminar motion (of the sort that was discussed in connection with Poiseuille's law, for example) at sufficiently high rates of shear, small periodic perturbations of this motion are liable to grow parasitically. Perturbations on a smaller scale still grow parasitically on those that are first established, until the flow pattern is so grossly disturbed that it is no longer useful to define a fluid velocity for each point in space; the description of the flow has to be a statistical one in terms of mean values and of correlated fluctuations about the mean. The flow is then said to be turbulent.

In the case (to which Poiseuille's law applies) of laminar flow through a uniform cylindrical pipe of diameter D, turbulence inevitably sets in when the Reynolds number R reaches a critical value that is about 10^5; in this context, the Reynolds number is defined (compare equation [174]) as

$$R = \frac{4\rho Q}{\pi D\eta} = \frac{\rho D<v>}{\eta}, \tag{175}$$

where Q is the rate of discharge and $<v>$ is the mean fluid velocity. Turbulence sets in at much lower velocities, however, if the end of the pipe where the fluid enters is not carefully flared. The critical value of the Reynolds number for a pipe with a bluff entry may be as low as 2300, and this corresponds to a rate of discharge through a pipe for which D is, say, two centimetres, of only about three litres per minute. Thus pipe flow in engineering practice is more often turbulent than not. Once turbulence has set in, Q increases less rapidly with pressure gradient than Poiseuille's equation—equation (150)—predicts; it increases roughly as the square root of the pressure gradient or slightly more rapidly than this if the internal surface of the pipe is very smooth.

Turbulence arises not only in pipes but also within boundary layers around solid obstacles when the rate of shear within the boundary layer becomes large enough. Curiously enough, the onset of turbulence in the boundary layer can reduce the drag force on obstacles. In the case of a spherical obstacle, the point at which the boundary layer separates from the rear surface of the sphere shifts backward when the boundary layer becomes turbulent, and the eddies attached to the sphere therefore become smaller. It is turbulence in the boundary layer that is responsible for the dramatic drop in the drag coefficient for both spheres and cylinders that occurs, when the Reynolds number is about 3×10^5. This drop enables golf balls to travel farther than they would do otherwise, and the dimples on the surface of golf balls are meant to encourage turbulence in the boundary layer. If swimsuits with rough surfaces help swimmers to move faster, as has been claimed, the same explanation may apply.

Where conditions for turbulence exist, flow rates of water through tubes may be increased and the drag forces exerted on obstacles by water diminished by dissolving small amounts of suitable polymers in the water. This is surprising, because such additives increase viscosity, and in the preturbulent regime to which Poiseuille's law applies, their effect on the flow rate is quite the reverse. As has already been stated, the small perturbations that arise in a turbulent fluid tend to collapse into smaller perturbations and then into smaller perturbations still, until the motion is turbulent on a very fine scale—i.e., on the scale of molecular dimensions—and until the energy stored in the perturbations is finally dissipated as heat. Polymer molecules seem to have the effect they do because, over the relatively large distances to which each such molecule extends, they impose a coherence on the fluid motion that would not otherwise be present.

CONVECTION

No attention has yet been paid to situations in which temperature differences are imposed upon a fluid by contact with hot and cold bodies. Consider first the case of two vertical plates with fluid between them, one at temperature T_1 and the other at T_2, in the presence of a vertical gravitational field. The hotter plate might be a domestic radiator and the colder plate the wall to which it is fixed. Thermal conduction ensures that the layer of air adjacent to the radiator is hotter than the rest of the air, and thermal expansion ensures that it is less dense. Consequently, the vertical pressure gradient which satisfies equation (123) in the rest of the air is too large to keep the layer adjacent to the radiator in equilibrium; that layer rises and, similarly, the cold layer adjacent to the wall falls. A circulating pattern of thermal convection is thereby established, and, because this brings colder air into contact with the radiator, the rate at which heat is lost from the radiator is enhanced. The heat loss, once convection has been established, depends in a complicated manner on the separation between the plates (D) and on the thermal diffusivity (κ), specific heat, density, thermal expansion coefficient (α), and viscosity of the fluid. The heat loss also depends on $(T_1 - T_2)$, of course, and it is worthwhile noting that the manner in which it does so is not linear; the heat loss increases more rapidly than the temperature difference. Newton's law of cooling, which postulates a linear relationship, is obeyed only in circumstances where convection is prevented or in circumstances where it is forced (when a radiator is fan-assisted, for example).

Imagine a situation in which the same two plates are horizontal rather than vertical. In such a case, no convection can occur if the hot plate is above the cold one, and it is not obvious that it occurs in the reverse situation.

Whether it does so or not depends on the magnitude of the temperature difference through a dimensionless combination of some of the relevant parameters, $\rho g \alpha D^3 (T_1 - T_2)/\eta \kappa$, which is known as the Rayleigh number. If the Rayleigh number is less than 1,708, the fluid is stable—or perhaps it would be more accurate to say that it is metastable— even though it is warmer at the bottom than at the top. However, when 1,708 is exceeded, a pattern of convective rolls known as Bénard cells is established between the plates. Evidence for the existence of such cells in the convecting atmosphere is sometimes seen in the regular columns of cloud that form over regions where the air is rising. Their periodicity can be astonishingly uniform.

Macroscopic instabilities of a convective nature, of which the formation of Bénard cells provides just one example, are a feature of the oceans as well as of the atmosphere and are frequently associated with gradients of salinity rather than gradients of temperature. A serious discussion of atmospheric and oceanic circulation on Earth, however, requires a more detailed examination of the dynamics of rotating fluids than is given here.

Gravity is the universal force of attraction acting between all matter. It is by far the weakest known force in nature and thus plays no role in determining the internal properties of everyday matter. On the other hand, through its long reach and universal action, it controls the trajectories of bodies in the solar system and elsewhere in the universe and the structures and evolution of stars, galaxies, and the whole cosmos. On Earth all bodies have a weight, or downward force of gravity, proportional to their mass, which Earth's mass exerts on them. Gravity is measured by the acceleration that it gives to freely falling objects. At Earth's surface the acceleration of gravity is about 9.8 metres (32 feet) per second per second. Thus, for every second an object is in free fall, its speed increases by about 9.8 metres per second. At the surface of the Moon the acceleration of a freely falling body is about 1.6 metres per second per second.

The works of Isaac Newton and Albert Einstein dominate the development of gravitational theory. Newton's classical theory of gravitational force held sway from his *Principia*, published in 1687, until Einstein's work in the early 20th century. Newton's theory is sufficient even today for all but the most precise applications. Einstein's theory of general relativity predicts only minute quantitative differences from the Newtonian theory except in a few special cases. The major significance of Einstein's theory is its radical conceptual departure from classical theory and its implications for further growth in physical thought.

The launch of space vehicles and developments of research from them have led to great improvements in measurements of gravity around Earth, other planets, and the Moon, and in experiments on the nature of gravitation.

DEVELOPMENT OF GRAVITATIONAL THEORY

Newton argued that the movements of celestial bodies and the free fall of objects on Earth are determined by the same force. The classical Greek philosophers, on the other hand, did not consider the celestial bodies to be affected by gravity, because the bodies were observed to follow perpetually repeating nondescending trajectories in the sky. Thus, Aristotle considered that each heavenly body followed a particular "natural" motion, unaffected by external causes or agents. Aristotle also believed that massive earthly objects possess a natural tendency to move toward the Earth's centre. Those Aristotelian concepts prevailed for centuries along with two others: that a body moving at constant speed requires a continuous force acting on it and that force must be applied by contact rather than interaction at a distance. These ideas were generally held until the 16th and early 17th centuries, thereby impeding an understanding of the true principles of motion and precluding the development of ideas about universal gravitation. This impasse began to change with several scientific contributions to the problem of earthly and celestial motion, which in turn set the stage for Newton's later gravitational theory.

EARLY CONCEPTS

The 17th-century German astronomer Johannes Kepler accepted the argument of Nicolaus Copernicus (which goes back to Aristarchus of Samos) that the planets orbit the Sun, not Earth. Using the improved measurements of planetary movements made by the Danish astronomer Tycho

Brahe during the 16th century, Kepler described the planetary orbits with simple geometric and arithmetic relations. Kepler's three quantitative laws of planetary motion are:

1. The planets describe elliptic orbits, of which the Sun occupies one focus (a focus is one of two points inside an ellipse; any ray coming from one of them bounces off a side of the ellipse and goes through the other focus).
2. The line joining a planet to the Sun sweeps out equal areas in equal times.
3. The square of the period of revolution of a planet is proportional to the cube of its average distance from the Sun.

During this same period the Italian astronomer and natural philosopher Galileo Galilei made progress in understanding "natural" motion and simple accelerated motion for earthly objects. He realized that bodies that are uninfluenced by forces continue indefinitely to move and that force is necessary to change motion, not to maintain constant motion. In studying how objects fall toward Earth, Galileo discovered that the motion is one of constant acceleration. He demonstrated that the distance a falling body travels from rest in this way varies as the square of the time. As noted earlier, the acceleration due to gravity at the surface of Earth is about 9.8 metres per second per second. Galileo was also the first to show by experiment that bodies fall with the same acceleration whatever their composition (the weak principle of equivalence).

NEWTON'S LAW OF GRAVITY

Newton discovered the relationship between the motion of the Moon and the motion of a body falling freely on Earth.

By his dynamical and gravitational theories, he explained Kepler's laws and established the modern quantitative science of gravitation. Newton assumed the existence of an attractive force between all massive bodies, one that does not require bodily contact and that acts at a distance. By invoking his law of inertia (bodies not acted upon by a force move at constant speed in a straight line), Newton concluded that a force exerted by Earth on the Moon is needed to keep it in a circular motion about Earth rather than moving in a straight line. He realized that this force could be, at long range, the same as the force with which Earth pulls objects on its surface downward. When Newton discovered that the acceleration of the Moon is 1/3,600 smaller than the acceleration at the surface of Earth, he related the number 3,600 to the square of the radius of Earth. He calculated that the circular orbital motion of radius R and period T requires a constant inward acceleration A equal to the product of $4\pi^2$ and the ratio of the radius to the square of the time:

$$A = \frac{4\pi^2 R}{T^2}. \qquad (1)$$

The Moon's orbit has a radius of about 384,000 km (239,000 miles; approximately 60 Earth radii), and its period is 27.3 days (its synodic period, or period measured in terms of lunar phases, is about 29.5 days). Newton found the Moon's inward acceleration in its orbit to be 0.0027 metre per second per second, the same as $(1/60)^2$ of the acceleration of a falling object at the surface of Earth.

In Newton's theory every least particle of matter attracts every other particle gravitationally, and on that basis he showed that the attraction of a finite body with spherical symmetry is the same as that of the whole mass at the centre of the body. More generally, the attraction of any body at a sufficiently great distance is equal to that of the whole mass at the centre of mass. He could thus relate the two accelerations, that of the Moon and that of a body falling freely on Earth, to a common interaction, a gravitational force between bodies that diminishes as the inverse square of the distance between them. Thus, if the distance between the bodies is doubled, the force on them is reduced to a fourth of the original.

Newton saw that the gravitational force between bodies must depend on the masses of the bodies. Since a body of mass M experiencing a force F accelerates at a rate F/M, a force of gravity proportional to M would be consistent with Galileo's observation that all bodies accelerate under gravity toward Earth at the same rate, a fact that Newton also tested experimentally. In Newton's equation

$$F_{12} = \frac{GM_1 M_2}{r_{12}^2} \qquad (2)$$

F_{12} is the magnitude of the gravitational force acting between masses M_1 and M_2 separated by distance r_{12}. The force equals the product of these masses and of G, a universal constant, divided by the square of the distance.

The constant G is a quantity with the physical dimensions (length)^3/(mass)(time)^2; its numerical value depends on the physical units of length, mass, and time used. (G is discussed more fully in subsequent sections.)

The force acts in the direction of the line joining the two bodies and so is represented naturally as a vector, F. If r is the vector separation of the bodies, then

$$\mathbf{F} = \frac{GM_1 M_2 \mathbf{r}}{r^3}. \qquad (3)$$

In this expression the factor r/r^3 acts in the direction of r and is numerically equal to $1/r^2$.

The attractive force of a number of bodies of masses M_I on a body of mass M is

$$F = \frac{GM\sum_1 M_1 r_1}{r_1^3},\qquad(4)$$

where $\sum_I$ means that the forces due to all the attracting bodies must be added together vectorially. This is Newton's gravitational law essentially in its original form. A simpler expression, equation (5), gives the surface acceleration on Earth. Setting a mass equal to Earth's mass M_E and the distance equal to Earth's radius r_E, the downward acceleration of a body at the surface g is equal to the product of the universal gravitational constant and the mass of Earth divided by the square of the radius:

$$g = \frac{GM_E}{r_E^2}.\qquad(5)$$

WEIGHT AND MASS

The weight W of a body can be measured by the equal and opposite force necessary to prevent the downward acceleration; that is M_g. The same body placed on the surface of the Moon has the same mass, but, as the Moon has a mass of about $\frac{1}{81}$ times that of Earth and a radius of just 0.27 that of Earth, the body on the lunar surface has a weight of only $\frac{1}{6}$ its Earth weight, as the Apollo program astronauts demonstrated. Passengers and instruments in orbiting satellites are in free fall. They experience weightless conditions even though their masses remain the same as on Earth.

Equations (1) and (2) can be used to derive Kepler's third law for the case of circular planetary orbits. By using the expression for the acceleration A in equation (1) for the force of gravity for the planet $GM_P M_S/R^2$ divided by the planet's mass M_p, the following equation, in which M_S is the mass of the Sun, is obtained:

$$\frac{GM_S}{R^2} = \frac{4\pi^2 R}{T^2}$$

or   (6)

$$R^3 = \left(\frac{GM_S}{4\pi^2}\right) T^2.$$

Kepler's very important second law depends only on the fact that the force between two bodies is along the line joining them.

Newton was thus able to show that all three of Kepler's observationally derived laws follow mathematically from the assumption of his own laws of motion and gravity. In all observations of the motion of a celestial body, only the product of G and the mass can be found. Newton first estimated the magnitude of G by assuming Earth's average mass density to be about 5.5 times that of water (somewhat greater than Earth's surface rock density) and by calculating Earth's mass from this. Then, taking M_E and r_E as Earth's mass and radius, respectively, the value of G was

$$G = \frac{g r_E^2}{M_E},$$ (7)

which numerically comes close to the accepted value of 6.6726×10^{-11} m³ s⁻² kg⁻¹, first directly measured by Henry Cavendish.

Comparing equation (5) for Earth's surface acceleration g with the R^3/T^2 ratio for the planets, a formula for the ratio of the Sun's mass M_S to Earth's mass M_E was obtained in terms of known quantities, R_E being the radius of Earth's orbit:

$$\frac{M_S}{M_E} = \frac{4\pi^2 R_E^3}{g T_E^2 r_E^2} \cong 325{,}000. \tag{8}$$

The motions of the moons of Jupiter (discovered by Galileo) around Jupiter obey Kepler's laws just as the planets do around the Sun. Thus, Newton calculated that Jupiter, with a radius 11 times larger than Earth's, was 318 times more massive than Earth but only ¼ as dense.

INTERACTION BETWEEN CELESTIAL BODIES

When two celestial bodies of comparable mass interact gravitationally, both orbit about a fixed point (the centre of mass of the two bodies). This point lies between the bodies on the line joining them at a position such that the products of the distance to each body with the mass of each body are equal. Thus, Earth and the Moon move in complementary orbits about their common centre of mass. The motion of Earth has two observable consequences. First, the direction of the Sun as seen from Earth relative to the very distant stars varies each month by about 12 arc seconds in addition to the Sun's annual motion. Second, the line-of-sight velocity from Earth to a freely moving spacecraft varies each month by 2.04 metres per second, according to very accurate data obtained from radio tracking. From these results the Moon is found to have a mass $\frac{1}{81}$ times that of Earth. With slight modifications Kepler's laws remain valid for systems of two comparable masses; the foci of the elliptical orbits are the two-body centre-of-mass positions, and, putting $M_1 + M_2$ instead of M_S in the expression of Kepler's third law, equation (6), the third law reads:

$$R^3 = \frac{G(M_1 + M_2)}{4\pi^2} T^2. \tag{9}$$

That agrees with equation (6) when one body is so small that its mass can be neglected. The rescaled formula can be used to determine the separate masses of binary stars (pairs of stars orbiting around each other) that are a known distance from the solar system. Equation (9) determines the sum of the masses; and, if R_1 and R_2 are the distances of the individual stars from the centre of mass, the ratio of the distances must balance the inverse ratio of the masses, and the sum of the distances is the total distance R. In symbols

$$\frac{R_1}{R_2} = \frac{M_2}{M_1}; \; R_1 + R_2 = R. \tag{10}$$

Those relations are sufficient to determine the individual masses. Observations of the orbital motions of double stars, of the dynamic motions of stars collectively moving within their galaxies, and of the motions of the galaxies themselves verify that Newton's law of gravity is valid to a high degree of accuracy throughout the visible universe.

Ocean tides, phenomena that mystified thinkers for centuries, were also shown by Newton to be a consequence of the universal law of gravitation, although the details of the complicated phenomena were not understood until comparatively recently. They are caused specifically by the gravitational pull of the Moon and, to a lesser extent, of the Sun.

Newton showed that the equatorial bulge of Earth was a consequence of the balance between the centrifugal forces of the rotation of Earth and the attractions of each particle of Earth on all others. The value of gravity at the surface of Earth increases in a corresponding way from the Equator to the poles. Among the data that Newton used to estimate the size of the equatorial bulge were the adjustments to his pendulum clock that the English astronomer Edmond Halley had to make in the course of his astronomical observations on the southern island of Saint Helena. Jupiter, which rotates faster than Earth, has a proportionally larger equatorial bulge, the difference between its polar and equatorial radii being about 10 percent. Another success of Newton's theory was his demonstration that comets move in parabolic orbits under the gravitational attraction of the Sun. In a thorough analysis in the *Principia*, he showed that the great comet of 1680–81 did indeed follow a parabolic path.

It was already known in Newton's day that the Moon does not move in a simple Keplerian orbit. Later, more-accurate observations of the planets also showed discrepancies from Kepler's laws. The motion of the Moon is particularly complex; however, apart from a long-term acceleration due to tides on Earth, the complexities can be accounted for by the gravitational attraction of the Sun and the planets. The gravitational attractions of the planets for each other explain almost all the features of their motions. The exceptions are nonetheless important. Uranus, the seventh planet from the Sun, was observed to undergo variations in its motion that could not be explained by perturbations from Saturn, Jupiter, and the other planets. Two 19th-century astronomers, John Couch Adams of Britain and Urbain-Jean-Joseph Le Verrier of France, independently assumed the presence of an unseen eighth planet that could produce the observed discrepancies. They calculated its position within a degree of where the planet Neptune was discovered in 1846. Measurements of the motion of the innermost planet, Mercury, over an extended period led astronomers to conclude that the major axis of this planet's elliptical orbit precesses in space at a rate 43 arc seconds per century faster than could be accounted for from perturbations of the other planets. In this case, however, no other bodies could be found that could produce this discrepancy, and very slight modification of Newton's law of gravitation seemed to be needed. Einstein's theory of relativity precisely predicts this observed behaviour of Mercury's orbit.

POTENTIAL THEORY

For irregular, nonspherical mass distributions in three dimensions, Newton's original vector equation (4) is inefficient, though theoretically it could be used for finding the resulting gravitational field. The main progress in classical gravitational theory after Newton was the development of potential theory, which provides the mathematical representation of gravitational fields. It allows practical as well as theoretical investigation of the gravitational variations in space and of the anomalies due to the irregularities and shape deformations of Earth.

Potential theory led to the following elegant formulation: the gravitational acceleration g is a function of position R, g(R), which at any point in space is given from a function Φ called the gravitational potential, by means of a generalization of the operation of differentiation:

$$g(R) = \frac{\partial \Phi}{\partial x} i + \frac{\partial \Phi}{\partial y} j + \frac{\partial \Phi}{\partial z} k, \qquad (11)$$

in which i, j, and k stand for unit basis vectors in a three-dimensional Cartesian coordinate system. The potential and therefore g are determined by an equation discovered by the French mathematician Siméon-Denis Poisson:

$$\left(\frac{\partial^2}{\partial x^2} + \frac{\partial^2}{\partial y^2} + \frac{\partial^2}{\partial z^2} \right) \Phi(R) = -4\pi G \rho(R). \qquad (12)$$

where $\rho(R)$ is the density at the vector position R.

The significance of this approach is that Poisson's equation can be solved under rather general conditions, which is not the case with Newton's equation. When the mass density ρ is nonzero, the solution is expressed as the definite integral:

$$\Phi(R) = G \int \frac{\rho(R')\,dR'}{|R - R'|}. \tag{13}$$

where the integral is a three-dimensional integral over the volume of all space. When $\rho = 0$ (in particular, outside Earth), Poisson's equation reduces to the simpler equation of Laplace.

The appropriate coordinates for the region outside the nearly spherical Earth are spherical polar coordinates: R, the distance from the centre of Earth; θ, the colatitude measured from the North Pole; and the longitude measured from Greenwich. The solutions are series of powers of R multiplied by trigonometric functions of colatitude and longitude, known as spherical harmonics; the first terms are:

$$\Phi(R) = \frac{GM_E}{R}\left[1 - J_2\left(\frac{R_E}{R}\right)^2 \frac{3\cos^2\theta - 1}{2}\right.$$

$$\left. - J_3\left(\frac{R_E}{R}\right)^3 \frac{5\cos^3\theta - 3\cos\theta}{2} + \dots\right], \tag{14}$$

The constants J_2, J_3, and so forth are determined by the detailed mass distribution of Earth; and, since Newton showed that for a spherical body all the J_n are zero, they must measure the deformation of Earth from a spherical shape. J_2 measures the magnitude of Earth's rotational equatorial bulge, J_3 measures a slight pear-shaped deformation of Earth, and so on. The orbits of spacecraft around Earth, other planets, and the Moon deviate from simple Keplerian ellipses in consequence of the various spherical harmonic terms in the potential. Observations of such deviations were made for the very first artificial spacecraft. The parameters J_2 and J_3 for Earth have been found to be 1,082.7 × 10^{-6} and -2.4 × 10^{-6}, respectively. Very many other harmonic terms have been found in that way for Earth and also for the Moon and for other planets. Halley had already pointed out in the 18th century that the motions of the moons of Jupiter are perturbed from simple ellipses by the variation of gravity around Jupiter.

The surface of the oceans, if tides and waves are ignored, is a surface of constant potential of gravity and rotation. If the only spherical harmonic term in gravity were that corresponding to the equatorial bulge, the sea surface would be just a spheroid of revolution (a surface

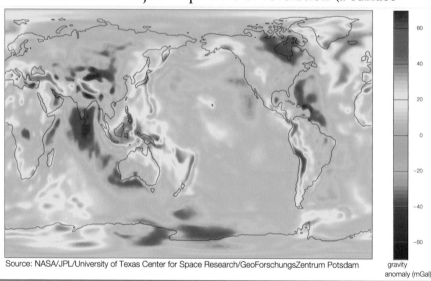

Source: NASA/JPL/University of Texas Center for Space Research/GeoForschungsZentrum Potsdam

gravity anomaly (mGal)

The variation in the gravitational field, given in milliGals (mGal), over the Earth's surface gives rise to an imaginary surface known as the geoid. The geoid expresses the height of an imaginary global ocean not subject to tides, currents, or winds. Such an ocean would vary by up to 200 metres (650 feet) in height because of regional variations in gravitation. Encyclopædia Britannica, Inc.

formed by rotating a two-dimensional curve about some axis; for example, rotating an ellipse about its major axis produces an ellipsoid). Additional terms in the potential give rise to departures of the sea surface from that simple form. The actual form may be calculated from the sum of the known harmonic terms, but it is now possible to measure the form of the sea surface itself directly by laser ranging from spacecraft. Whether found indirectly by calculation or directly by measurement, the form of the sea surface may be shown as contours of its deviation from the simple spheroid of revolution.

EFFECTS OF LOCAL MASS DIFFERENCES

Spherical harmonics are the natural way of expressing the large-scale variations of potential that arise from the deep structure of Earth. However, spherical harmonics are not suitable for local variations due to more-superficial structures. Not long after Newton's time, it was found that the gravity on top of large mountains is less than expected on the basis of their visible mass. The idea of isostasy was developed, according to which the unexpectedly low acceleration of gravity on a mountain is caused by low-density rock 30 to 100 km (19–62 miles) underground, which buoys up the mountain. Correspondingly, the unexpectedly high force of gravity on ocean surfaces is explained by dense rock 10 to 30 km (6–19 miles) beneath the ocean bottom.

Portable gravimeters, which can detect variations of one part in 10^9 in the gravitational force, are in wide use today for mineral and oil prospecting. Unusual underground deposits reveal their presence by producing local gravitational variations.

WEIGHING EARTH

The mass of Earth can be calculated from its radius and g if G is known. G was measured by the English physicist-chemist Henry Cavendish and other early experimenters, who spoke of their work as "weighing the Earth." The mass of Earth is about 5.98×10^{24} kg, while the mean densities of Earth, the Sun, and the Moon are, respectively, 5.52, 1.43, and 3.3 times that of water.

ACCELERATION AROUND EARTH, THE MOON, AND OTHER PLANETS

The value of the attraction of gravity or of the potential is determined by the distribution of matter within Earth or other celestial body. In turn, as seen above, the distribution of matter determines the shape of the surface on which the potential is constant. Measurements of gravity and the potential are thus essential both to geodesy, which is the study of the shape of Earth, and to geophysics, the study of its internal structure. For geodesy and global geophysics, it is best to measure the potential from the orbits of artificial satellites. Surface measurements of gravity are best for local geophysics, which deals with the structure of mountains and oceans and the search for minerals.

VARIATIONS DUE TO LOCATION AND TIME

The acceleration g varies by about $\frac{1}{2}$ of 1 percent with position on Earth's surface, from about 9.78 metres per second per second at the Equator to approximately 9.83 metres per second per second at the poles. In addition to this broad-scale variation, local variations of a few parts in 10^6 or smaller are caused by variations in the density of Earth's crust as well as height above sea level.

The gravitational potential at the surface of Earth is due mainly to the mass and rotation of Earth, but there are also small contributions from the distant Sun and

Moon. As Earth rotates, those small contributions at any one place vary with time, and so the local value of g varies slightly. Those are the diurnal and semidiurnal tidal variations. For most purposes it is necessary to know only the variation of gravity with time at a fixed place or the changes of gravity from place to place; then the tidal variation can be removed. Accordingly, almost all gravity measurements are relative measurements of the differences from place to place or from time to time.

MEASUREMENTS OF g

Because gravity changes are far less than 1 metre per second per second, it is convenient to have a smaller unit for relative measurements. The gal (named after Galileo) has been adopted for this purpose; a gal is one-hundredth metre per second per second. The unit most commonly used is the milligal, which equals 10^{-5} metre per second per second—i.e., about one-millionth of the average value of g.

ABSOLUTE MEASUREMENTS

Two basic ways of making absolute measurements of gravity have been devised: timing the free fall of an object and timing the motion under gravity of a body constrained in some way, almost always as a pendulum. In 1817 the English physicist Henry Kater, building on the work of the German astronomer Friedrich Wilhelm Bessel, was the first to use a reversible pendulum to make absolute measurements of g. If the periods of swing of a rigid pendulum about two alternative points of support are the same, then the separation of those two points is equal to the length of the equivalent simple pendulum of the same period. By careful construction, Kater was able to measure the separation very accurately. The so-called reversible pendulum was used for absolute measurements of gravity from Kater's day until the 1950s. Since that time, electronic instruments have enabled investigators to measure with high precision the half-second time of free fall of a body (from rest) through one metre. It is also possible to make extremely accurate measurements of position by using interference of light. Consequently, direct measurements of free fall have replaced the pendulum for absolute measurements of gravity.

Nowadays, lasers are the sources of light for interferometers, while the falling object is a retroreflector that returns a beam of light back upon itself. The falling object can be timed in simple downward motion, or it can be projected upward and timed over the upward and downward path. Transportable versions of such apparatuses have been used in different locations to establish a basis for measuring differences of gravity over the entire Earth. The accuracy attainable is about one part in 10^8.

More recently, interferometers using beams of atoms instead of light have given absolute determinations of gravity. Interference takes place between atoms that have been subject to different gravitational potentials and so have different energies and wavelengths. The results are comparable to those from bodies in free fall.

RELATIVE MEASUREMENTS

From the time of Newton, measurements of differences of gravity (strictly, the ratios of values of gravity) were made by timing the same pendulum at different places. During the 1930s, however, static gravimeters replaced pendulums for local measurements over small ranges of gravity. Today, free-fall measurements have rendered the pendulum obsolete for all purposes.

Spring gravimeters balance the force of gravity on a mass in the gravity field to be measured against the elastic force of the spring. Either the extension of the spring is measured, or a servo system restores it to a constant amount. High sensitivity is achieved through electronic or mechanical means. If a thin wire is stretched by a mass hung from it, the tension in the wire, and therefore the frequency of transverse oscillations, will vary with the force of gravity upon the mass. Such vibrating string gravimeters were originally developed for use in submarines and were later employed by the *Apollo 17* astronauts on the Moon to conduct a gravity survey of their landing site. Another relatively recent development is the superconducting gravimeter, an instrument in which the position of a magnetically levitated superconducting sphere is sensed to provide a measure of g. Modern gravimeters may have sensitivities better than 0.005 milligal, the standard deviation of observations in exploration surveys being of the order of 0.01–0.02 milligal.

Differences in gravity measured with gravimeters are obtained in quite arbitrary units—divisions on a graduated dial, for example. The relation between these units and milligals can be determined only by reading the instrument at a number of points where g is known as a result of absolute or relative pendulum measurements. Further, because an instrument will not have a completely linear response, known points must cover the entire range of gravity over which the gravimeter is to be used.

Since g is an acceleration, the problem of its measurement from a vehicle that is moving, and therefore accelerating relative to Earth, raises a number of fundamental problems. Pendulum, vibrating-string, and spring-gravimeter observations have been made from submarines; using gyro-stabilized platforms, relative gravity measurements with accuracies approaching a few milligals have been and are being made from surface ships. Experimental measurements with various gravity sensors on fixed-wing aircraft as well as on helicopters have been carried out.

Gravimetric Surveys and Geophysics

As a result of combining all available absolute and relative measurements, it is now possible to obtain the most probable gravity values at a large number of sites to high accuracy. The culmination of gravimetric work begun in the 1960s has been a worldwide gravity reference system having an accuracy of at least one part in 10^7 (0.1 milligal or better).

The value of gravity measured at the terrestrial surface is the result of a combination of factors:

1. The gravitational attraction of Earth as a whole
2. Centrifugal force caused by Earth's rotation
3. Elevation
4. Unbalanced attractions caused by surface topography
5. Tidal variations
6. Unbalanced attractions caused by irregularities in underground density distributions

Most geophysical surveys are aimed at separating out the last of these in order to interpret the geologic structure. It is therefore necessary to make proper allowance for the other factors. The first two factors imply a variation of gravity with latitude that can be calculated for an assumed shape for Earth. The third factor, which is the decrease in gravity with elevation, due to increased distance from the centre of Earth, amounts to -0.3086 milligal per metre. This value, however, assumes that material of zero density occupies the whole space between the point of observation and sea level, and it is therefore termed the free-air correction factor. In practice the mass of rock material that occupies part or all of this space must be considered. In an area where the topography is reasonably flat, this is usually calculated by assuming the presence of an infinite slab of thickness equal to the height of the station h and having an appropriate density σ; its value is +0.04185 σh milligal per metre. This is commonly called the Bouguer correction factor.

Terrain or topographical corrections also can be applied to allow for the attractions due to surface relief if the densities of surface rocks are known. Tidal effects (the amplitudes are less than 0.3 milligal) can be calculated and allowed for.

THE MOON AND THE PLANETS

Although the Apollo astronauts used a gravimeter at their lunar landing site, most scientific knowledge about the gravitational attractions of the Moon and the planets has been derived from observations of their effects upon the accelerations of spacecraft in orbit around or passing close to them. Radio tracking makes it possible to determine the accelerations of spacecraft very accurately, and the results can be expressed either as terms in a series of spherical harmonics or as the variation of gravity over the surface. As in the case of Earth, spherical harmonics are more effective for studying gross structure, while the variation of gravity is more useful for local features. Spacecraft must descend close to the surface or remain in orbit for extended periods in order to detect local gravity variations; such data had been obtained for the Moon, Venus, Mars, and Jupiter by the end of the 20th century.

The Moon's polar flattening is much less than that of Earth, while its equator is far more elliptical. There are also large, more-local irregularities from visible and concealed structures. Mars also exhibits some large local variations, while the equatorial bulges of Mercury and Venus are very slight.

By contrast, the major planets, all of which rotate quite fast, have large equatorial bulges, and their gravity is dominated by a large increase from equator to pole. The polar flattening of Jupiter is about 10 percent and was first estimated from telescopic observation by Gian Domenico Cassini about 1664. As mentioned above, Edmond Halley subsequently realized that the corresponding effect on gravity would perturb the orbits of the satellites of Jupiter (those discovered by Galileo). The results of gravity measurements are crucial to understanding the internal properties of the planets.

The Newtonian theory of gravity is based on an assumed force acting between all pairs of bodies—i.e., an action at a distance. When a mass moves, the force acting on other masses had been considered to adjust instantaneously to the new location of the displaced mass. That, however, is inconsistent with special relativity, which is based on the axiom that all knowledge of distant events comes from electromagnetic signals. Physical quantities have to be defined in such a way that certain combinations of them—in particular, distance, time, mass, and momentum—are independent of choice of space-time coordinates. This theory, with the field theory of electrical and magnetic phenomena, has met such empirical success that most modern gravitational theories are constructed as field theories consistent with the principles of special relativity. In a field theory the gravitational force between bodies is formed by a two-step process: (1) One body produces a gravitational field that permeates all surrounding space but has weaker strength farther from its source. A second body in that space is then acted upon by this field and experiences a force. (2) The Newtonian force of reaction is then viewed as the response of the first body to the gravitational field produced by the second body, there being at all points in space a superposition of gravitational fields due to all the bodies in it.

FIELD THEORIES OF GRAVITATION

In the 1970s the physicists Abdus Salam of Pakistan and Steven Weinberg and Sheldon L. Glashow of the United

States were able to show that the electromagnetic forces and the weak force responsible for beta decay were different manifestations of the same basic interaction. That was the first successful unified field theory. Physicists are actively seeking other possible unified combinations. The possibility that gravitation might be linked with the other forces of nature in a unified theory of forces greatly increased interest in gravitational field theories during the 1970s and '80s. Because the gravitational force is exceedingly weak compared with all others and because it seems to be independent of all physical properties except mass, the unification of gravitation with the other forces remains the most difficult to achieve. That challenge has provided a tremendous impetus to experimental investigations to determine whether there may be some failure of the apparent independence.

The prime example of a field theory is Einstein's general relativity, according to which the acceleration due to gravity is a purely geometric consequence of the properties of space-time in the neighbourhood of attracting masses. In a whole class of more-general theories, these and other effects not predicted by simple Newtonian theory are characterized by free parameters; such formulations are called parameterized post-Newtonian (PPN) theories. There is now considerable experimental and observational evidence for limits to the parameters. So far, no deviation from general relativity has been demonstrated convincingly.

Field theories of gravity predict specific corrections to the Newtonian force law, the corrections taking two basic forms: (1) When matter is in motion, additional gravitational fields (analogous to the magnetic fields produced by moving electric charges) are produced; also, moving bodies interact with gravitational fields in a motion-dependent way. (2) Unlike electromagnetic field theory, in which two or more electric or magnetic fields superimpose by simple addition to give the total fields, in gravitational field theory nonlinear fields proportional to the second and higher powers of the source masses are generated, and gravitational fields proportional to the products of different masses are created. Gravitational fields themselves become sources for additional gravitational fields. The acceleration A of a moving particle of negligible mass that interacts with a mass M, which is at rest, is given in the following formula, derived from Einstein's gravitational theory.

The expression for A now has, as well as the Newtonian expression from equation (1), further terms in higher powers of GM/R^2 — that is, in G^2M^2/R^4. As elsewhere, V is the particle's velocity vector, A is its acceleration vector, R is the vector from the mass M, and c is the speed of light. When written out, the sum is

$$A = -\frac{GMR}{R^3} + 2\frac{G^2M^2R}{c^2R^2} - \frac{3}{2}\frac{GMR}{R^3}\left(\frac{V^2}{c^2}\right)$$

$$-\frac{V \cdot AV}{c^2} - \frac{1}{2}\frac{V^2}{c^2}A + \dots.$$

(15)

This expression gives only the first post-Newtonian corrections; terms of higher power in $1/c$ are neglected. For planetary motion in the solar system, the $1/c^2$ terms are smaller than Newton's acceleration term by at least a factor of 10^{-8}, but some of the consequences of these correction terms are measurable and important tests of Einstein's theory. It should be pointed out that prediction of new observable gravitational effects requires particular care; Einstein's pioneer work in gravity has shown that gravitational fields affect the basic measuring instruments of experimental physics—clocks, rulers, light rays—with which any experimental result in physics is established. Some of these effects are listed below:

- The rate at which clocks run is reduced by proximity of massive bodies; i.e., clocks near the Sun will run slowly compared with identical clocks farther away from it.
- In the presence of gravitational fields, the spatial structure of physical objects is no longer describable precisely by Euclidean geometry; for example, in the arrangement of three rigid rulers to form a triangle, the sum of the subtended angles will not equal 180°. A more-general type of geometry, Riemannian geometry, seems required to describe the spatial structure of matter in the presence of gravitational fields.
- Light rays do not travel in straight lines, the rays being deflected by gravitational fields. To distant observers the light-propagation speed is observed to be reduced near massive bodies.

GRAVITATIONAL FIELDS AND THE THEORY OF GENERAL RELATIVITY

In Einstein's theory of general relativity, the physical consequences of gravitational fields are stated in the following way. Space-time is a four-dimensional non-Euclidean continuum, and the curvature of the Riemannian geometry of space-time is produced by or related to the distribution of matter in the world. Particles and light rays travel along the geodesics (shortest paths) of this four-dimensional geometric world.

There are two principal consequences of the geometric view of gravitation: (1) the accelerations of bodies depend only on their masses and not on their chemical or nuclear constitution, and (2) the path of a body or of light in the neighbourhood of a massive body (the Sun, for example) is slightly different from that predicted by Newton's theory. The first is the weak principle of equivalence. Newton himself performed experiments with pendulums that demonstrated the principle to better than one part in 1,000 for a variety of materials, and, at the beginning of the 20th century, the Hungarian physicist Roland, Baron von Eötvös, showed that different materials accelerate in Earth's field at the same rate to within one part in 10^9. More-recent experiments have shown the equality of accelerations in the field of the Sun to within one part in 10^{11}. Newtonian theory is in accord with these results because of the postulate that gravitational force is proportional to a body's mass.

Inertial mass is a mass parameter giving the inertial resistance to acceleration of the body when responding to all types of force. Gravitational mass is determined by the strength of the gravitational force experienced by the body when in the gravitational field g. The Eötvös experiments therefore show that the ratio of gravitational and inertial mass is the same for different substances.

In Einstein's theory of special relativity, inertial mass is a manifestation of all the forms of energy in a body, according to his fundamental relationship $E = mc^2$, E being the total energy content of a body, m the inertial mass of the body, and c the speed of light. Dealing with gravitation, then, as a field phenomenon, the weak principle of equivalence indicates that all forms of nongravitational energy must identically couple to or interact with the gravitational field, because the various materials in nature possess different fractional amounts of nuclear, electrical, magnetic, and kinetic energies, yet they accelerate at identical rates.

In the theory of general relativity, the gravitational field also interacts with gravitational energy in the same manner as with other forms of energy, an example of that theory's universality not possessed by most other theories of gravitation.

The Sun has an appreciable fraction of internal gravitational energy, and the repetitions of the Eötvös experiments during the 1970s, with the Sun instead of Earth as the attracting mass, revealed that bodies accelerate at identical rates in the Sun's field as well as in that of Earth. Extremely accurate laser measurements of the distance of the Moon from Earth have made possible a further test of the weak principle of equivalence. The chemical constitutions of Earth and the Moon are not the same, and so, if the principle did not hold, they might accelerate at different rates under the Sun's attraction. No such effect has been detected.

Newton's third law of dynamics states that every force implies an equal and opposite reaction force. Modern field theories of force contain this principle by requiring every entity that is acted upon by a field to be also a source of the field. An experiment by the American physicist Lloyd Kreuzer established to within 1 part in 20,000 that different materials produce gravitational fields with a strength the same as that of gravitational fields acting upon them. In this experiment a sphere of solid material was moved through a liquid of identical weight density. The absence of a gravitational effect on a nearby Cavendish balance instrument during the sphere's motion is interpreted as showing that the two materials had equal potency in producing a local gravitational-field anomaly.

Other experiments have confirmed Einstein's predictions to within a few percent. Using the Mössbauer effect to monitor the nuclear reabsorption of resonant gamma radiation, a shift of wavelength of the radiation that traveled vertically tens of metres in Earth's gravitational field was measured, and the slowing of clocks (in this case the nuclear vibrations are clocks) as predicted by Einstein was confirmed to 1 percent precision. If v and Δv are clock frequency and change of frequency, respectively, h is the height difference between clocks in the gravitational field g. Then

$$\frac{\Delta v}{v} = -\frac{gh}{c^2}. \qquad (16)$$

THE PATHS OF PARTICLES AND LIGHT

The idea that light should be deflected by passing close to a massive body had been suggested by the British astronomer and geologist John Michell in the 18th century. However, Einstein's general relativity theory predicted twice as much deflection as Newtonian physics. Quick confirmation of Einstein's result came from measuring the direction of a star close to the Sun's direction during an expedition led by the British astronomer Sir Arthur Stanley Eddington to observe the solar eclipse of 1919. Optical determinations of the change of direction of a star are subject to many systematic errors, and far better results have been obtained of the directions of spacecraft

Earth   Moon   Sun   apparent position / true position   (distance and objects not to scale)

Experimental evidence for general relativity. In 1919, observation of a solar eclipse confirmed Einstein's prediction that light is bent in the presence of mass. This experimental support for his general theory of relativity garnered him instant worldwide acclaim. Encyclopædia Britannica, Inc.

with radio interferometers of very long baselines. The effect comes from the decrease in the speed of light near a massive object (the Sun). That decrease has also been found directly from the round-trip travel times for radar pulses between Earth and other inner planets or artificial satellites passing behind the Sun and has confirmed to about 4 percent the prediction of an additional time delay Δt given by the following formula, in which M_S is the Sun's mass, R_1 and R_2 are the distances from the Sun to Earth and to the other reflecting body, and D is the distance of closest approach of the radar pulses to the Sun (ln stands for natural logarithm):

$$\Delta t = \frac{4 G M_S}{c^3} \ln \frac{4 R_1 R_2}{D^2}. \qquad (17)$$

The additional precession of the orbit of Mercury of 43 arc seconds per century was known before the development of the theory of general relativity. With radar measurements of the distances to the planets, similar anomalous precessions have been estimated for Venus and Earth and have been found to agree with general relativity.

GRAVITATIONAL RADIATION

According to general relativity, the curvature of space-time is determined by the distribution of masses, while the motion of masses is determined by the curvature. In consequence, variations of the gravitational field should be transmitted from place to place as waves, just as variations of an electromagnetic field travel as waves. If the masses that are the source of a field change with time, they should radiate energy as waves of curvature of the field. There are strong grounds for believing that such radiation exists. One particular double-star system has a pulsar as one of its components, and, from measurements of the shift of the pulsar frequency due to the Doppler effect, precise estimates of the period of the orbit show that the period is changing, corresponding to a decrease in the energy of the orbital motion. Gravitational radiation is the only known means by which that could happen.

Double stars in their regular motions (such as that for which a change in period has been detected) and massive stars collapsing as supernovas have been suggested as sources of gravitational radiation, and considerable theoretical effort has gone into calculating the signals to be expected from those and other sources.

Three types of detectors are being developed to look for gravitational radiation, which is expected to be very weak. The changes of curvature would correspond to a dilation in one direction and a contraction at right angles to that direction. One scheme, first tried out about 1960, employs a massive cylinder that might be set in mechanical oscillation by a gravitational signal. The authors of this apparatus argued that signals had been detected, but their claim has not been substantiated. In later developments the cylinder has been cooled by liquid helium, and great attention has been paid to possible disturbances. In a second scheme an optical interferometer is set up with freely suspended reflectors at the ends of long paths that are at right angles to each other. Shifts of interference fringes corresponding to an increase in length of one arm and a decrease in the other would indicate the passage of gravitational waves. A third scheme is planned that uses three separate, but not independent, interferometers located in three spacecraft located at the corners of a triangle with sides of some 5 million km (3 million miles). Some extremely sensitive instruments have been built or are still being developed, but so far gravitational radiation has not been observed with certainty.

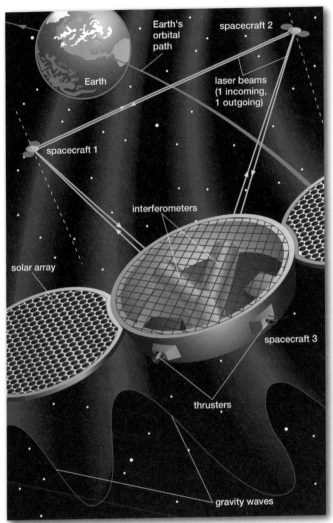

Laser Interferometer Space Antenna (LISA) a Beyond Einstein Great Observatory, is scheduled for launch in 2015. Jointly funded by the National Aeronautics and Space Administration (NASA) and the European Space Agency (ESA), LISA will consist of three identical spacecraft that will trail the Earth in its orbit by about 50 million km (30 million miles). The spacecraft will contain thrusters for maneuvering them into an equilateral triangle, with sides of approximately 5 million km (3 million miles), such that the triangle's centre will be located along the Earth's orbit. By measuring the transmission of laser signals between the spacecraft (essentially a giant Michelson interferometer in space), scientists hope to detect and accurately measure gravity waves. Encyclopædia Britannica, Inc.

SOME ASTRONOMICAL ASPECTS OF GRAVITATION

As stated earlier, studies of gravity allow the masses and densities of celestial bodies to be estimated and thereby make it possible to investigate the physical constitutions of stars and planets. Because gravitation is a very weak force, however, its distinctive effects appear only when masses are extremely large. The idea that light might be attracted gravitationally had been suggested by Michell and examined by the French mathematician and astronomer Pierre-Simon Laplace. Predictions by classical physics and general relativity that light passing close to the Sun might be deflected are described above. There are two further consequences for astronomy. Light from a distant object may pass close to objects other than the Sun and be deflected by them. In particular, they may be deflected by a massive galaxy. If some object is behind a massive galaxy, as seen from Earth, deflected light may reach Earth by more than one path. Operating like a lens that focuses light along different paths, the gravity of the galaxy may make the object appear multiple; examples of such apparently double objects have been found.

Both Michell and Laplace pointed out that the attraction of a very dense object upon light might be so great that the light could never escape from the object, rendering it invisible. Such a phenomenon is a black hole. The relativistic theory of black holes has been thoroughly developed in recent years, and astronomers have conducted an intense search for them. One possible class of black holes comprises very large stars that have used up all of their nuclear energy so that they are no longer held up by radiation pressure and have collapsed into black holes (less-massive stars may collapse into neutron stars). Black holes are thought to exist at the centres of most galaxies.

Black holes, from which no radiation is able to escape, cannot be seen by their own light, but there may be observable secondary effects. If a black hole were one component of a double star, the orbital motion of the pair and the mass of the invisible member might be derived from the oscillatory motion of a visible companion. Because black holes attract matter, any gas in the vicinity of an object of this kind would fall into it and acquire, before vanishing into the hole, a high velocity and consequently a high temperature. The gas may become hot enough to produce X-rays and gamma rays from around the hole. While there is still no definite proof, such a mechanism may be the origin of at least some powerful X-ray and radio astronomical sources, including those at the centres of galaxies and quasars.

Only astronomical objects are sufficiently massive to produce detectable gravitational radiation. As already mentioned, gravitational radiation is probably responsible for changes in the orbits of some double stars, and so, in the very long term, it may have an effect on the stability of celestial objects. If and when gravitational radiation is detected, new astronomical phenomena will no doubt be discovered.

EXPERIMENTAL STUDY OF GRAVITATION

The essence of Newton's theory of gravitation is that the force between two bodies is proportional to the product of their masses and the inverse square of their separation and that the force depends on nothing else. With a small modification, the same is true in general relativity. Newton himself tested his assumptions by experiment and observation. He made pendulum experiments to confirm the principle of equivalence and checked the inverse square law as applied to the periods and diameters of the orbits of the satellites of Jupiter and Saturn.

During the latter part of the 19th century, many experiments showed the force of gravity to be independent of temperature, electromagnetic fields, shielding by other matter, orientation of crystal axes, and other factors. The revival of such experiments during the 1970s was the result of theoretical attempts to relate gravitation to other forces of nature by showing that general relativity was an incomplete description of gravity. New experiments on the equivalence principle were performed, and experimental tests of the inverse square law were made both in the laboratory and in the field.

There also has been a continuing interest in the determination of the constant of gravitation, although it must be pointed out that G occupies a rather anomalous position among the other constants of physics. In the first place, the mass M of any celestial object cannot be determined independently of the gravitational attraction that it exerts. Thus, the combination GM, not the separate value of M, is the only meaningful property of a star, planet, or galaxy. Second, according to general relativity and the principle of equivalence, G does not depend on material properties but is in a sense a geometric factor. Hence, the determination of the constant of gravitation does not seem as essential as the measurement of quantities like the electronic charge or Planck's constant. It is also much less well determined experimentally than any of the other constants of physics.

Experiments on gravitation are in fact very difficult, as a comparison of experiments on the inverse square law of electrostatics with those on gravitation will show. The electrostatic law has been established to within one part in 10^{16} by using the fact that the field inside a closed conductor is zero when the inverse square law holds. Experiments with very sensitive electronic devices have failed to detect any residual fields in such a closed cavity. Gravitational forces have to be detected by mechanical means, most often the torsion balance, and, although the sensitivities of mechanical devices have been greatly improved, they are still far below those of electronic detectors. Mechanical arrangements also preclude the use of a complete gravitational enclosure. Last, extraneous disturbances are relatively large because gravitational forces are very small (something that Newton first pointed out). Thus, the inverse square law is established over laboratory distances to no better than one part in 10^4.

THE INVERSE SQUARE LAW

Recent interest in the inverse square law arose from two suggestions. First, the gravitational field itself might have a mass, in which case the constant of gravitation would change in an exponential manner from one value for small distances to a different one for large distances over a characteristic distance related to the mass of the field. Second, the observed field might be the superposition of two or more fields of different origin and different strengths, one of which might depend on chemical or nuclear constitution. Deviations from the inverse square law have been sought in three ways:

1. The law has been checked in the laboratory over distances up to about 1 metre.
2. The effective value of G for distances between 100 metres and 1 km has been estimated from geophysical studies.
3. There have been careful comparisons of the value of the attraction of Earth as measured on the surface and as experienced by artificial satellites.

Early in the 1970s an experiment by the American physicist Daniel R. Long seemed to show a deviation from the inverse square law at a range of about 0.1 metre. Long compared the maximum attractions of two rings upon a test mass hung from the arm of a torsion balance. The maximum attraction of a ring occurs at a particular point on the axis and is determined by the mass and dimensions of the ring. If the ring is moved until the force on the test mass is greatest, the distance between the test mass and the ring is not needed. Two later experiments over the same range showed no deviation from the inverse square law. In one, conducted by the American physicist Riley Newman and his colleagues, a test mass hung on a torsion balance was moved around in a long hollow cylinder. The cylinder approximates a complete gravitational enclosure and, allowing for a small correction because it is open at the ends, the force on the test mass should not depend on its location within the cylinder. No deviation from the inverse square law was found. In the other experiment, performed in Cambridge, Eng., by Y.T. Chen and associates, the attractions of two solid cylinders of different mass were balanced against a third cylinder so that only the separations of the cylinders had to be known; it was not necessary to know the distances of any from a test mass. Again no deviation of more than one part in 10^4 from the inverse square law was found. Other, somewhat less-sensitive experiments at ranges up to one metre or so also have failed to establish any greater deviation.

The geophysical tests go back to a method for the determination of the constant of gravitation that had been used in the 19th century, especially by the British astronomer Sir George Airy. Suppose the value of gravity g is measured at the top and bottom of a horizontal slab of rock of thickness t and density d. The values for the top and bottom will be different for two reasons. First, the top of the slab is t farther from the centre of Earth, and so the measured value of gravity will be less by $2(t/R)g$, where R is the radius of Earth. Second, the slab itself attracts objects above and below it toward its centre; the difference between the downward and upward attractions of the slab is $4\pi Gtd$. Thus, a value of G may be estimated. Frank D. Stacey and his colleagues in Australia made such measurements at the top and bottom of deep mine shafts and claimed that there may be a real difference between their value of G and the best value from laboratory experiments. The difficulties lie in obtaining reliable samples of the density and in taking account of varying densities at greater depths. Similar uncertainties appear to have afflicted measurements in a deep bore hole in the Greenland ice sheet.

New measurements have failed to detect any deviation from the inverse square law. The most thorough investigation was carried out from a high tower in Colorado. Measurements were made with a gravimeter at different heights and coupled with an extensive survey of gravity around the base of the tower. Any variations of gravity over the surface that would give rise to variations up the height of the tower were estimated with great care. Allowance was also made for deflections of the tower and for the accelerations of its motions. The final result was that no deviation from the inverse square law could be found.

A further test of the inverse square law depends on the theorem that the divergence of the gravity vector should vanish in a space that is free of additional gravitational sources. An experiment to test this was performed by M.V. Moody and H.J. Paik in California with a three-axis superconducting gravity gradiometer that measured the gradients of gravity in three perpendicular directions. The sum of the three gradients was zero within the accuracy of the measurements, about one part in 10^4.

The absolute measurements of gravity described earlier, together with the comprehensive gravity surveys made over the surface of Earth, allow the mean value of gravity over Earth to be estimated to about one part in 10^6. The techniques of space research also have given the mean value of the radius of Earth and the distances of artificial satellites to the same precision; thus, it has been possible to compare the value of gravity on Earth with that acting on an artificial satellite. Agreement to about one part in 10^6 shows that, over distances from the surface of Earth to close satellite orbits, the inverse square law is followed.

Thus far, all of the most reliable experiments and observations reveal no deviation from the inverse square law.

THE PRINCIPLE OF EQUIVALENCE

Experiments with ordinary pendulums test the principle of equivalence to no better than about one part in 10^5. Eötvös obtained much better discrimination with a torsion balance. His tests depended on comparing gravitational forces with inertial forces for masses of different composition. Eötvös set up a torsion balance to compare, for each of two masses, the gravitational attraction of Earth with the inertial forces due to the rotation of Earth about its polar axis. His arrangement of the masses was not optimal, and he did not have the sensitive electronic means of control and reading that are now available. Nonetheless, Eötvös found that the weak equivalence principle was satisfied to within one part in 10^9 for a number of very different chemicals, some of which were quite exotic. His results were later confirmed by the Hungarian physicist János Renner. Renner's work has been analyzed recently in great detail because of the suggestion that it could provide evidence for a new force.

It seems that the uncertainties of the experiments hardly allow such analyses.

Eötvös also suggested that the attraction of the Sun upon test masses could be compared with the inertial forces of Earth's orbital motion about the Sun. He performed some experiments, verifying equivalence with an accuracy similar to that which he had obtained with his terrestrial experiments. The solar scheme has substantial experimental advantages, and the American physicist Robert H. Dicke and his colleagues, in a careful series of observations in the 1960s (employing up-to-date methods of servo control and observation), found that the weak equivalence principle held to about one part in 10^{11} for the attraction of the Sun on gold and aluminum. A later experiment by the Russian researcher Vladimir Braginski, with very different experimental arrangements, gave a limit of about one part in 10^{12} for platinum and aluminum.

Galileo's supposed experiment of dropping objects from the Leaning Tower of Pisa has been reproduced in the laboratory with apparatuses used to determine the absolute value of gravity by timing a falling body. Two objects, one of uranium, the other of copper, were timed as they fell. No difference was detected.

Laser-ranging observations of the Moon in the LAGEOS (*la*ser *geo*dynamic *s*atellites) experiment have also failed to detect deviations from the principle of equivalence. Earth and the Moon have different compositions, the Moon lacking the iron found in Earth's core. Thus, if the principle of equivalence were not valid, the accelerations of Earth and the Moon toward the Sun might be different. The very precise measurements of the motion of the Moon relative to Earth could detect no such difference.

By the start of the 21st century, all observations and experiments on gravitation had detected that there are no deviations from the deductions of general relativity, that the weak principle of equivalence is valid, and that the inverse square law holds over distances from a few centimetres to thousands of kilometres. Coupled with observations of electromagnetic signals passing close to the Sun and of images formed by gravitational lenses, those observations and experiments make it very clear that general relativity provides the only acceptable description of gravitation at the present time.

THE CONSTANT OF GRAVITATION

The constant of gravitation has been measured in three ways:

1. The comparison of the pull of a large natural mass with that of the Earth
2. The measurement with a laboratory balance of the attraction of Earth upon a test mass
3. The direct measurement of the force between two masses in the laboratory

The first approach was suggested by Newton; the earliest observations were made in 1774 by the British astronomer Nevil Maskelyne on the mountain of Schiehallion in Scotland. The subsequent work of Airy and more-recent developments are noted above. The laboratory balance method was developed in large part by the British physicist John Henry Poynting during the late 1800s, but all the most recent work has involved the use of the torsion balance in some form or other for the direct laboratory measurement of the force between two bodies. The torsion balance was devised by Michell, who died before he could use it to measure G. Cavendish adapted Michell's design to make the first reliable measurement of G in 1798; only in comparatively recent times have clearly better results been obtained. Cavendish measured the change in deflection of the balance when attracting masses were moved from one side to the other of the torsion beam. The method of deflection was analyzed most thoroughly in the late 1800s by Sir Charles Vernon Boys, an English physicist, who carried it to its highest development, using a delicate suspension fibre of fused silica for the pendulum. In a variant of that method, the deflection of the balance is maintained constant by a servo control.

The second scheme involves the changes in the period of oscillation of a torsion balance when attracting masses are placed close to it such that the period is shortened in one position and lengthened in another. Measurements of period can be made much more precisely than those of deflection, and the method, introduced by Carl Braun of Austria in 1897, has been used in many subsequent determinations. In a third scheme the acceleration of the suspended masses is measured as they are moved relative to the large attracting masses.

In another arrangement a balance with heavy attracting masses is set up near a free test balance and adjusted so that it oscillates with the same period as the test balance. The latter is then driven into resonant oscillations with an amplitude that is a measure of the constant of gravitation. The technique was first employed by J. Zahradnicek of Czechoslovakia during the 1930s and was effectively used again by C. Pontikis of France some 40 years later.

Suspensions for two-arm balances for the comparison of masses and for torsion balances have been studied intensively by T.J. Quinn and his colleagues at the International Bureau of Weights and Measures, near Paris, and they have found that suspensions with thin ribbons of metal rather than wires provide the most stable systems. They have used balances with such suspensions to look for deviations from the predictions of general relativity and have most recently used a torsion balance with ribbon suspension in two new determinations of the constant of gravitation.

Many new determinations of G were made in the five years from 1996 to 2001. However, despite the great attention given to systematic errors in those experiments, it is clear from the range of the results that serious discrepancies, much greater than the apparent random errors, still afflict determinations of G. In 2001 the best estimate of G was taken to be 6.67553×10^{-11} m^3 s^{-2} kg^{-1}. Results before 1982 indicate a lower value, perhaps 6.670, but those from 1996 onward suggest a higher value.

THE VARIATION OF THE CONSTANT OF GRAVITATION WITH TIME

The 20th-century English physicist P.A.M. Dirac, among others, suggested that the value of the constant of gravitation might be proportional to the age of the universe; other rates of change over time also have been proposed. The rates of change would be extremely small, one part in 10^{11} per year if the age of the universe is taken to be 10^{11} years; such a rate is entirely beyond experimental capabilities at present. There is, however, the possibility of looking for the effects of any variation upon the orbit of a celestial body, in particular the Moon. It has been claimed from time to time that such effects may have been detected. As yet, there is no certainty.

FUNDAMENTAL CHARACTER OF G

The constant of gravitation is plainly a fundamental quantity, since it appears to determine the large-scale structure of the entire universe. Gravity is a fundamental quantity whether it is an essentially geometric parameter, as in general relativity, or the strength of a field, as in one aspect of a more-general field of unified forces. The fact that, so far as is known, gravitation depends on no other physical factors makes it likely that the value of G reflects a basic restriction on the possibilities of physical measurement, just as special relativity is a consequence of the fact that, beyond the shortest distances, it is impossible to make separate measurements of length and time.

CONCLUSION

In this book we examined the subjects of thermodynamics and the various branches of mechanics. These branches include the mechanics of solids and fluid mechanics. The force of gravity was also studied in detail. These subjects are associated with simple laws, those of thermodynamics and Newton's laws of motion and gravity.

The 20th-century English scientist and novelist C.P. Snow explained the first three laws of thermodynamics, respectively, as:

1. You cannot win (i.e., one cannot get something for nothing, because of the conservation of matter and energy).
2. You cannot break even (i.e., one cannot return to the same energy state, because entropy, or disorder, always increases).
3. You cannot get out of the game (i.e., absolute zero is unattainable because no perfectly pure substance exists).

The sweeping generality of the constraints imposed by the laws of thermodynamics makes the number of potential applications so large that it is impractical to catalog every possible formula that might come into use, even in detailed textbooks on the subject. For this reason, students and practitioners in the field must be proficient in mathematical manipulations involving partial derivatives and in understanding their physical content.

The principles of mechanics have been applied to many different phenomena. The motions of such celestial bodies as stars, planets, and satellites can be predicted with great accuracy thousands of years before they occur through knowledge of Newton's law of gravity. (The theory of relativity predicts some deviations from the motion according to classical, or Newtonian, mechanics; however, these are so small as to be observable only with very accurate techniques, except in problems involving all or a large portion of the detectable universe.) The law of gravity has been used to determine the mass of Earth. Even the internal structure of the planets has been studied using the principles of mechanics. Ordinary objects on Earth down to microscopic size (moving at speeds much lower than that of light) are properly described by classical mechanics without significant corrections. The engineer who designs bridges or aircraft may use the Newtonian laws of classical mechanics with confidence, even though the forces may be very complicated, and the calculations lack the beautiful simplicity of celestial mechanics. Such complications were addressed in the sections on solids, stress and strain, and liquids.

CHAPTER 12

BIOGRAPHIES

I n this section, biographies of some of the notable people who studied thermodynamics and mechanics are presented. Some names, such as Sir Isaac Newton and Galileo, are familiar worldwide. Others, such as Sophie Germain and J. Willard Gibbs, are not so prominent, but interesting for their important contributions to physics.

LUDWIG EDUARD BOLTZMANN

(b. Feb. 20, 1844, Vienna, Austria—d. Sept. 5, 1906, Duino, Italy)

Ludwig Eduard Boltzmann was a physicist whose greatest achievement was in the development of statistical mechanics, which explains and predicts how the properties of atoms (such as mass, charge, and structure) determine the visible properties of matter (such as viscosity, thermal conductivity, and diffusion).

After receiving his doctorate from the University of Vienna in 1866, Boltzmann held professorships in mathematics and physics at Vienna, Graz, Munich, and Leipzig.

In the 1870s Boltzmann published a series of papers in which he showed that the second law of thermodynamics, which concerns energy exchange, could be explained by applying the laws of mechanics and the theory of probability to the motions of the atoms. In so doing, he made clear that the second law is essentially statistical and that a system approaches a state of thermodynamic equilibrium (uniform energy distribution throughout) because equilibrium is overwhelmingly the most probable state of a material system. During these investigations Boltzmann worked out the general law for the distribution of energy among the various parts of a system at a specific temperature and derived the theorem of equipartition of energy (Maxwell-Boltzmann distribution law). This law states that the average amount of energy involved in each different direction of motion of an atom is the same. He derived an equation for the change of the distribution of energy among atoms due to atomic collisions and laid the foundations of statistical mechanics.

Boltzmann was also one of the first continental scientists to recognize the importance of the electromagnetic theory proposed by James Clerk Maxwell of England. Though Boltzmann's work on statistical mechanics was strongly attacked and long-misunderstood, his conclusions were finally supported by the discoveries in atomic physics that began shortly before 1900 and by recognition that fluctuation phenomena, such as Brownian motion (random movement of microscopic particles suspended in a fluid), could be explained only by statistical mechanics.

SADI CARNOT

(b. June 1, 1796, Paris, France—d. Aug. 24, 1832, Paris)

French scientist Nicolas-Léonard-Sadi Carnot described the Carnot cycle, relating to the theory of heat engines.

Carnot was the eldest son of the French Revolutionary figure Lazare Carnot and was named for a medieval Persian poet and philosopher, Sa'dī of Shīrāz. His early years were a period of unrest, and the family suffered many changes of fortune. His father fled into exile soon after Sadi's birth; in 1799 he returned to be appointed Napoleon's minister of war but was soon forced to resign. A writer on mathematics and mechanics as well as military and political matters, the elder Carnot now had the leisure to direct his son's early education.

Nicolas-Léonard-Sadi Carnot. SSPL via Getty Images

Sadi entered the École Polytechnique in 1812, an institution providing an exceptionally fine education, with a faculty of famous scientists aware of the latest developments in physics and chemistry, which they based on a rigorous mathematics. By the time Sadi graduated in 1814, Napoleon's empire was being rolled back, and European armies were invading France. Soon Paris itself was besieged, and the students, Sadi among them, fought a skirmish on the outskirts of the city.

During Napoleon's brief return to power in 1815, Lazare Carnot was minister of the interior, but, following the emperor's final abdication, he fled to Germany, never to return to France.

Sadi remained an army officer for most of his life, despite disputes about his seniority, denial of promotion, and the refusal to employ him in the job for which he had been trained. In 1819 he transferred to the recently formed General Staff but quickly retired on half pay, living in Paris on call for army duty. Friends described him as reserved, almost taciturn, but insatiably curious about science and technical processes.

The mature, creative period of his life now began. Sadi attended public lectures on physics and chemistry provided for workingmen. He was also inspired by long discussions with the prominent physicist and successful industrialist Nicolas Clément-Desormes, whose theories he further clarified by his insight and ability to generalize.

The problem occupying Carnot was how to design good steam engines. Steam power already had many uses — draining water from mines, excavating ports and rivers, forging iron, grinding grain, and spinning and weaving cloth — but it was inefficient. The import into France of advanced engines after the war with Britain showed Carnot how far French design had fallen behind. It irked him particularly that the British had progressed so far through the genius of a few engineers who lacked formal scientific education. British engineers had also accumulated and published reliable data about the efficiency of many types of engines under actual running conditions; and they vigorously argued the merits of low- and high-pressure engines and of single-cylinder and multicylinder engines.

Convinced that France's inadequate utilization of steam was a factor in its downfall, Carnot began to write a nontechnical work on the efficiency of steam engines. Other workers before him had examined the question of improving the efficiency of steam engines by comparing the expansion and compression of steam with the production of work and consumption of fuel. In his essay, *Réflexions sur la puissance motrice du feu et sur les machines propres à développer cette puissance (Reflections on the Motive Power of Fire)*, published in 1824, Carnot tackled the essence of the process, not concerning himself as others had done with its mechanical details.

Carnot saw that, in a steam engine, motive power is produced when heat "drops" from the higher temperature of the boiler to the lower temperature of the condenser, just as water, when falling, provides power in a waterwheel. He worked within the framework of the caloric theory of heat, assuming that heat was a gas that could be neither created nor destroyed. Though the assumption was incorrect and Carnot himself had doubts about it even while he was writing, many of his results were nevertheless true, notably the prediction that the efficiency of an idealized engine depends only on the temperature of its hottest and coldest parts and not on the substance (steam or any other fluid) that drives the mechanism.

Although formally presented to the Academy of Sciences and given an excellent review in the press, the work was completely ignored until 1834, when Émile Clapeyron, a railroad engineer, quoted and extended

Carnot's results. Several factors might account for this delay in recognition; the number of copies printed was limited and the dissemination of scientific literature was slow, and such a work was hardly expected to come from France when the leadership in steam technology had been centred in England for a century. Eventually Carnot's views were incorporated by the thermodynamic theory as it was developed by Rudolf Clausius in Germany (1850) and William Thomson (later Lord Kelvin) in Britain (1851).

Little is known of Carnot's subsequent activities. In 1828 he described himself as a "constructor of steam engines, in Paris." When the Revolution of 1830 in France seemed to promise a more liberal regime, there was a suggestion that Carnot be given a government position, but nothing came of it. He was also interested in improving public education. When absolutist monarchy was restored, he returned to scientific work, which he continued until his death in the cholera epidemic of 1832 in Paris.

HENRY CAVENDISH

(b. Oct. 10, 1731, Nice, France—d. Feb. 24, 1810, London, Eng.)

Natural philosopher Henry Cavendish was the greatest experimental and theoretical English chemist and physicist of his age. Members of the Cavendish family were distinguished for their great accuracy and precision. His experiment to weigh Earth has come to be known as the Cavendish experiment.

Cavendish had no title, although his father was the third son of the duke of Devonshire, and his mother (née Ann Grey) was the fourth daughter of the duke of Kent. Henry went to the Hackney Academy, a private school near London, and in 1748 entered Peterhouse College, Cambridge, where he remained for three years before he left without taking a degree (a common practice). He then lived with his father in London, where he soon had his own laboratory.

Cavendish took virtually no part in politics, but, like his father, he lived a life of service to science, both through his researches and through his participation in scientific organizations. Cavendish was a shy man who was uncomfortable in society and avoided it when he could. He conversed little, always dressed in an old-fashioned suit, and developed no known deep personal attachments outside his family.

In 1783 Cavendish published a paper on the production of water by burning inflammable air (that is, hydrogen) in dephlogisticated air (now known to be oxygen), the latter a constituent of atmospheric air. Cavendish concluded that dephlogisticated air was dephlogisticated water and that hydrogen was either pure phlogiston or phlogisticated water.

In 1783 he published a paper on the temperature at which mercury freezes and in that paper made use of the idea of latent heat, although he did not use the term because he believed that it implied acceptance of a material theory of heat. He made his objections explicit in his 1784 paper on air. He went on to develop a general theory of heat, which was at once mathematical and mechanical; it contained the principle of the conservation of heat (later understood as an instance of conservation of energy) and even contained the concept (although not the label) of the mechanical equivalent of heat.

The most famous of Cavendish's experiments, published in 1798, was to determine the density of Earth. His apparatus for weighing the world was a modification of the Englishman John Michell's torsion balance. The balance had two small lead balls suspended from the arm of a torsion balance and two much larger stationary lead balls. Cavendish calculated the attraction between the balls from the period of oscillation of the torsion balance, and then he used this value to calculate the density of Earth. What was extraordinary about Cavendish's experiment was its elimination of every source of error and every factor that could disturb the experiment and its precision in measuring an astonishingly small attraction, a mere 1/50,000,000 of the weight of the lead balls. The result that Cavendish obtained for the density of Earth is within 1 percent of the currently accepted figure. The combination of painstaking care, precise experimentation, thoughtfully modified apparatus, and fundamental theory carries Cavendish's unmistakable signature. Cavendish remained active in science and healthy in body almost until the end.

RUDOLF CLAUSIUS

(b. Jan. 2, 1822, Köslin, Prussia—d. Aug. 24, 1888, Bonn)

German mathematical physicist Julius Emanuel Rudolf Clausius formulated the second law of thermodynamics and is credited with making thermodynamics a science.

Clausius was appointed professor of physics at the Artillery and Engineering School at Berlin in 1850, the same year in which he presented a paper stating the second law of thermodynamics in the well-known form: "Heat cannot of itself pass from a colder to a hotter body." He applied his results to an exhaustive development of the theory of the steam engine, stressing the concept of entropy (dissipation of available energy). He became professor of physics at Zürich Polytechnikum in 1855, and, two years later, contributed to the theory of electrolysis (the breaking down of a compound by electricity) by suggesting that molecules are made up of continually interchanging atoms and that electric force does not cause but simply directs the interchange. This view later was used as the basis of the theory of electrolytic dissociation (breakdown of molecules into charged atoms or ions).

He became professor of physics at the University of Würzburg in 1867 and at the University of Bonn in 1869. In molecular physics, Clausius restated the French physicist Sadi Carnot's principle concerning efficiency of heat engines and thus provided a much sounder basis for the theory of heat.

GUSTAVE-GASPARD CORIOLIS

(b. May 21, 1792, Paris, France—d. Sept. 19, 1843, Paris)

French engineer and mathematician Gustave-Gaspard Coriolis first described what would be termed the Coriolis force, an effect of motion on a rotating body, of paramount importance to meteorology, ballistics, and oceanography.

An assistant professor of analysis and mechanics at the École Polytechnique, Paris (1816–38), he introduced the terms "work" and "kinetic energy" in their modern scientific meanings in his first major book, *Du calcul de l'effet des machines* (1829; "On the Calculation of Mechanical Action"), in which he attempted to adapt theoretical principles to applied mechanics.

In 1835 Coriolis published a paper, "Sur les équations du mouvement relatif des systèmes de corps" ("On the Equations of Relative Motion of Systems of Bodies"), in which he showed that on a rotating surface, in addition to the ordinary effects of motion of a body, there is an inertial force acting on the body at right angles to its direction of motion. This force results in a curved path for a body that would otherwise travel in a straight line. The Coriolis force on Earth determines the general wind directions and is responsible for the rotation of hurricanes and tornadoes. His other works include *Traité de la mécanique des corps solides* (1844; "Treatise on the Mechanics of Solid Bodies") and *Théorie mathématique des effets du jeu de billiard* (1835; "Mathematical Theory of the Game of Billiards").

The effect of the Coriolis force

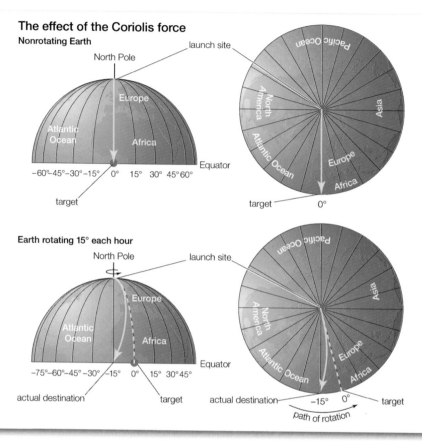

Encyclopædia Britannica, Inc.

GALILEO

(b. Feb. 15, 1564, Pisa [Italy]—d. Jan. 8, 1642, Arcetri, near Florence)

Italian astronomer and mathematician Galileo Galilei contributed to the sciences of motion, astronomy, and strength of materials and to the development of the scientific method. His formulation of (circular) inertia, the law of falling bodies, and parabolic trajectories marked the beginning of a fundamental change in the study of motion.

In 1581 Galileo matriculated at the University of Pisa, where he was to study medicine but instead became enamoured with mathematics. In 1585 Galileo left the university without having obtained a degree, and for several years he gave private lessons in mathematics. During this period he designed a new form of hydrostatic balance for weighing small quantities. He also began his studies on motion.

Galileo obtained the chair of mathematics at the University of Pisa in 1589. There he demonstrated, by dropping bodies of different weights from the top of the famous Leaning Tower, that the speed of fall of a heavy object is not proportional to its weight, as Aristotle had claimed. The tract *De motu* (*On Motion*), finished during this period, shows that Galileo was abandoning Aristotelian notions about motion. But his attacks on Aristotle made him unpopular, and in 1592 his contract was not renewed. His patrons, however, secured him the chair of mathematics at the University of Padua, where he taught from 1592 until 1610.

Galileo continued his research on motion, and by 1609 he had determined that the distance fallen by a body is proportional to the square of the elapsed time (the law of falling bodies) and that the trajectory of a projectile is a parabola, both conclusions that contradicted Aristotelian physics.

At this point, however, Galileo's career took a dramatic turn. In the spring of 1609 he heard that in the Netherlands an instrument had been invented that showed distant things as though they were nearby. By trial and error, he quickly figured out the secret of the invention and made his own telescope from lenses for sale in spectacle makers' shops. In the fall of 1609 Galileo began observing the heavens. In December he drew the Moon's phases, showing that the Moon's surface is not smooth, as had been thought, but is rough and uneven. In January 1610 he discovered four

Galileo Galilei. Hulton Archive/Getty Images

moons revolving around Jupiter. He also found that the telescope showed many more stars than are visible with the naked eye. These discoveries were earthshaking.

Galileo went on to discover that Venus goes through phases just as the Moon does. Although these discoveries did not prove that Earth is a planet orbiting the Sun, they nevertheless undermined Aristotelian cosmology: the absolute difference between the corrupt earthly region and the perfect and unchanging heavens was proved wrong by the mountainous surface of the Moon, the moons of Jupiter showed that there had to be more than one centre of motion in the universe, and the phases of Venus showed that it revolves around the Sun. As a result, Galileo was confirmed in his belief that the Sun is the centre of the universe and that Earth is a planet, as Copernicus had argued. Galileo's conversion to Copernicanism would be a key turning point in the scientific revolution.

Galileo's increasingly overt Copernicanism began to cause trouble for him. In 1615, Inquisition consultants pronounced the Copernican theory heretical. Galileo was admonished by Robert Cardinal Bellarmine not to "hold or defend" the Copernican theory. An improperly pre-pared document placed in the Inquisition files at this time states that Galileo was admonished "not to hold, teach, or defend" the Copernican theory.

Galileo was thus effectively muzzled, but he slowly recovered from this setback. *Il saggiatore* (*The Assayer*), published in 1623, was a brilliant exposition of the new scientific method.

Publication of *Il saggiatore* came at an auspicious moment, for Maffeo Cardinal Barberini, a friend of Galileo, was named Pope Urban VIII as the book was going to press. In 1624 Galileo had six interviews with Urban VIII. Galileo told the pope about his theory of the tides, which he put forward as proof of the annual and diurnal motions of Earth. The pope gave Galileo permission to write a book about theories of the universe but warned him to treat the Copernican theory only hypothetically. The book, *Dialogo sopra i due massimi sistemi del mondo, tolemaico e copernicano* (*Dialogue Concerning the Two Chief World Systems, Ptolemaic & Copernican*), was finished in 1630 and appeared in 1632 with a preface in which Galileo professed that what followed was written hypothetically.

In the *Dialogue*'s witty conversation between Salviati (representing Galileo), Sagredo (the intelligent layman), and Simplicio (the Aristotelian), Galileo gathered together all the arguments for the Copernican theory. However, he gave Simplicio the final word, that God could have made the universe any way he wanted to and still made it appear to us the way it does, thus putting Urban VIII's favourite argument in the mouth of the person who had been ridiculed throughout the dialogue. The reaction against the book was swift. The pope convened a special commission that recommended that a case be brought against Galileo by the Inquisition. During Galileo's first appearance before the Inquisition, he was confronted with the 1616 edict recording that he was forbidden to discuss the Copernican theory. In his defense Galileo produced a letter from Cardinal Bellarmine, by then dead, stating that he was admonished only not to hold or defend the theory. The case was at somewhat of an impasse, and, in what can only be called a plea bargain, Galileo confessed to having overstated his case. He was condemned to life imprisonment and was made to abjure formally. There is no evidence that at this time he whispered, "Eppur si muove" ("And yet it moves"). It should be noted that Galileo was never in a dungeon or tortured; during the trial he stayed mostly at the house of the Tuscan ambassador to the Vatican. After the process he moved into a villa near Florence.

Galileo was then 70 years old. Yet he kept working. He had begun a new book on the sciences of motion and strength of materials. The book was published in Leiden, the Netherlands, in 1638 under the title *Discorsi e dimostrazioni matematiche intorno a due nuove scienze attenenti alla meccanica* (*Dialogues Concerning Two New Sciences*). Galileo here treated for the first time the bending and breaking of beams and summarized his mathematical and experimental investigations of motion, including the law of falling bodies and the parabolic path of projectiles as a result of the mixing of two motions, constant speed, and uniform acceleration.

SOPHIE GERMAIN

(b. April 1, 1776, Paris, France—d. June 27, 1831, Paris)

French mathematician Marie-Sophie Germain contributed notably to the study of acoustics, elasticity, and the theory of numbers.

Sophie Germain, as engraved by 19th century French sculptor and painter Zacharie Astruc. Boyer/Roger Viollet/Getty Images

As a girl Germain read widely in her father's library and then later, using the pseudonym of M. Le Blanc, managed to obtain lecture notes for courses from the newly organized École Polytechnique in Paris. It was through the École Polytechnique that she met the mathematician Joseph-Louis Lagrange, who remained a strong source of support and encouragement to her for several years. Germain's early work was in number theory, her interest having been stimulated by Adrien-Marie Legendre's *Théorie des nombres* (1789) and by Carl Friedrich Gauss's *Disquisitiones Arithmeticae* (1801). This subject occupied her throughout her life and eventually provided her most significant result. In 1804 Germain initiated a correspondence with Gauss under her male pseudonym. Gauss only learned of her true identity when Germain, fearing for Gauss's safety as a result of the French occupation of Hannover in 1807, asked a family friend in the French army to ascertain his whereabouts and ensure that he would not be ill-treated.

In 1809 the French Academy of Sciences offered a prize for a mathematical account of the phenomena exhibited in experiments on vibrating plates conducted by the German physicist Ernst F.F. Chladni. In 1811 Germain submitted an anonymous memoir, but the prize was not awarded. The competition was reopened twice more, once in 1813 and again in 1816, and Germain submitted a memoir on each occasion. Her third memoir, for which she finally won the prize, treated vibrations of general curved as well as plane surfaces and was published privately in 1821. During the 1820s she worked on generalizations of her research but, isolated from the academic community on account of her gender and thus largely unaware of new developments taking place in the theory of elasticity, she made little real progress. In 1816 Germain met Joseph Fourier, whose friendship and position in the Academy helped her to participate more fully in Parisian scientific life, but his reservations about her work on elasticity eventually led him to distance himself from her professionally, although they remained close friends.

Meanwhile Germain had actively revived her interest in number theory and in 1819 wrote to Gauss outlining her strategy for a general solution to Fermat's last theorem, which states that there is no solution for the equation $xn + yn = zn$ if n is an integer greater than 2 and x, y, and z are nonzero integers. She proved the special case in which x, y, z, and n are all relatively prime (have no common divisor except for 1) and n is a prime smaller than 100, although she did not publish her work. Her result first appeared in 1825 in a supplement to the second edition of Legendre's *Théorie des nombres*. She corresponded extensively with Legendre, and her method formed the basis for his proof of the theorem for the case $n = 5$. The theorem was proved for all cases by the English mathematician Andrew Wiles in 1995.

J. WILLARD GIBBS

(b. Feb. 11, 1839, New Haven, Conn., U.S.—d. April 28, 1903, New Haven)

Theoretical physicist and chemist Josiah Willard Gibbs was one of the greatest scientists in the United States in the 19th century. His application of thermodynamic theory converted a large part of physical chemistry from an empirical into a deductive science.

Gibbs was the fourth child and only son of Josiah Willard Gibbs, Sr., professor of sacred literature at Yale University. There were college presidents among his ancestors and scientific ability in his mother's family. Facially and mentally, Gibbs resembled his mother. He was a friendly youth but was also withdrawn and intellectually absorbed.

This circumstance and his delicate health kept him from participating much in student and social life. He was educated at the local Hopkins Grammar School and in 1854 entered Yale, where he won a succession of prizes. After graduating, Gibbs pursued research in engineering. His thesis on the design of gearing was distinguished by the logical rigour with which he employed geometrical methods of analysis. In 1863 Gibbs received the first doctorate of engineering to be conferred in the United States. He was appointed a tutor at Yale in the same year. He devoted some attention to engineering invention.

Gibbs lost his parents rather early, and he and his two older sisters inherited the family home and a modest fortune. In 1866 he and his sisters went to Europe, remaining there nearly three years while Gibbs attended the lectures of European masters of mathematics and physics, whose intellectual technique he assimilated. He returned more a European than an American scientist in spirit—one of the reasons why general recognition in his native country came so slowly. Gibbs applied his increasing command of theory to the improvement of James Watt's steam-engine governor. In analyzing its equilibrium, Gibbs began to develop the method by which the equilibriums of chemical processes could be calculated.

He was appointed professor of mathematical physics at Yale in 1871, before he had published his fundamental work. His first major paper was "Graphical Methods in the Thermodynamics of Fluids," which appeared in 1873. It was followed in the same year by "A Method of Geometrical Representation of the Thermodynamic Properties of Substances by Means of Surfaces" and in 1876 by his most famous paper, "On the Equilibrium of Heterogeneous Substances." The importance of his work was immediately recognized by the Scottish physicist James Clerk Maxwell in England, who constructed a model of Gibbs's thermodynamic surface with his own hands and sent it to him.

He remained a bachelor, living in his surviving sister's household. In his later years he was a tall, dignified gentleman, with a healthy stride and ruddy complexion, performing his share of household chores, approachable and kind (if unintelligible) to students.

Gibbs was highly esteemed by his friends, but U.S. science was too preoccupied with practical questions to make much use of his profound theoretical work during his lifetime. He lived out his quiet life at Yale, deeply admired by a few able students but making no immediate impression on U.S. science commensurate with his genius. He never even became a member of the American Physical Society. He seems to have been unaffected by this. He was aware of the significance of what he had done and was content to let posterity appraise him.

The contemporary historian Henry Adams called Gibbs "the greatest of Americans, judged by his rank in science." Gibbs's application of thermodynamics to physical processes led him to develop the science of statistical mechanics; his treatment of it was so general that it was later found to apply as well to quantum mechanics as to the classical physics from which it had been derived.

SIR WILLIAM ROWAN HAMILTON

(b. Aug. 3/4, 1805, Dublin, Ire.—d. Sept. 2, 1865, Dublin)

Irish mathematician Sir William Rowan Hamilton contributed to the development of optics, dynamics, and algebra—in particular, discovering the algebra of quaternions.

Hamilton was the son of a solicitor. At five he was already making progress with Latin, Greek, and Hebrew, broadening his studies to include Arabic, Sanskrit, Persian, Syriac, French, and Italian before he was 12.

A serious interest in mathematics was awakened on reading the *Analytic Geometry* of Bartholomew Lloyd at the age of 16. Further reading included works of the French mathematicians Pierre-Simon Laplace and Joseph-Louis Lagrange.

Hamilton entered Trinity College, Dublin, in 1823. He excelled as an undergraduate in mathematics and physics, while he continued with his own mathematical investigations. In 1827, while still an undergraduate, Hamilton was appointed professor of astronomy at Trinity College and Royal Astronomer of Ireland.

Hamilton's first published mathematical paper begins by proving that a system of light rays filling a region of space can be focused down to a single point by a suitably curved mirror if and only if those light rays are orthogonal to some series of surfaces. Moreover, the latter property is preserved under reflection in any number of mirrors. Hamilton's innovation was to associate with such a system of rays a characteristic function, constant on each of the surfaces to which the rays are orthogonal, which he employed in the mathematical investigation of the foci and caustics of reflected light.

The theory of the characteristic function of an optical system was further developed in three supplements. In the third of these, the characteristic function depends on the Cartesian coordinates of two points (initial and final) and measures the time taken for light to travel through the optical system from one to the other. If the form of this function is known, then basic properties of the optical system can easily be obtained.

From 1833 onward, Hamilton adapted his optical methods to the study of dynamics. He created an elegant theory that associated a characteristic function with any system of attracting or repelling point particles. If the form of this function is known, then the solutions of the equations of motion of the system can easily be obtained. The equations of motion of a dynamical system are expressed in a particularly pleasing form (Hamilton's equations of motion). The significance of Hamilton's approach became apparent in the development of celestial mechanics and quantum mechanics. Hamiltonian mechanics underlies contemporary mathematical research the theory of dynamical systems.

Hamilton had a deep interest in the fundamental principles of algebra. Complex numbers were then represented as "algebraic couples"—i.e., ordered pairs of real numbers. For many years Hamilton sought to construct a theory of triplets, analogous to complex numbers, that would be applicable to the study of three-dimensional geometry. Then, on Oct. 16, 1843, while walking with his wife beside the Royal Canal on his way to Dublin, Hamilton suddenly realized that the solution lay not in triplets but in quadruplets, or quaternions. Thrilled by his inspiration, he stopped to carve the fundamental equations of this algebra on a stone of a bridge they were passing.

Hamilton devoted the last 22 years of his life to the development of the theory of quaternions and related systems. Many basic concepts and results in vector analysis have their origin in Hamilton's papers on quaternions.

HERMANN VON HELMHOLTZ

(b. Aug. 31, 1821, Potsdam, Prussia [Germany]—d. Sept. 8, 1894, Charlottenburg, Berlin, Ger.)

German scientist and philosopher Hermann Ludwig Ferdinand von Helmholtz made fundamental contributions to physiology, optics, electrodynamics, mathematics, and meteorology. He is best known for his statement of the law of the conservation of energy.

Helmholtz was the eldest of four children and because of his delicate health was confined to home for his first seven years. After graduating from the gymnasium, Helmholtz in 1838 entered the Friedrich Wilhelm Medical Institute in Berlin, where he received a free medical education on the condition that he serve eight years as an army doctor. At the institute he did research under the greatest German physiologist of the day, Johannes Müller. Helmholtz attended physics lectures, worked his way through the standard textbooks of higher mathematics, and learned to play the piano with a skill that later helped him in his work on the sensation of tone.

Upon graduation from medical school in 1843, Helmholtz was assigned to a regiment at Potsdam. Because his army duties were few, he did experiments in a makeshift laboratory he set up in the barracks. Before long, Helmholtz's obvious scientific talents led to his release from military duties. In 1848 he was appointed assistant at the Anatomical Museum and lecturer at the Academy of Fine Arts in Berlin, moving the next year to Königsberg, in East Prussia (now Kaliningrad), to become assistant professor and director of the Physiological Institute. In 1855 he became professor of anatomy and physiology at the University of Bonn, moving in 1858 to Heidelberg. During these years his scientific interests progressed from physiology to physics. His growing scientific stature was further recognized in 1871 by the offer of the professorship of physics at the University of Berlin; in 1882, by his elevation to the nobility; and, in 1888, by his appointment as first director of the Physico-Technical Institute at Berlin, the post that he held for the rest of his life.

The variety of positions Helmholtz held reflects his interests and competence but does not reflect the way in which his mind worked. He did not start out in medicine, shift to physiology, then drift into mathematics and physics. Rather, he was able to coordinate the insights he had acquired from his experience in these disciplines and to apply them to every problem he examined.

Hermann Ludwig Ferdinand von Helmholtz. SSPL via Getty Images

The general theme that runs through most, if not all, of Helmholtz's work may be traced to his rejection of the then-prevalent "Nature philosophy." Nature philosophy derived from Immanuel Kant, who in the 1780s had suggested that the concepts of time, space, and causation were not products of sense experience but mental attributes by which it was possible to perceive the world. Therefore, the mind did not merely record order in nature; rather, the mind organized the world of perceptions so that it could deduce the system of the world from a few basic principles. Helmholtz opposed this view by insisting that all knowledge came through the senses. Furthermore, in his view, all science could and should be reduced to the laws of classical mechanics.

Helmholtz's approach to nature was evident in the very first scientific researches he undertook while working for his doctorate in Müller's laboratory. Like most biologists, Müller was a vitalist who was convinced that it was impossible to reduce living processes to the ordinary mechanical laws of physics and chemistry.

In Müller's laboratory Helmholtz met a group of young men, among whom were Emil Heinrich Du Bois-Reymond, the founder of experimental neurophysiology, and Ernst Wilhelm von Brücke, who later became an expert on the operations of the human eye. Du Bois-Reymond expressed their opposition to Müller's views in a statement that fully expressed Helmholtz's own position. "Brücke and I," Du Bois-Reymond wrote, "we have sworn to each other to validate the basic truth that in an organism no other forces have any effect than the common physiochemical ones."

It was with this attitude that Helmholtz began his doctoral thesis in 1842 on the connection between nerve fibres and nerve cells. This soon led him to a broader field of inquiry, namely, the source of animal heat. Recent publications in France had cast doubt upon the earlier confident assertion that all the heat produced in an animal body was the result of the heats of combination of the various chemical elements involved, particularly carbon, hydrogen, and oxygen. Having mastered both physics and mathematics, Helmholtz could do what no other physiologist of the time could even attempt—subject the problem to a mathematical and physical analysis. He supposed that, if vital heat were not the sum of all the heats of the substances involved in chemical reactions within the organic body, there must be some other source of heat not subject to physical laws. This, of course, was precisely what the vitalists argued. But such a source, Helmholtz went on, would permit the creation of a perpetual motion machine if the heat could, somehow, be harnessed. Hence, Helmholtz concluded, vital heat must be the product of mechanical forces within the organism. From there he went on to generalize his results to state that all heat was related to ordinary forces and, finally, to state that force itself could never be destroyed. His paper "On the Conservation of Force," which appeared in 1847, marked an epoch in both the history of physiology and the history of physics. For physiology, it provided a fundamental statement about organic nature that permitted physiologists henceforth to perform the same kind of material and energy balances as their colleagues in physics and chemistry. For the physical sciences, it provided one of the first, and certainly the clearest, statements of the principle of the conservation of energy.

Helmholtz attacked and solved equations that had long frustrated physicists and mathematicians. In 1858 he published the paper "On the Integrals of Hydrodynamic Equations to Which Vortex Motions Conform." One of the consequences that flowed from Helmholtz' mathematical analysis was that vortices of an ideal fluid were amazingly stable; they could collide elastically with one another, intertwine to form complex knotlike structures, and undergo tensions and compressions, all without losing their identities.

Helmholtz's work was the end product of the development of classical mechanics. He pushed it as far as it could go. When Helmholtz died, the world of physics was poised on the brink of revolution. The discovery of X rays, radioactivity, and relativity led to a new kind of physics in which Helmholtz's achievements, although impressive, had little to offer the new generation.

ROBERT HOOKE

(b. July 18, 1635, Freshwater, Isle of Wight, Eng.—d. March 3, 1703, London)

English physicist Robert Hooke discovered the law of elasticity, known as Hooke's law, and who did research in a remarkable variety of fields.

In 1655 Hooke was employed by Robert Boyle to construct the Boylean air pump. Five years later, Hooke discovered his law of elasticity, which states that the stretching of a solid body (e.g., metal or wood) is proportional to the force applied to it. The law laid the basis for studies of stress and strain and for understanding of elastic materials. He applied these studies in his designs for the balance springs of watches. In 1662 he was appointed curator of experiments to the Royal Society of London and was elected a fellow the following year.

One of the first men to build a Gregorian reflecting telescope, Hooke discovered the fifth star in the Trapezium, an asterism in the constellation Orion, in 1664 and first suggested that Jupiter rotates on its axis. His detailed sketches of Mars were used in the 19th century to determine that planet's rate of rotation. In 1665 he was appointed professor of geometry in Gresham College. In *Micrographia* (1665; "Small Drawings") he included his studies and illustrations of the crystal structure of snowflakes, discussed the possibility of manufacturing artificial fibres by a process similar to the spinning of the silkworm, and first used the word "cell" to name the microscopic honeycomb cavities in cork. His studies of microscopic fossils led him to become one of the first proponents of a theory of evolution.

Hooke suggested that the force of gravity could be measured by utilizing the motion of a pendulum (1666) and attempted to show that Earth and the Moon follow an elliptical path around the Sun. In 1672 he discovered the phenomenon of diffraction (the bending of light rays around corners); to explain it, he offered the wave theory of light. He stated the inverse square law to describe planetary motions in 1678, a law that Newton later used in modified form. Hooke complained that he was not given sufficient credit for the law and became involved in bitter controversy with Newton. Hooke was the first man to state in general that all matter expands when heated and that air is made up of particles separated from each other by relatively large distances.

WILLIAM THOMSON, BARON KELVIN

(b. June 26, 1824, Belfast, County Antrim, Ire. [now in Northern Ireland]—d. Dec. 17, 1907, Netherhall, near Largs, Ayrshire, Scot.)

William Thomson, Baron Kelvin of Largs, was a Scottish engineer, mathematician, and physicist, who profoundly influenced the scientific thought of his generation.

Thomson's contributions to science included a major role in the development of the second law of thermodynamics;

the absolute temperature scale (measured in kelvins); the dynamical theory of heat; the mathematical analysis of electricity and magnetism, including the basic ideas for the electromagnetic theory of light; the geophysical determination of the age of Earth; and fundamental work in hydrodynamics. His theoretical work on submarine telegraphy and his inventions for use on submarine cables aided Britain in capturing a preeminent place in world communication during the 19th century.

William Thomson was the fourth child in a family of seven. His mother died when he was six years old. His father, James Thomson taught mathematics, first in Belfast and later as a professor at the University of Glasgow; he taught his sons the most recent mathematics, much of which had not yet become a part of the British university curriculum.

William, age 10, matriculated at the University of Glasgow in 1834. There he was introduced to the advanced and controversial thinking of Jean-Baptiste-Joseph Fourier when one of the young student's professors loaned him Fourier's path-breaking book *The Analytical Theory of Heat*, which applied abstract mathematical techniques to the study of heat flow through any solid object. Thomson's first two published articles, which appeared when he was 16 and 17 years old, were a defense of Fourier's work, which was then under attack by British scientists. Thomson was the first to promote the idea that Fourier's mathematics, although applied solely to the flow of heat, could be used in the study of other forms of energy—whether fluids in motion or electricity flowing through a wire.

Thomson entered Cambridge in 1841 and took his B.A. degree four years later with high honours. In 1845 he was given a copy of George Green's *An Essay on the Application of Mathematical Analysis to the Theories of Electricity and*

Magnetism. That work and Fourier's book were the components from which Thomson shaped his worldview and which helped him create his pioneering synthesis of the mathematical relationship between electricity and heat.

The chair of natural philosophy (later called physics) at the University of Glasgow fell vacant in 1846. Thomson's father then mounted a carefully planned and energetic campaign to have his son named to the position, and at the age of 22 William was unanimously elected to it. Thomson remained at Glasgow for the rest of his career.

Thomson's scientific work was guided by the conviction that the various theories dealing with matter and energy were converging toward one great, unified theory. He pursued the goal of a unified theory even though he doubted that it was attainable in his lifetime—or ever. The basis for Thomson's conviction was the cumulative impression obtained from experiments showing the interrelation of forms of energy. By the middle of the 19th century it had been shown that magnetism and electricity, electromagnetism, and light were related, and Thomson had shown by mathematical analogy that there was a relationship between hydrodynamic phenomena and an electric current flowing through wires. James Prescott Joule also claimed that there was a relationship between mechanical motion and heat, and his idea became the basis for the science of thermodynamics.

In 1847 Thomson first heard Joule's theory about the interconvertibility of heat and motion at a meeting of the British Association for the Advancement of Science. Joule's theory went counter to the accepted knowledge of the time, which was that heat was an imponderable substance (caloric) and could not be, as Joule claimed, a form of motion. Thomson was open-minded enough to discuss with Joule the implications of the new theory. At the

William Thomson, Baron Kelvin. Photos.com/Getty Images

time, though he could not accept Joule's idea, Thomson was willing to reserve judgment, especially since the relation between heat and mechanical motion fit into his own view of the causes of force. By 1851 Thomson was able to give public recognition to Joule's theory, along with a cautious endorsement in a major mathematical treatise, "On the Dynamical Theory of Heat." Thomson's essay contained his version of the second law of thermodynamics, which was a major step toward the unification of scientific theories.

Thomson's work on electricity and magnetism also began during his student days at Cambridge. When, much later, James Clerk Maxwell decided to undertake research in magnetism and electricity, he read all of

Thomson's papers on the subject and adopted Thomson as his mentor. Maxwell—in his attempt to synthesize all that was known about the interrelationship of electricity, magnetism, and light—developed his monumental electromagnetic theory of light, probably the most significant achievement of 19th-century science. This theory had its genesis in Thomson's work, and Maxwell readily acknowledged his debt.

Thomson's contributions to 19th-century science were many. He advanced the ideas of Michael Faraday, Fourier, Joule, and others. Using mathematical analysis, Thomson drew generalizations from experimental results. He formulated the concept that was to be generalized into the dynamic theory of energy. He also collaborated with a number of leading scientists of the time, among them Sir George Gabriel Stokes, Hermann von Helmholtz, Peter Guthrie Tait, and Joule. With these partners, Thomson advanced the frontiers of science in several areas, particularly hydrodynamics. Furthermore, he originated the mathematical analogy between the flow of heat in solid bodies and the flow of electricity in conductors.

In an 1884 series of lectures at Johns Hopkins University on the state of scientific knowledge, Thomson wondered aloud about the failures of the wave theory of light to explain certain phenomena. His interest in the sea, roused aboard his yacht, the *Lalla Rookh*, resulted in a number of patents: a compass that was adopted by the British Admiralty; a form of analog computer for measuring tides in a harbour and for calculating tide tables for any hour, past or future; and sounding equipment. He established a company to manufacture these items and a number of electrical measuring devices. Like his father, he published a textbook, *Treatise on Natural Philosophy* (1867), a work on physics coauthored with Tait that helped shape the thinking of a generation of physicists.

JOHANNES KEPLER

(b. Dec. 27, 1571, Weil der Stadt, Württemberg [Germany] — d. Nov. 15, 1630, Regensburg)

German astronomer Johannes Kepler discovered three major laws of planetary motion, conventionally designated as follows: (1) the planets move in elliptical orbits with the Sun at one focus; (2) the time necessary to traverse any arc of a planetary orbit is proportional to the area of the sector between the central body and that arc (the "area law"); and (3) there is an exact relationship between the squares of the planets' periodic times and the cubes of the radii of their orbits (the "harmonic law"). Kepler himself did not call these discoveries "laws," as would become customary after Isaac Newton derived them from a new and quite different set of general physical principles. He regarded them as celestial harmonies that reflected God's design for the universe. Kepler's discoveries turned Nicolaus Copernicus's Sun-centred system into a dynamic universe, with the Sun actively pushing the planets around in noncircular orbits. And it was Kepler's notion of a physical astronomy that fixed a new problematic for other important 17th-century world-system builders, the most famous of whom was Newton.

Kepler came from a very modest family in a small German town called Weil der Stadt and was one of the beneficiaries of the ducal scholarship; it made possible his attendance at the Lutheran *Stift*, or seminary, at the University of Tübingen, where he began his university studies in 1589. Kepler had planned to become a theologian.

His life did not work out quite as he expected. At Tübingen, the professor of mathematics was Michael Maestlin, one of the most talented astronomers in Germany and also, privately, one of the few adherents of the Copernican theory in the late 16th century.

JOANNIS KEPPLERI,
Mathematici Cæsarei
hanc Imaginem,
ARGENTORATENSI BIBLIOTHECÆ.
Confecr.

Johannes Kepler. Rischgitz/Hulton Archive/Getty Images

Maestlin lent Kepler his own heavily annotated copy of Copernicus's 1543 book, *De revolutionibus orbium coelestium libri vi* ("Six Books Concerning the Revolutions of the Heavenly Orbs"). Kepler quickly grasped the main ideas in Copernicus's work and was tutored in its complex details by Maestlin.

The ideas that Kepler would pursue for the rest of his life were already present in his first work, *Mysterium cosmographicum* (1596; "Cosmographic Mystery"). In 1595, it struck him suddenly that the spacing among the six Copernican planets might be explained by circumscribing and inscribing each orbit with one of the five regular polyhedrons. Since Kepler knew Euclid's proof that there can be five and only five such mathematical objects made up of congruent faces, he decided that such self-sufficiency must betoken a perfect idea. If now the ratios of the mean orbital distances agreed with the ratios obtained from circumscribing and inscribing the polyhedrons, then, Kepler felt confidently, he would have discovered the architecture of the universe. Remarkably, Kepler did find agreement within 5 percent, with the exception of Jupiter, at which, he said, "no one will wonder, considering such a great distance."

Had Kepler's investigation ended with the establishment of this architectonic principle, he might have continued to search for other sorts of harmonies; but his work would not have broken with the ancient Greek notion of uniform circular planetary motion. Kepler posited the hypothesis that a single force from the Sun accounts for the increasingly long periods of motion as the planetary distances increase. Kepler did not yet have an exact mathematical description for this relation, but he intuited a connection. A few years later he acquired William Gilbert's groundbreaking book *De Magnete, Magneticisque Corporibus, et de Magno Magnete Tellure* (1600;

"On the Magnet, Magnetic Bodies, and the Great Magnet, the Earth"), and he immediately adopted Gilbert's theory that Earth is a magnet. From this Kepler generalized to the view that the universe is a system of magnetic bodies in which the rotating Sun sweeps the planets around. The solar force, attenuating inversely with distance in the planes of the orbits, was the major physical principle that guided Kepler's struggle to construct a better orbital theory for Mars.

But there was something more: the standard of empirical precision that Kepler held for himself was unprecedented for his time. The great Danish astronomer Tycho Brahe (1546–1601) had set himself the task of amassing a completely new set of planetary observations—a reform of the foundations of practical astronomy. In 1600 Tycho invited Kepler to join his court at Castle Benátky near Prague. When Tycho died suddenly in 1601, Kepler quickly succeeded him as imperial mathematician to Holy Roman emperor Rudolf II. In his lifetime Tycho had been stingy in sharing his observations. After his death, although there was a political struggle with Tycho's heirs, Kepler was ultimately able to work with data accurate to within 2′ of arc. Without data of such precision to back up his solar hypothesis, Kepler would have been unable to discover his "first law" (1605), that Mars moves in an elliptical orbit. At one point, for example, as he tried to balance the demand for the correct heliocentric distances predicted by his physical model with a circular orbit, an error of 6′ or 8′ appeared in the octants (assuming a circle divided into eight equal parts). Kepler exclaimed, "Because these 8′ could not be ignored, they alone have led to a total reformation of astronomy."

Finally, Kepler published the first textbook of Copernican astronomy, *Epitome Astronomiae Copernicanae* (1618–21; *Epitome of Copernican Astronomy*). The title mimicked Maestlin's traditional-style textbook, but the content could not have been more different. The *Epitome* began with the elements of astronomy but then gathered together all the arguments for Copernicus's theory and added to them Kepler's harmonics and new rules of planetary motion. This work would prove to be the most important theoretical resource for the Copernicans in the 17th century. Galileo and Descartes were probably influenced by it. It was capped by the appearance of *Tabulae Rudolphinae* (1627; "Rudolphine Tables"). The *Epitome* and the Rudolphine Tables cast heliostatic astronomy and astrology into a form where detailed and extensive counterargument would force opponents to engage with its claims or silently ignore them to their disadvantage. Eventually Newton would simply take over Kepler's laws while ignoring all reference to their original theological and philosophical framework.

JOSEPH-LOUIS LAGRANGE

(b. Jan. 25, 1736, Turin, Sardinia-Piedmont [Italy]—d. April 10, 1813, Paris, France)

Italian-French mathematician Joseph-Louis Lagrange, comte de l'Empire, made great contributions to number theory and to analytic and celestial mechanics. His most important book, *Mécanique analytique* (1788; "Analytic Mechanics"), was the basis for all later work in this field.

Lagrange was from a well-to-do family of French origin on his father's side. His father was treasurer to the king of Sardinia and lost his fortune in speculation. Lagrange later said, "If I had been rich, I probably would not have devoted myself to mathematics." His interest in mathematics was aroused by the chance reading of a memoir by the English astronomer Edmond Halley. At 19 (some say 16) he was teaching mathematics at the artillery school of Turin (he would later be instrumental in founding the

Turin Academy of Sciences). Lagrange's early publications, on the propagation of sound and on the concept of maxima and minima, were well received; the Swiss mathematician Leonhard Euler praised Lagrange's version of his theory of variations.

By 1761 Lagrange was already recognized as one of the greatest living mathematicians. In 1764 he was awarded a prize offered by the French Academy of Sciences for an essay on the libration of the Moon (i.e., the apparent oscillation that causes slight changes in position of lunar features on the face that the Moon presents to Earth). In this essay he used the equations that now bear his name. His success encouraged the academy in 1766 to propose, as a problem, the theory of the motions of the satellites of Jupiter. The prize was again awarded to Lagrange, and he won the same distinction in 1772, 1774, and 1778. In 1766, on the recommendation of Euler and the French mathematician Jean d'Alembert, Lagrange went to Berlin to fill a post at the academy vacated by Euler, at the invitation of Frederick the Great, who expressed the wish of "the greatest king in Europe" to have "the greatest mathematician in Europe" at his court.

Lagrange stayed in Berlin until 1787. His productivity in those years was prodigious: he published papers on the three-body problem, which concerns the evolution of three particles mutually attracted according to Sir Isaac Newton's law of gravity; differential equations; prime number theory; the fundamentally important number-theoretic equation that has been identified (incorrectly by Euler) with John Pell's name; probability; mechanics; and the stability of the solar system. In his long paper "Réflexions sur la résolution algébrique des équations" (1770; "Reflections on the Algebraic Resolution of Equations"), Lagrange inaugurated a new period in algebra and inspired Évariste Galois to his group theory.

A kind and quiet man, living only for science, Lagrange had little to do with the factions and intrigues around the king. When Frederick died, Lagrange preferred to accept Louis XVI's invitation to Paris. He was given apartments in the Louvre, was continually honoured, and was treated with respect throughout the French Revolution. From the Louvre he published his classic *Mécanique analytique*, a lucid synthesis of the hundred years of research in mechanics since Newton, based on his own calculus of variations, in which certain properties of a mechanistic system are inferred by considering the changes in a sum (or integral) that are due to conceptually possible (or virtual) displacements from the path that describes the actual history of the system. This led to independent coordinates that are necessary for the specifications of a system of a finite number of particles, or "generalized coordinates." It also led to the so-called Lagrangian equations for a classical mechanical system in which the kinetic energy of the system is related to the generalized coordinates, the corresponding generalized forces, and the time. The book was typically analytic; he stated in his preface that "one cannot find any figures in this work."

The French Revolution, which began in 1789, pressed Lagrange into work on the committee to reform the metric system. When the great chemist Antoine-Laurent Lavoisier was guillotined, Lagrange commented, "It took them only an instant to cut off that head, and a hundred years may not produce another like it." When the École Centrale des Travaux Publics (later renamed the École Polytechnique) was opened in 1794, he became, with Gaspard Monge, its leading professor of mathematics. His lectures were published as *Théorie des fonctions analytiques* (1797; "Theory of Analytic Functions") and *Leçons sur le calcul des fonctions* (1804; "Lessons on the Calculus of Functions") and were the first textbooks on real analytic functions. In them Lagrange tried to substitute an algebraic foundation for the existing and problematic analytic foundation of calculus—although ultimately unsuccessful, his criticisms spurred others to develop the modern analytic foundation. Lagrange also continued to work on his *Mécanique analytique*, but the new edition appeared only after his death.

Napoleon honoured the aging mathematician, making him a senator and a count of the empire, but he remained the quiet, unobtrusive academician—a venerable figure wrapped in his thoughts.

HORACE LAMB

(b. Nov. 27, 1849, Stockport, near Manchester, Eng.—d. Dec. 4, 1934, Cambridge, Cambridgeshire)

Sir Horace Lamb was an English mathematician who contributed to the field of mathematical physics.

In 1872 Lamb was elected a fellow and lecturer of Trinity College, Cambridge, and three years later he became professor of mathematics at Adelaide University, Australia. He returned to England in 1885 to become professor of mathematics at Victoria University, Manchester (now the University of Manchester). Lamb wrote the *Mathematical Theory of the Motion of Fluids* (1878) which was enlarged and transformed into *Hydrodynamics* (1895); the latter was, for many years, the standard work on hydrodynamics. His many papers, principally on applied mathematics, detailed his researches on wave propagation, electrical induction, earthquake tremors, and the theory of tides and waves.

Lamb made valuable studies of airflow over aircraft surfaces for the Aeronautical Research Committee from 1921 to 1927. He was made a fellow of the Royal Society of London in 1884 and was knighted in 1931. His other publications include *Infinitesimal Calculus* (1897), *Dynamical*

Theory of Sound (1910), *Statics* (1912), *Dynamics* (1914), and *Higher Mechanics* (1920).

Lamb was elected to the Royal Society in 1884, and was president of the London Mathematical Society (1902-1904). He was awarded many honours and was knighted in 1931.

JAMES CLERK MAXWELL

(b. June 13, 1831, Edinburgh, Scot. — d. Nov. 5, 1879, Cambridge, Cambridgeshire, Eng.)

Scottish physicist James Clerk Maxwell was best known for his formulation of electromagnetic theory. He also contributed to the study of thermodynamics.

Maxwell was an only child. A dull and uninspired tutor was engaged who claimed that James was slow at learning, though in fact he displayed a lively curiosity at an early age and had a phenomenal memory. Fortunately the young Maxwell was rescued by his aunt Jane Cay and from 1841 was sent to school at the Edinburgh Academy.

Maxwell's interests ranged far beyond the school syllabus, and he did not pay particular attention to examination performance. His first scientific paper, published when he was only 14 years old, described a generalized series of oval curves that could be traced with pins and thread by analogy with an ellipse.

At age 16 he entered the University of Edinburgh, where he read voraciously on all subjects and published two more scientific papers. In 1850 he went to the University of Cambridge, where his exceptional powers began to be recognized. His mathematics teacher, William Hopkins, was a well-known "wrangler maker" (a wrangler is one who takes first-class honours in the mathematics examinations at Cambridge). Of Maxwell, Hopkins is reported to have said that he was the most extraordinary man he had ever met and that it seemed impossible for him to think wrongly on any physical subject.

In 1854 Maxwell was second wrangler. He was elected to a fellowship at Trinity, but, because his father's health was deteriorating, he wished to return to Scotland. In 1856 he was appointed to the professorship of natural philosophy at Marischal College, Aberdeen, but before the appointment was announced his father died. This was a great personal loss, for Maxwell had had a close relationship with his father. In 1860 he was appointed to the professorship of natural philosophy at King's College, London.

The next five years were undoubtedly the most fruitful of his career. During this period his two classic papers on the electromagnetic field were published, and his demonstration of colour photography took place. His theoretical and experimental work on the viscosity of gases also was undertaken during these years and culminated in a lecture to the Royal Society in 1866.

In 1865 Maxwell resigned his professorship at King's College and retired to the family estate in Glenlair. Most of his energy during this period was devoted to writing his famous treatise on electricity and magnetism.

It was Maxwell's research on electromagnetism that established him among the great scientists of history. In the preface to his *Treatise on Electricity and Magnetism* (1873), the best exposition of his theory, Maxwell stated that his major task was to convert Michael Faraday's physical ideas into mathematical form. In attempting to illustrate Faraday's law of induction (that a changing magnetic field gives rise to an induced electromagnetic field), Maxwell constructed a mechanical model. He found that the model gave rise to a corresponding "displacement current" in the dielectric medium, which could then be the seat of transverse waves. On calculating the velocity of these waves, he found that they were very close to the velocity of light. Maxwell concluded that he could "scarcely avoid the inference that light consists in the transverse undulations of the same medium which is the cause of electric and magnetic phenomena."

In addition to his electromagnetic theory, Maxwell made major contributions to other areas of physics. The Maxwell relations of equality between different partial derivatives of thermodynamic functions are included in every standard textbook on thermodynamics. Though Maxwell did not originate the modern kinetic theory of gases, he was the first to apply the methods of probability and statistics in describing the properties of an assembly of molecules. Thus he was able to demonstrate that the velocities of molecules in a gas, previously assumed to be equal, must follow a statistical distribution (known subsequently as the Maxwell-Boltzmann distribution law). In later papers Maxwell investigated the transport properties of gases—i.e., the effect of changes in temperature and pressure on viscosity, thermal conductivity, and diffusion.

Maxwell was far from being an abstruse theoretician. He was skillful in the design of experimental apparatus, as was shown early in his career during his investigations of colour vision. He devised a colour top with adjustable sectors of tinted paper to test the three-colour hypothesis of Thomas Young and later invented a colour box that made it possible to conduct experiments with spectral colours rather than pigments. His investigations of the colour theory led him to conclude that a colour photograph could be produced by photographing through filters of the three primary colours and then recombining the images. He demonstrated his supposition in a lecture to the Royal Institution of Great Britain in 1861 by projecting through filters a colour photograph of a tartan ribbon that had been taken by this method.

In addition to these well-known contributions, a number of ideas that Maxwell put forward quite casually have since led to developments of great significance. The hypothetical intelligent being known as Maxwell's demon was a factor in the development of information theory. Maxwell's analytic treatment of speed governors is generally regarded as the founding paper on cybernetics, and his "equal areas" construction provided an essential constituent of the theory of fluids developed by Johannes Diederik van der Waals. His work in geometrical optics led to the discovery of the fish-eye lens. From the start of his career to its finish, his papers are filled with novelty and interest. He also was a contributor to the ninth edition of *Encyclopædia Britannica*.

In 1871 Maxwell was elected to the new Cavendish professorship at Cambridge. He set about designing the Cavendish Laboratory and supervised its construction. Maxwell had few students, but they were of the highest calibre and included William D. Niven, Ambrose (later Sir Ambrose) Fleming, Richard Tetley Glazebrook, John Henry Poynting, and Arthur Schuster.

During the Easter term of 1879 Maxwell took ill on several occasions; he returned to Glenlair in June, but his condition did not improve. He died on November 5, after a short illness. Maxwell received no public honours and was buried quietly in a small churchyard in the village of Parton, in Scotland.

ISAAC NEWTON

(b. Dec. 25, 1642 [Jan. 4, 1643, New Style], Woolsthorpe, Lincolnshire, Eng.—d. March 20 [March 31], 1727, London)

English physicist and mathematician Sir Isaac Newton was the culminating figure of the scientific revolution of the 17th century. His three laws of motion, the basic principles of modern physics, resulted in the formulation of the law of universal gravitation.

A tiny and weak baby, Newton was not expected to survive his first day of life, much less 84 years. Deprived of a father before birth, he soon lost his mother when she remarried and her husband, the well-to-do minister Barnabas Smith, left young Isaac with his grandmother. For nine years, Isaac was effectively separated from his mother, and his pronounced psychotic tendencies have been ascribed to this traumatic event.

After his mother was widowed again, she determined that Newton should manage her now considerable property, but he could not bring himself to concentrate on rural affairs—set to watch the cattle, he would curl up under a tree with a book. Fortunately, the mistake was recognized, and Newton was sent to the grammar school in Grantham to prepare for the university.

When Newton arrived in Cambridge in 1661, the scientific revolution was well advanced. Yet the universities of Europe, including Cambridge, continued to be the strongholds of outmoded Aristotelianism, which rested on a geocentric view of the universe.

Newton began his higher education by immersing himself in Aristotle's work. However, on his own, without formal guidance, Newton had sought out the new philosophy and the new mathematics and made them his own, but he had confined the progress of his studies to his notebooks. Then, in 1665, the plague closed the university, and for most of the following two years he was forced to stay at his home. During the plague years he examined the elements of circular motion and, applying his analysis to the Moon and the planets, derived the inverse square relation that the radially directed force acting on a planet decreases with the square of its distance from the Sun—which was later crucial to the law of universal gravitation. The world heard nothing of this discovery.

About 1679, Newton began to ascribe puzzling phenomena—chemical affinities, the generation of heat in chemical reactions, surface tension in fluids, capillary action, and the cohesion of bodies—to attractions and repulsions between particles of matter. Newton originally applied the idea of attractions and repulsions solely to the range of terrestrial phenomena mentioned above. But late in 1679, another application was suggested in a letter from Robert Hooke, who was seeking to renew correspondence. Hooke mentioned his analysis of planetary motion. Newton bluntly refused to correspond but, nevertheless, mentioned an experiment to demonstrate the rotation of Earth: let a body be dropped from a tower; because the tangential velocity at the top of the tower is greater than that at the foot, the body should fall slightly to the east. He sketched the path of fall as part of a spiral ending at the centre of Earth. This was a mistake, as Hooke pointed out; according to Hooke's theory of planetary motion, the path should be elliptical, so that if Earth were split and separated to allow the body to fall, it would rise again to its original location. Newton corrected Hooke's figure using the assumption that gravity is constant. Hooke then countered by replying that, although Newton's figure was correct for constant gravity, his own assumption was that gravity decreases as the square of the distance. Several years later, this letter became the basis for Hooke's charge of plagiarism. He was mistaken in the charge. His knowledge of the inverse square relation rested only on intuitive grounds. Moreover, unknown to him, Newton had so derived the relation more than ten years earlier.

Nearly five years later, in August 1684, Newton was visited by the British astronomer Edmond Halley, who was also troubled by the problem of orbital dynamics.

Upon learning that Newton had solved the problem, he extracted Newton's promise to send the demonstration. Three months later he received a short tract entitled *De Motu* ("On Motion"). Already Newton was at work improving and expanding it. In two and a half years, the tract *De Motu* grew into *Philosophiae Naturalis Principia Mathematica*,

Sir Isaac Newton. Hulton Archive/Getty Images

which is not only Newton's masterpiece but also the fundamental work for the whole of modern science.

The mechanics of the *Principia* was an exact quantitative description of the motions of visible bodies. It rested on Newton's three laws of motion: (1) that a body remains in its state of rest unless it is compelled to change that state by a force impressed on it; (2) that the change of motion (the change of velocity times the mass of the body) is proportional to the force impressed; (3) that to every action there is an equal and opposite reaction. The analysis of circular motion in terms of these laws yielded a formula of the quantitative measure, in terms of a body's velocity and mass, of the centripetal force necessary to divert a body from its rectilinear path into a given circle. When Newton substituted this formula into Kepler's third law, he found that the centripetal force holding the planets in their given orbits about the Sun must decrease with the square of the planets' distances from the Sun. Because the satellites of Jupiter also obey Kepler's third law, an inverse square centripetal force must also attract them to the centre of their orbits. Newton was able to show that a similar relation holds between Earth and its Moon. The distance of the Moon is approximately 60 times the radius of Earth. Newton compared the distance by which the Moon, in its orbit of known size, is diverted from a tangential path in one second with the distance that a body at the surface of Earth falls from rest in one second. When the latter distance proved to be 3,600 (60 × 60) times as great as the former, he concluded that one and the same force, governed by a single quantitative law, is operative in all three cases, and from the correlation of the Moon's orbit with the measured acceleration of gravity on the surface of Earth, he applied the ancient Latin word *gravitas* (literally, "heaviness" or "weight") to it. The law of universal gravitation states that every particle of matter in the universe attracts every other particle with a force that is proportional to the product of their masses and inversely proportional to the square of the distance between their centres.

The *Principia* immediately raised Newton to international prominence. In their continuing loyalty to the mechanical ideal, Continental scientists rejected the idea of action at a distance for a generation, but even in their rejection they could not withhold their admiration for the technical expertise revealed by the work. Young British scientists spontaneously recognized him as their model. Within a generation the limited number of salaried positions for scientists in England were monopolized by the young Newtonians of the next generation.

LUDWIG PRANDTL

(b. Feb. 4, 1875, Freising, Ger.—d. Aug. 15, 1953, Göttingen)

German physicist Ludwig Prandtl is considered to be the father of aerodynamics.

In 1901 Prandtl became professor of mechanics at the Technical Institute of Hannover, where he continued his earlier efforts to provide a sound theoretical basis for fluid mechanics. From 1904 to 1953, he served as professor of applied mechanics at the University of Göttingen, where he established a school of aerodynamics and hydrodynamics that achieved world renown. In 1925 he became director of the Kaiser Wilhelm (later the Max Planck) Institute for Fluid Mechanics. His discovery (1904) of the boundary layer, which adjoins the surface of a body moving in air or water, led to an understanding of skin friction drag and of the way in which streamlining reduces the drag of airplane wings and other moving bodies. His work on wing theory, which followed similar work by a British physicist, Frederick W. Lanchester, but was carried out independently, elucidated the process of airflow over airplane wings of finite span. That body of work is known as the Lanchester-Prandtl wing theory.

Prandtl made decisive advances in boundary-layer and wing theories, and his work became the fundamental material of aerodynamics. He was an early pioneer in streamlining airships, and his advocacy of monoplanes greatly advanced heavier-than-air aviation. He contributed the Prandtl-Glaubert rule for subsonic airflow to describe the compressibility effects of air at high speeds. In addition to his important advances in the theories of supersonic flow and turbulence, he made notable innovations in the design of wind tunnels and other aerodynamic equipment. He also devised a soap-film analogy for analyzing the torsion forces of structures with noncircular cross sections.

WILLIAM JOHN MACQUORN RANKINE

(b. July 5, 1820, Edinburgh, Scot.—d. Dec. 24, 1872, Glasgow)

Scottish engineer and physicist William John Macquorn Rankine was one of the founders of the science of thermodynamics, particularly in reference to steam-engine theory.

Trained as a civil engineer under Sir John Benjamin MacNeill, Rankine was appointed to the Queen Victoria chair of civil engineering and mechanics at the University of Glasgow (1855). One of Rankine's first scientific works, a paper on fatigue in metals of railway axles (1843), led to new methods of construction. His *Manual of Applied Mechanics* (1858) was of considerable help to designing engineers and architects. His classic *Manual of the Steam Engine and Other Prime Movers* (1859) was the first attempt at a systematic treatment of steam-engine theory. Rankine worked out a thermodynamic cycle of events (the so-called Rankine cycle) used as a standard for the performance of steam-power installations in which a condensable vapour provides the working fluid.

In soil mechanics his work on earth pressures and the stability of retaining walls was a notable advance, particularly his paper "On the Thermodynamic Theory of Waves of Finite Longitudinal Disturbance."

BENJAMIN THOMPSON

(b. March 26, 1753, Woburn, Mass. [U.S.]—d. Aug. 21, 1814, Auteuil, France)

Sir Benjamin Thompson, count von Rumford, was an American-born British physicist, government administrator, and a founder of the Royal Institution of Great Britain, London. His investigations of heat overturned the theory that heat is a liquid form of matter and established the beginnings of the modern theory that heat is a form of motion.

In 1772 Thompson married a wealthy widow, Sarah Walker, and lived in Rumford (now Concord), N.H. Loyal to the British crown, he served as a spy after the outbreak of the American Revolution, but in 1776 he was forced to flee to London, leaving his wife and daughter behind. There he served for a time as a government clerk and undersecretary of state. As a lieutenant colonel he later commanded a British regiment in New York, but with the end of the war he resigned himself to exile.

Knighted by King George III in 1784, Thompson subsequently received the crown's permission to enter the Bavarian civil service and became war and police minister and grand chamberlain to the elector of Bavaria. He introduced numerous social reforms and brought James

Watt's steam engine into common use. Thompson's work resulted in improved fireplaces and chimneys, and among his inventions are a double boiler, a kitchen range, and a drip coffeepot. He also introduced the potato as a staple food. He was created a count of the Holy Roman Empire in 1791. Interest in gunpowder and weaponry stimulated his physical investigations, and in 1798 he began his studies of heat and friction. He reported some of his findings in the classic paper "An Experimental Enquiry Concerning the Source of the Heat which is Excited by Friction" (1798) and made one of the earliest measurements of the equivalence of heat and mechanical energy.

Thompson returned to England in 1798 and continued his researches on heat. In 1799, with Sir Joseph Banks, he helped establish the Royal Institution of Great Britain and chose the British chemist Sir Humphry Davy as lecturer. He established the Rumford professorship at Harvard College as well as the Rumford medals of the Royal Society (London) and the American Academy of Arts and Sciences, Boston.

abjure To renounce.

adiabatic Occurring without loss or gain of heat.

aneurysm Blood-filled protrusion in the wall of a blood vessel (usually an artery, and particularly the aorta).

anisotropic Exhibiting properties with different values when measured in different directions.

anomalous Inconsistent with or deviating from what is usual, normal, or expected.

architectonic Of, relating to, or according with the principles of architecture.

attenuating To lessen the amount, force, magnitude, or value of.

cavitate To form cavities or bubbles.

centripetal Proceeding or acting in a direction toward a centre or axis.

cesium-133 An isotope of cesium used especially in atomic clocks and one of whose atomic transitions is used as a scientific time standard. (Cesium is a silver-white soft ductile element of the alkali metal group that is the most electropositive element known and that is used especially in photoelectric cells.)

diatomic Consisting of two atoms.

differential The product of the derivative of a function of one variable by the increment of the independent variable.

dilatational The state of being expanded.

dissipate To cause to spread thin or scatter and gradually vanish.

ducal Of or relating to a duke or dukedom.

ductile Capable of being fashioned into a new form.

enthalpy The sum of the internal energy of a body or system and the product of its volume multiplied by the pressure.

entropy Measure of a system's energy that is unavailable for work; the degree of disorder or uncertainty in a system.

equinox Either of two moments in the year when the Sun is exactly above the Equator and day and night are of equal length all over Earth.

foehn A warm dry wind blowing down the side of a mountain.

geoid The surface within or around the earth that is everywhere normal to the direction of gravity and coincides with mean sea level in the oceans.

hertz A unit of frequency equal to one cycle per second—abbreviation Hz.

inertia A property of matter by which it remains at rest or in uniform motion in the same straight line unless acted upon by some external force.

interferometer An apparatus that utilizes the interference of waves (as of light) for precise determinations (as of distance or wavelength).

isentropic Of or relating to equal or constant entropy; especially: taking place without change of entropy.

isothermal Of, relating to, or marked by equality of temperature.

isotropic Exhibiting properties (as velocity of light transmission) with the same values when measured along axes in all directions.

joule A unit of work or energy equal to the work done by a force of one newton acting through a distance of one metre.

kilojoule One thousand joules; also: a unit in nutrition equivalent to 0.239 calorie.

kinematic A branch of dynamics that deals with aspects of motion apart from considerations of mass and force.

lamina A thin plate or scale (plural laminae).

libration An oscillation in the apparent aspect of a secondary body (as a planet or a satellite) as seen from the primary object around which it revolves.

macroscopic Involving large units or elements.

meniscus The curved upper surface of a column of liquid.

milligal A unit of acceleration equivalent to 1/1000 gal.

monatomic Consisting of one atom.

newton That force necessary to provide a mass of 1 kilogram with an acceleration of 1 metre per second per second.

orthogonal Intersecting or lying at right angles.

oscillate To swing backward and forward like a pendulum.

paradoxical Seemingly contradictory or opposed to common sense, yet perhaps true.

parallelepiped A 6-faced polyhedron all of whose faces are parallelograms lying in pairs of parallel planes.

parameter Any of a set of physical properties whose values determine the characteristics or behaviour of something.

pascal A unit of pressure in the metre-kilogram-second system equivalent to one newton per square metre.

pedantic Unimaginative, pedestrian.

phlogiston The hypothetical principle of fire regarded formerly as a material substance.

piezoelectricity Electricity or electric polarity due to pressure especially in a crystalline substance (as quartz).

polyatomic Containing more than one and especially more than two atoms.

postulate A hypothesis advanced as an essential presupposition, condition, or premise of a train of reasoning.

prototype A standard or typical example.

proximate Very near, close.

quaternion A generalized complex number that is composed of a real number and a vector and that depends on one real and three imaginary units.

radian A unit of plane angular measurement that is equal to the angle at the centre of a circle subtended by an arc whose length equals the radius or approximately 57.3 degrees.

reactant A substance that enters into and is altered in the course of a chemical reaction.

resonance The enhancement of an atomic, nuclear, or particle reaction or a scattering event by excitation of internal motion in the system.

Roman legion A soldier from ancient Rome, upon whose pace the mile is based.

scalar A quantity (as mass or time) that has a magnitude describable by a real number and no direction.

seismology Scientific discipline that is concerned with the study of earthquakes.

solicitor One of the two types of practicing lawyers in England, the other being the barrister, who pleads cases before the court. The solicitors carry on most of the office work in law.

supersonic Of, being, or relating to speeds from one to five times the speed of sound in air.

synodic Relating to the period between two successive conjunctions of the same celestial bodies (as the moon and the sun).

torque A force that produces or tends to produce rotation or torsion (twisting).

trajectory The curve that a body (as a planet or comet in its orbit or a rocket) describes in space.

translational Changing from one form to another.

undulatory Moving in or resembling waves.

vector A quantity that has magnitude and direction and that is commonly represented by a directed line segment whose length represents the magnitude and whose orientation in space represents the direction.

viscosity The property of resistance to flow in a fluid or semifluid.

vorticity A vector measure of local rotation in a fluid flow.

THERMODYNAMICS

H.C. Van Ness, *Understanding Thermodynamics* (1969, reissued 1983), is an informal introduction to the basic concepts of thermodynamics; in particular, the first few chapters are accessible to high-school students. Enrico Fermi, *Thermodynamics*, new ed. (1956), is a compact and beautifully written introduction to classical thermo-dynamics for those with a basic knowledge of calculus, including partial differentiation.

Herbert B. Callen, *Thermodynamics and an Introduction to Thermostatistics*, 2nd ed. (1987), provides a widely cited postulational formulation for thermodynamics. Dilip Kondepudi and Ilya Prigogine, *Modern Thermodynamics: From Heat Engines to Dissipative Structures* (1998), gives a modern treatment of equilibrium and nonequilibrium thermodynamics; the text makes extensive use of com-puter exercises and Internet resources.

Good engineering textbooks, which tend to focus more on applications, include Yunus A. Çengel and Michael A. Boles, *Thermodynamics: An Engineering Approach*, 5th ed. (2005); and Richard E. Sonntag, Claus Borgnakke, and Gordon J. Van Wylen, *Fundamentals of Thermodynamics*, 3rd ed. (2003).

Donald T. Haynie, *Biological Thermodynamics* (2001), is an informal introduction intended for students of biol-ogy and biochemistry. Sven E. Jørgensen and James Kay, *Thermodynamics and Ecological Modeling* (2000), discusses appli-cations of thermodynamics principles to living ecosystems.

MECHANICS

The history of classical mechanics is chronicled in
I. Bernard Cohen, *The Newtonian Revolution* (1980);
and E.J. Dijksterhuis, *The Mechanization of the World
Picture* (1961; originally published in Dutch, 1950). All
introductory physics textbooks contain a portion on
classical mechanics; recent examples include Hans C.
Ohanian, *Physics*, 2nd ed. (1989); and Robert Resnick,
David Halliday, and Kenneth S. Krane, *Physics*, 4th ed.
(1992). The principal reference for classical mechanics
is S. Frautschi et al., *The Mechanical Universe: Mechanics
and Heat*, advanced ed. (1986). Other texts include, at
an introductory level, A.P. French, *Newtonian Mechanics*
(1971); and at a more advanced, graduate-school level,
Herbert Goldstein, *Classical Mechanics*, 2nd ed. (1980), a
standard text that contains a lengthy, detailed bibliog-
raphy of more specialized books dealing with specific
aspects of the subject.

SOLIDS MECHANICS

There are a number of works on the history of the subject. A.E.H. Love, *A Treatise on the Mathematical Theory
of Elasticity*, 4th ed. (1927, reprinted 1944), has a well-
researched chapter on the origin of elasticity up to the
early 1900s. Stephen P. Timoshenko, *History of Strength
of Materials: With a Brief Account of the History of Theory
of Elasticity and Theory of Structures* (1953, reprinted
1983), provides good coverage of most subfields of solid
mechanics up to the period around 1940, including in
some cases detailed but quite readable accounts of specific developments and capsule biographies of major
figures. C. Truesdell, *Essays in the History of Mechanics*
(1968), summarizes his studies of original source

materials on Jakob Bernoulli (1654–1705), Leonhard
Euler, Leonardo da Vinci, and others and connects those
contributions to some of the developments in what he
calls "rational mechanics" as of the middle 1900s. Two
articles in *Handbuch der Physik* provide historical back-
ground: C. Truesdell and R.A. Toupin, "The Classical
Field Theories," vol. 3, pt. 1 (1960); and C. Truesdell and
W. Noll, "The Nonlinear Field Theories of Mechanics,"
vol. 3, pt. 3 (1965).

There are many good books for beginners on the
subject, intended for the education of engineers; one that
stands out for its coverage of inelastic solid mechanics
as well as the more conventional topics on elementary
elasticity and structures is Stephen H. Crandall, Norman
C. Dahl, and Thomas J. Lardner (eds.), *An Introduction
to the Mechanics of Solids*, 2nd ed., with SI units (1978).
Those with an interest in the physics of materials might
begin with A.H. Cottrell, *The Mechanical Properties of
Matter* (1964, reprinted 1981). Some books for beginners aim for a more general introduction to continuum
mechanics, including solids and fluids; one such text is
Y.C. Fung, *A First Course in Continuum Mechanics*, 2nd ed.
(1977). A readable introduction to continuum mechanics at a more advanced level, such as might be used by
scientists and engineers from other fields or by first-year
graduate students, is Lawrence E. Malvern, *Introduction
to the Mechanics of a Continuous Medium* (1969). The article
by Truesdell and Toupin, mentioned above, provides a
comprehensive, perhaps overwhelming, treatment of
continuum mechanics fundamentals.

For more specialized treatment of linear elasticity, the
classics are the work by Love, mentioned above; Stephen
P. Timoshenko and J.N. Goodier, *Theory of Elasticity*, 3rd
ed. (1970); and N.I. Muskhelishvili, *Some Basic Problems*

of the Mathematical Theory of Elasticity, 2nd ed. (1963, reprinted 1977; originally published in Russian, 4th corrected and augmented ed., 1954). The article by Truesdell and Noll noted above is a good source on finite elasticity and also on viscoelastic fluids; a standard reference on the latter is R. Byron Bird et al., *Dynamics of Polymeric Liquids,* vol. 1, *Fluid Mechanics*, 2nd ed. (1987). Other books generally regarded as classics in their subfields are R. Hill, *The Mathematical Theory of Plasticity* (1950, reissued 1983); J.C. Jaeger and N.G. Cook, *Fundamentals of Rock Mechanics*, 3rd ed. (1979). John Price Hirth and Jens Lothe, *Theory of Dislocations*, 2nd ed. (1982); and Keiiti Aki and Paul G. Richards, *Quantitative Seismology*, 2 vol. (1980). Other aspects of stress waves in solids are covered by J.D. Achenbach, *Wave Propagation in Elastic Solids* (1973). In addition, the scope of finite element analysis in solid mechanics and many other areas can be gleaned from O.C. Zienkiewicz and R.L. Taylor, *The Finite Element Method*, 4th ed., 2 vol. (1989–91); and that of fracture mechanics from Melvin F. Kanninen and Carl H. Popelar, *Advanced Fracture Mechanics* (1985). Structural mechanics and issues relating to stability and elastic-plastic stress-strain relations in a way that updates the book by Hill are presented by Zdeněk P. Baˇzant and Luigi Cedolin, *Stability of Structures: Elastic, Inelastic, Fracture, and Damage Theories* (1991).

Fluid Mechanics

A classic text that enshrines all the results of 19th-century fluid dynamics is Horace Lamb, *Hydrodynamics*, 6th ed. (1932, reissued 1993). This remains useful, but many later books, besides being more up-to-date, provide a better-balanced perspective of the subject and have better illustrations. N. Curle and Hubert J. Davies, *Modern Fluid Dynamics: Incompressible Flow*, vol. 1 (1968, reissued 2000); and G.K. Batchelor, *An Introduction to Fluid Dynamics* (1967, reissued 1973), can both be recommended to serious students who are not put off by mathematics. D.J. Tritton, *Physical Fluid Dynamics*, 2nd ed. (1988), adopts a somewhat different approach and contains interesting material on turbulence and convective instabilities. B.S. Massey, *Mechanics of Fluids*, 8th ed. (2005), covers practical aspects of the subject, including hydrostatics, from an engineering perspective. The development of the subject as a practical science is traced in Hunter Rouse and Simon Ince, *History of Hydraulics* (1957, reissued 1980).

Gravitation

General Introductions to Gravitation

Isaac Newton, *The Principia: Mathematical Principles of Natural Philosophy*, trans. by I. Bernard Cohen and Anne Whitman (1999), often referred to as the *Principia*, is the origin of all fundamental work on gravity. Stephen W. Hawking and W. Israel (eds.), *Three Hundred Years of Gravitation* (1987, reissued 1989), provides many authoritative review articles in commemoration of the tercentenary of the publication of Newton's *Principia*. Stephen W. Hawking, *A Brief History of Time: From the Big Bang to Black Holes* (1988), is a nonmathematical book by an outstanding author that features a chapter on black holes. Expositions of theory and the results of relevant experiments are presented in Ignazio Ciufolini and John Archibald Wheeler, *Gravitation and Inertia* (1995). Alan

Cook, *The Motion of the Moon* (1988), discusses theories of the lunar orbit, with a chapter on applications that includes an account of gravitational studies.

GRAVITY FIELDS AROUND EARTH, THE MOON, AND THE PLANETS

Alan Cook, *Physics of the Earth and Planets* (1973), includes a chapter on methods and results of gravity measurements, and *Interiors of the Planets* (1980) summarizes knowledge of the gravity fields of the planets and their interpretation.

GRAVITATIONAL EXPERIMENTS

Henry Cavendish, "Experiments to Determine the Density of the Earth," *Philosophical Transactions of the Royal Society of London*, 88:469–526 (June 21, 1798), details the first measurement of *G*. Clifford M. Will, *Theory and Experiment in Gravitational Physics*, rev. ed. (1993), is a thorough treatment. Y.T. Chen and Alan Cook, *Gravitational Experiments in the Laboratory* (1993), includes a detailed discussion of experimental methods, their design, and sources of error.

INDEX

S

T